WELCOME

Both a dreamer and a pragmatist, Ho Chi Minh, leader of the revolution that shook off the yoke of European colonialism and after years of strife established Vietnam as an independent socialist republic, was firm in his conviction.

"You will kill 10 of our men, and we will kill one of yours, and in the end, it will be you who tire of it," he wrote prophetically. The long, bloody saga of war in Vietnam spanned three decades, from the end of Japanese occupation and French dominion to the withdrawal of US fighting forces and the fall of Saigon, 1945-1975. While historians acknowledge that the path to independence was arduous for Vietnam under the leadership of its communist party officials, the consequences of the war were far reaching – well beyond the boundaries of this territory of Southeast Asia.

The outcome of the Vietnam conflict shook the world. The United States, a mighty superpower, was riven to its core as its perspective on the conflict evolved. In his book *The Best and the Brightest*, an in-depth work on the origins of the Vietnam war, eminent historian and author David Halberstam wrote, "…by 1950, caught up increasingly in our own global vision of anti-Communism, we chose not to see this war as primarily a colonial/anticolonial war, and we had begun to underwrite most of the French costs. Where our money went our rhetoric soon followed. We adjusted our public statements, and much of our journalism, to make it seem as if this was a war of Communists against anti-Communists, instead, as the people of Vietnam might have seen it, a war of a colonial power against an indigenous nationalist force."

The greatest bastion of capitalism the world had ever seen was brought eventually

ABOVE: Before a map of North Vietnam and neighbouring Laos, President Kennedy addresses a conference at the US State Department, March 22, 1961. (Executive Office of the President of the United States via Wikimedia Commons)

low in defeat by the tenacious, relentless will and total commitment of the North Vietnamese Army, its allied Viet Cong guerrillas throughout the Central Highlands and coastal plains of South Vietnam, and the dedication of the people who embraced the concept of their own independence in the context of a Marxist-Leninist government. In the end, the Vietnamese communists were willing to fight and to die for as long as required to achieve their once seemingly improbable goal.

For the United States, the very foundation of its bright and shining torch of freedom had been tarnished amid the long downward spiral in which the flower of a generation was committed. Vietnam, as far as the US government was concerned, was the line in

the sand against the spread of communism throughout Southeast Asia and perhaps elsewhere around the globe. Guided by the principle of the Domino Theory, the country's march of folly engulfed its people at home and abroad. And then, irretrievably, the nation wallowed in the wake of a war lost along with its veneer of invincibility and idealism.

In the depths of the Cold War, the turbulence of Vietnam brought the contending super powers into conflict, the United States backing a rigid and often corrupt South Vietnamese government that was solidly anti-communist while the Soviet Union and the neighbouring People's Republic of China funnelled supplies, weapons, and ammunition into the hands of the North Vietnamese and Viet Cong. All the while, one of the costliest conflicts in human history wore on, its ghastly toll reaching a shocking crescendo with millions of military and civilian dead or maimed. Other countries of Southeast Asia, Cambodia, and Laos, were also brought into a widening war, suffering as well.

Across the decades, the Vietnam war continues to fascinate and horrify, to amaze and to dismay. Its history is one of lost opportunity, of clashing visions of world order, and of tremendous cost in lives and treasure. A thorough exploration of its impact almost defies the attempt. Still, from the halls of power to the rice paddies and jungles, the embattled skies, and the villages in flames, the spectre of the conflict begs for analysis.

Welcome to *Vietnam: The Long Journey*. Step into this survey, assessment, and consideration of the conflict that continues to shape the modern geopolitical landscape even to this day.

ABOVE: Soldiers of the US 27th Infantry Regiment, 25th Infantry Division, cross a small stream during a patrol near Fire Base Kien, August 21, 1970. (NARA photo 111-CCV-613-CC73170 by SP4 Peter Finnegan via Wikimedia Commons)

ABOVE: Smoke billows from fires after an attack by Viet Cong guerrillas in the South Vietnamese capital of Saigon, February 1968. (National Archives and Records Administration via Wikimedia Commons)

MAIN COVER IMAGE: Operation Oregon, Vietnam, April 24, 1967. (DPA Picture Alliance/Alamy Stock Photo)

CONTENTS

ABOVE: Notre Dame Cathedral of Saigon bears silent witness to the influence of France and Roman Catholicism during the colonial era of Vietnam. (Haut commissariat de France pour l'Indochine via Wikimedia Commons)

ABOVE: Ho Chi Minh (right) stands with his brilliant communist associate and military leader Vo Nguyen Giap in 1945. (Executive Office of the President of the United States via Wikimedia Commons)

ABOVE: Captured by US Army troops in 1967, a terrified Viet Cong guerrilla sits blindfolded awaiting interrogation. (PFC David Epstein US Army via Wikimedia Commons)

ABOVE: Private First Class Robert Chale, Headquarters Company, 1st Battalion, 327th Infantry Regiment, 101st Airborne Division, reflects the stress of an all-night patrol on return to base at Tuy Hon, South Vietnam. (Photo by SFC Peter P. Ruplenas, US Army Sp Photo Det, Pacific via Wikimedia Commons)

ABOVE: South Vietnamese soldiers man a defensive position during fighting in a South Vietnamese street.
(National Archives and Records Administration via Wikimedia Commons)

ABOVE: US and Vietnamese sailors manipulate a fire hose during the visit of the guided missile destroyer USS John S. McCain to Vietnam in 2014. (US Navy via Wikimedia Commons)

ISBN: 978 1 80282 981 5
Editor: Mike Haskew
Senior editor, specials: Roger Mortimer
Email: roger.mortimer@keypublishing.com
Cover Design: Steve Donovan
Design: SJmagic DESIGN SERVICES, India
Advertising Sales Manager: Sam Clark
Email: sam.clark@keypublishing.com
Tel: 01780 755131
Advertising Production: Becky Antoniades
Email: Rebecca.antoniades@keypublishing.com

SUBSCRIPTION/MAIL ORDER
Key Publishing Ltd, PO Box 300, Stamford, Lincs, PE9 1NA
Tel: 01780 480404
Subscriptions email: subs@keypublishing.com
Mail Order email: orders@keypublishing.com
Website: www.keypublishing.com/shop

PUBLISHING
Group CEO and Publisher: Adrian Cox

Published by
Key Publishing Ltd, PO Box 100, Stamford, Lincs, PE9 1XQ
Tel: 01780 755131
Website: www.keypublishing.com

PRINTING
Precision Colour Printing Ltd, Haldane, Halesfield 1, Telford, Shropshire. TF7 4QQ

DISTRIBUTION
Seymour Distribution Ltd, 2 Poultry Avenue, London, EC1A 9PU
Enquiries Line: 02074 294000.

FRENCH COLONIAL ERA

The independent countries of Vietnam, the Laotian Kingdom, and the Khmer Empire, collectively known as Indochina, existed well before the coming of European influence in Southeast Asia. Hundreds of years of rule by China, the colossus to the north, had finally been overthrown in Vietnam, and the territories of Cochinchina to the south, central Annam, and northern Tonkin had been historically linked together.

The first Frenchmen to venture to China, perhaps as early as the mid-17th century, were Roman Catholic missionaries intent on spreading the Christian gospel and converting the indigenous peoples to their faith. Inevitably, during this era known for exploration, territorial expansion, and European colonisation around the world, there were merchants and business people who sought to exploit the resources of these new lands, open their ports to trade, and in turn reap huge profits from the raw materials, exotic wares, rubber, tea, rice, and even manpower made available. The French government also sought to strategically establish a diplomatic and military presence in Southeast Asia, enhancing its status among the nations of imperial Europe.

Life in the villages of Vietnam was generally peaceful, although there was a tradition of willingness to take up arms against foreigners bent on domination and the occupation of their lands. A succession of emperors had ruled the country, but often only as figureheads as real authority resided with the individual villagers, their leaders chosen based on their own merit.

Although their primary religion was Buddhism, the Vietnamese usually welcomed the French missionaries, who moved north and south and into the interior of the country. Representatives of the French East India Company, a quasi-governmental enterprise established in France to compete with English and Dutch economic interests in the East Indies, promoted Catholicism while simultaneously establishing a flourishing trade with the indigenous people, exchanging technical expertise, modern weapons, and finished goods for available resources.

For the next 350 years, French influence steadily increased in Indochina. The domination of Southeast Asia did not occur overnight, but gradually, as the French military, administrative personnel, and religious officials arrived in ever-increasing numbers. They took tremendous pride in exporting their own 'civilization' to peoples perceived as backward. Vietnamese children were taught the French language, and they learned to read and write. They

ABOVE: French soldiers stationed in Indochina during the colonial era pause for a photograph.
(Creative Commons G. Garitan via Wikimedia Commons)

were educated with the same curricula taught to children in France, while the most gifted youths were given opportunities to attend universities established in the region or even to travel to France to further their education. However, when unrest periodically emerged the long shadow of the French Army fell across the event. If French nationals were killed, revenge was swift and brutal. If fighting broke out between rival Vietnamese factions, the French intervened, backing the group that was likely to further their own interests.

Gradually but inexorably, French territorial control expanded. French bureaucrats and political functionaries replaced local Vietnamese officials. By the early 20th century, approximately 5,000 French representatives occupied virtually all of the meaningful leadership offices in French Indochina, which had grown to include all of Vietnam, Laos, and Cambodia. They brought the Napoleonic Code, their European system of law, to Indochina, and the cities even took on a

ABOVE: Well-dressed French women toss coins among an eager group of Vietnamese children in 1901.
(Gabriel Veyre via Wikimedia Commons)

resemblance to the great metropolises of the homeland with crowded open-air cafes and wide tree-lined boulevards.

FRENCH INFRASTRUCTURE

The French were builders, and they brought modern infrastructure to Vietnam. An impressive rail line ran the length of the country from the capital of Hanoi in the north to the bustling population centre of Saigon in the south. Roads, bridges, gleaming buildings, and thriving markets were outwardly symbolic of French ingenuity, national pride, and benevolence.

Nevertheless, there were those whose nationalistic fervour could never be completely pacified. And when patriotism manifested itself in civil unrest, retribution was swift. At the same time, French economic investment had risen steadily, even to the point that deficit spending supported the continued influx of French wealth to Vietnam. By the 1890s, the government in Paris had decided to right size the imbalance. The tool it sanctioned for the purpose was opium, reminiscent of the control exerted by Europeans over contemporary China after the two disastrous Opium Wars of the mid-19th century had crippled that nation's ability to resist European exploitation.

When opium use became widespread among the people of Indochina, the French levied a substantial tax on its consumption to raise revenue. They also taxed such staples as salt and wine. In the event, those subsistence farmers or small business owners who were unable to pay these high taxes suffered the loss of their property and

ABOVE: French administrators and other officials pose for a portrait at a school in Hue, June 1912.
(Les Annales coloniales 1913-06-03 via Wikimedia Commons)

ABOVE: This image of the Boulevard Francis Garnier in Hanoi, taken in 1931, is indicative of French influence in the cities of Vietnam. (Creative Commons Maurice Lambert (1910 - 2004), titulaire du droit moral des photographies via Wikimedia Commons)

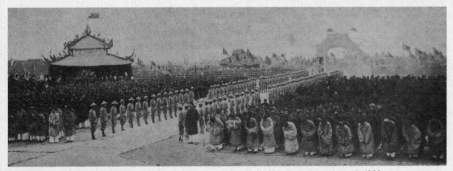

ABOVE: Puppet Emperor Bao Dai completes a pilgrimage to the tomb of his dynastic ancestors in 1932.
(Creative Commons VARCHIV author unknown via Wikimedia Commons)

repercussions. In the mid-19th century, figurehead Emperor Tu-Duc had attempted to eradicate Christianity in his nominal realm, but the government of Emperor Napoleon III had responded by sending large numbers of French soldiers into the south of Vietnam, landing in the vast delta of the Mekong River, and pressing on to Saigon.

In 1883, resistance to French rule boiled over in the north, and Admiral Amédée Courbet led a fleet of French warships that bombarded fortresses occupied by the Black Flag Army of Liu Yongfu at the mouth of the Perfume River near the provincial capital of Hue, resulting in heavy loss of life. The episode was indicative of the strife that occurred during the so-called Tonkin Campaign, which persisted into 1886. The treaty that France foisted on the Vietnamese included significant territorial concessions and such French expansion sparked another brief war with China. The Sino-French War of 1884-1885 ended once again with negotiations favourable to the Europeans.

During this period of unrest, reports of French cruelty, the execution of rebel wounded and prisoners, and men pressed into forced labour, circulated widely. For the next half century, the French military presence in Indochina was significant, marked by the introduction of Foreign Legion soldiers and troops from the country's colonial possessions in North Africa. Continual French repression kept the flame of Vietnamese nationalism alive, and various movements ebbed and flowed across the region. Civil strife was always simmering just below the surface of society.

THE CREEP OF COMMUNISM

Numerous resistance cells were linked to Marxist-Communist political thought. Ironically, European education and opportunities for travel had exposed many young Vietnamese men to these political ideals. One such individual, born Nguyen Sinh Cung, in May 1890, would emerge as a skilled and formidable opposition leader with the sobriquet Ho Chi Minh, translating literally into English as "He Who Enlightens."

With the fall of France to the Nazis in the spring of 1940, Imperial Japan seized the opportunity to occupy areas of Indochina. The puppet government of Vichy France acquiesced to the Japanese expansion that later included all of Vietnam, cooperating with the Axis throughout its existence during the World War Two years. Meanwhile, the League for the Independence of Vietnam (Viet Nam Doc Lap Dong Minh Hoi) was formed under Ho's leadership in 1941, its name popularly shortened to Viet Minh.

homes. The French government, in turn, confiscated these lands and leased them to the former owners for cultivation on behalf of the regime. French Indochina became a leading global exporter of rice, but the producers were rarely paid a living wage. Naturally, such hardship nurtured resentment of the Europeans and fuelled an armed resistance to the French ruling class in Indochina throughout the colonial period.

Armed resistance to French rule flashed into open rebellion from time to time, and in each case the French military responded with an iron fist. Persecution of Catholic missionaries also erupted, and the murders or beatings of French citizens prompted ruthless

ABOVE: The French built the presidential palace in Hanoi to house the governor-general of Indochina.
(Creative Commons Jorge Lascar via Wikimedia Commons)

The Viet Minh saw opportunity in the fragility of the Vichy government, whose officials the Japanese had maintained in office during their occupation of Indochina. Vichy forces brutally suppressed the nationalistic movement. Prisoners were shot, dissidents imprisoned, and one unfortunate group of captives was observed tied together with lengths of wire piercing the palms of their hands. The Viet Minh fought both the Vichy French and the Japanese, and with the end of World War Two in the Pacific they proclaimed the independence of Vietnam.

Prior to their evacuation and/or surrender in Southeast Asia, the Japanese had toppled the Vichy regime and installed a puppet government under Emperor Bao Dai. However, moving with alacrity, Viet Minh troops under Vo Nguyen Giap seized Hanoi and issued their own proclamation of Vietnamese independence. Negotiations among the Allied powers at Potsdam in early 1945 had specified that the Chinese Nationalists under Chiang Kai-shek would take the surrender of the Japanese in the north. Often, though, the Japanese surrendered to the Giap and the Viet Minh. By the summer of 1945, the Viet Minh controlled six provinces of northern Vietnam and were on the verge of 'liberating' four more.

Still, the newly-established postwar government in Paris, led by Charles de Gaulle, intended to exert dominion over its colonies in Southeast Asia once again. With support from Great Britain, the French proceeded. American policy was initially against the return of colonial rule to Vietnam; however, US perspective was altered within months as concern over the spread of communism trumped more altruistic attitudes toward ending European colonialism in the Far East.

HAIPHONG INCIDENT

Although significant inroads had been made, the Viet Minh faced rival factions, particularly in the south. At the same time, British troops under Major General Douglas Gracey, including the 22,000-strong 20th Indian Division, assumed control of southern Vietnam, taking remaining Japanese troops into custody, extinguishing the Vietnamese uprising in the region, and soon returning control there to the French. As US policy

supported the reintroduction of French government in Indochina, the French struck a deal with Ho Chi Minh in the spring of 1946 that appeared to possibly ensure lasting peace. The withdrawal of the French and Chinese from Vietnam was underway that autumn, but the so-called 'Haiphong Incident' caused the agreement to crumble.

On November 23, 1946, the French seized a Chinese junk allegedly carrying contraband. Although the event was innocuous enough, Vietnamese troops fired on the French and killed 23 soldiers. A French burial party was later ambushed by Vietnamese nationalists, and six more men were killed. Violence raged across the area, and the French cruiser *Suffren* led a fierce bombardment of the Vietnamese port of Haiphong, killing an estimated 6,000 nationalist troops and civilians.

Unfortunately, cooler heads did not prevail, and soon lasting peace was

Thông-Chê đã nói : Đại-Pháp khắng khít với thái bình, như dân quê với đất ruộng.

ABOVE: This French propaganda poster linking France to dynastic Vietnamese rule was produced during World War Two.
(Probably the government of French Indochina via Wikimedia Commons)

ABOVE: French troops salute their Tricolore during the occupation of Trat, a town on the border of Siam with Cambodia, in 1904.
(Le Petit Journal - N° (Quatrième de couverture) du 26 Février 1905)

irretrievable. General Jean Étienne Valluy, commander of French forces in Indochina, received a terse message from the high command in Paris. It read: "It appears clear that we are up against premeditated aggressions carefully staged by the Vietnamese regular army ... The moment has come to give a severe lesson to those who have treacherously attacked you. Use all the means at your disposal to make yourself complete master of Haiphong."

The Haiphong Incident is generally considered the opening clash of the modern war for Vietnamese independence. Although some historians prefer to divide the conflict into two phases, the first involving the French and the second primarily the United States along with anti-communist Vietnamese forces, others consider the ensuing years a protracted period of warfare, paused briefly, but spanning approximately 30 years.

ABOVE: During a 19th century uprising against colonial rule, French forces capture a fort occupied by Vietnamese nationalists. (Musée national de la Marine via Wikimedia Commons)

HO CHI MINH

From humble beginnings, Ho Chi Minh grew to be larger than life, the champion of a relentless movement and the father of a Vietnam united at last as one nation rapt in the rhetoric and promise of idyllic communist philosophy.

Born Nguyen Sinh Cung in the village of Kim Lien on May 19, 1890, he was the son of Nguyen Sinh Huy, a local magistrate in the coastal Binh Khe district. His mother was Hoang Thi Loan, the daughter of a teacher who had made Nguyen Sinh Huy his adopted son. Life was difficult, and the boy's father was said to have been demoted from his lower-level civil position after a landlord he had ordered punished was beaten to death.

The boy overcame the wretchedness of his early existence and journeyed around the world. He later became an ardent Vietnamese nationalist and embraced Marxist philosophy, meanwhile taking the name of Ho Chi Minh, "He Who Enlightens," and promulgating the innovative amalgam of communism and nationalism to win the decades-long battle for Vietnamese independence. In doing so, his will and magnetic persona drew the people to him as their leader, their 'Uncle Ho', the father figure who embodied these lustrous ideals.

Ho Chi Minh did not live to see Vietnam thoroughly independent. He died at the age of 79 on September 2, 1969, five years prior to the final military victory. However, even in death he was the prime mover in the revolution that first stood firm against the French and then wore the mighty American nation down, compelling its withdrawal.

Although details of his early years are somewhat nebulous, it is known that Huy attended primary school in the city of Hue, once the nation's capital and seat of the powerful Nguyen dynasty, in central Vietnam. He later taught school at Phan Thiet and then became a technical school apprentice in Saigon. By 1911, he apparently had become disenchanted with such a life and boarded a steamer under the assumed name of Ba, after taking a job as a cook. He travelled extensively, visiting Africa, Europe, and the United States, before settling in London during World War One and then moving on to France, where he did odd jobs and became acquainted with the socialist community.

Again changing his name, this time to Nguyen Ai Quoc, "Nguyen the Patriot," he became the leader of a group of expatriate Vietnamese and found the courage to formulate a petition of eight points to present to the delegates at Versailles, then negotiating the terms of the treaty that ended the Great War. The petition urged the delegates to require the French government to bestow on its Vietnamese subjects the same rights as citizens of France. Although there was no formal response, a political career was born.

SOVIET INFLUENCE

The French Socialist Party fractured in 1920, the left-wing communists striking out on their own, and with them went Nguyen the Patriot, enthralled with the success of the 1917 Russian Revolution. He travelled to Moscow in 1923 and attended the Fifth Congress of the Communist International, or Comintern. A year later, under the pseudonym of Ly Thuy, the passionate revolutionary travelled to Canton, China, where he met with other communists – some of whom had been exiled from Vietnam for their activities. He soon became their leader, and the Viet Nam Thanh Nien Cach Menh Dong Chi Hoi, "Vietnamese Revolutionary Youth Association," was organized.

The nationalist government of Generalissimo Chiang Kai-shek expelled the Vietnamese communists from China in 1927, and while his associates went into hiding there, young Ho spent the next two years in the Soviet Union and then travelling from Belgium to France and then Siam as a representative of the Comintern. By the spring of 1929, the expatriate communists were reunited in Hong Kong, and on February 3, 1930, the company proclaimed the founding of the Indochinese Communist Party (PCI).

ABOVE: Ho Chi Minh was the pragmatic and inspirational leader of the Vietnamese communist and nationalist revolution. (Creative Commons Dutch National Archives via Wikimedia Commons)

During the early days of the party, Ho was a steadying and pragmatic influence. He was careful not to offend the paternalistic government of the Soviet Union. He was aware of the obstacles that would be confronted, and he understood that internal strife and factionalism were counterproductive. Therefore, he proved adept at mediation and sustaining singular purpose. He maintained contact with the Soviets and attended the Seventh Congress of the Communist International in Moscow in 1935, later temporarily moderating the anti-colonial stance of the PCI as the political landscape dictated.

With the coming of World War Two, the communists envisioned a great opportunity. Formally adopting the name Ho Chi Minh, their leader crossed the border from China into Vietnam along with associates Vo Nguyen Giap and Pham Van Dong, ready to advance their cause in their homeland. Eight ardent communist-nationalists, Ho, Giap, and Dong at their head, founded the Viet Nam Doc Lap Dong Minh Hoi (League for the Independence of Vietnam), better known as the Viet Minh, and emphasised their nationalistic goal. However, even as Ho sought aid from China, Chiang felt threatened by the communist

ABOVE: Ho Chi Minh greets a group of Vietnamese children in 1950. (Musée Annam via Wikimedia Commons)

ABOVE: Ho Chi Minh and communist associates exit a meeting sometime prior to 1969.
(Creative Commons Phuongminhminh via Wikimedia Commons)

leader and had him arrested. After 18 months in prison, Ho was released when friends made a clandestine arrangement with a warlord in southern China.

JAPANESE OCCUPATION

Meanwhile, Japanese forces had occupied French Indochina. When the fortunes of war turned against them, the Japanese removed officials of the Vichy government previously allowed to remain in their offices. When the Japanese were finally defeated, it appeared that two great obstacles to Vietnamese independence – the French and the Japanese – had been removed. Ho had already contacted the United States government and worked in concert with its Office of Strategic Services (OSS), the forerunner of the modern Central Intelligence Agency (CIA), against the Japanese.

On August 19, 1945, with Viet Minh soldiers in control of Hanoi, Ho proclaimed an independent Vietnam, his announcement conjuring comparisons to the American Declaration of Independence. "All men are born equal: the Creator has given us inviolable rights, life, liberty, and happiness… The whole Vietnamese people, animated by a common purpose, are determined to fight against any attempt by the French colonialists to reconquer their country…."

Nevertheless, what Ho and his cohorts had thus far achieved was in danger of being bargained away at the negotiating table. At Potsdam, Allied leaders had agreed that Chiang's Chinese troops would take the surrender of the Japanese and occupy Vietnam north of the 16th parallel. In the south, the French returned in force, General Jacques Leclerc leading a strong contingent of troops and tanks representing the government of Charles de Gaulle.

Facing overwhelming odds, Ho chose negotiations over renewed fighting. Months of diplomatic wrangling finally led to an agreement that would allow Vietnam, having made concessions of its own, to hold the status of a free state within the French Union. A second agreement was concluded in the spring of 1946, but the tenuous peace was broken

ABOVE: Ho Chi Minh stands third from left with agents of the US Office of Strategic Services in the Vietnamese jungle, 1945. (US Army via Wikimedia Commons)

when violence erupted during the French withdrawal from the port city of Haiphong. Thousands of Vietnamese were killed, and even Ho could not prevent the coming of war.

The Viet Minh waged a guerrilla war with the French and the weak government of puppet Emperor Bao Dai for nearly eight years, controlling much of the countryside through intimidation and terror tactics until they won the decisive victory over the Europeans at Dien Bien Phu in the spring of 1954.

After Dien Bien Phu, the French and Vietnamese negotiated the Geneva Accords, which divided Vietnam at the 17th parallel, the communist North and the South under Bao Dai. Ho was represented by Pham Van Dong at the peace talks, but his influence is apparent in the outcome. Reunification was to take place in 1956, the succeeding government to be determined by the outcome of free elections. However, the United States and the government of the newly-created and ostensibly democratic South Vietnam subsequently opposed the elections. As tensions grew, Ho sought continuing economic assistance from both the Soviet Union and the People's Republic of China, whose relationship was adversarial at the time. Ho skilfully maintained good relations with both and obtained tremendous economic and military aid from them.

VIET CONG

By 1959, a growing insurgency known as the National Liberation Front of South Vietnam, better known as the Viet Cong, was prosecuting a guerrilla war below the 17th parallel. A number of Viet Cong leaders were former Viet Minh fighters, and their appeal to North Vietnam for support did not fall on deaf ears. That summer, the central committee of the North Vietnamese Communist Party approved a resolution that effectively combined the establishment of communism in North Vietnam with the objective of full national unification, guaranteeing military support for

the Viet Cong. The third Party Congress in Hanoi later endorsed the political stance.

As this Party Congress concluded, Ho handed responsibilities of secretary-general to his close associate Le Duan, although he retained the title of President. He still wielded tremendous influence over the government amid the growing US support for South Vietnam. Although American military advisors had been on the ground in the South for some years, the US military presence steadily increased in the mid-1960s. Devastating air strikes began in 1965 and gradually intensified.

In ill health, Ho rallied his people in the summer of 1967 with the statement that became their motto in the long struggle against the South Vietnamese Army, its Saigon-based leaders, and their US benefactors. "Nothing," he declared, "is as dear to the heart of the Vietnamese as independence and liberation."

ABOVE: With his close associate Pham Van Dong seated at right, Ho Chi Minh watches a football game in 1958. (Vietnam National Museum of History via Wikimedia Commons)

ABOVE: This portrait of Ho Chi Minh was taken in 1946 as he asserted authority in the effort to unify Vietnam under communist rule. (Unknown Author via Wikimedia Commons)

DIEN BIEN PHU

The French had trained troops, tanks, aircraft, and big guns. Both Ho Chi Minh and his trusted senior military commander, General Vo Nguyen Giap, knew the odds were long when they embarked on a war against their European oppressor that intended to reassert control of Indochina in the post-World War Two era.

However, Ho and Giap also recognised a blueprint that might lead to eventual victory. In China, the communists under Mao Tse-tung had waged a lengthy guerrilla war and at last defeated the nationalists under Chiang Kai-shek in 1949. Mao's forces had achieved their lofty goal through guerrilla tactics. They had won the support of the people throughout the countryside, skilfully using hit-and-run tactics to keep their enemy off-balance, striking swiftly with great force and then melting away, and they had exercised extreme patience with a long view to triumph.

Perhaps the Viet Minh might do the same to the French. True enough, the Viet Minh enjoyed popular support across rural areas of Vietnam and neighbouring Laos. French power was concentrated in population centres. Despite their military might, though, the French could not bring the communists to engage in a decisive major battle where their superior firepower might quash the insurgency for good. A succession of French generals had tried and been frustrated in the attempt.

Two of these, Philippe Leclerc de Hauteclocque and Jean de Lattre de Tassigny, were heroes of World War Two. Leclerc had actually brokered a deal with the Viet Minh but received little support for a negotiated peace. In fact, he had been derided by Admiral Georges Thierry d'Argenlieu, French high

BELOW: Viet Minh troops plant their flag atop the French headquarters at Dien Bien Phu on May 7, 1954. (Vietnam People's Army via Wikimedia Commons)

commissioner for Indochina, who chided, "I am amazed – yes, that is the word, amazed, that France's fine expeditionary corps in Indochina is commanded by officers who would rather negotiate than fight." Leclerc was killed in a plane crash in 1947, and with him died the last real hope of a diplomatic solution in Indochina.

De Lattre had brough new resolution to the French cause, actually defeating the Viet Minh in battles at Vinh Yen and Mao Khe in early 1951. He was appointed high commissioner and commander-in-chief of the French Far East Expeditionary Corps later in the year, but his heart was broken when his son was killed at the Battle of the Day River in May. Poor health forced de Lattre to return to France for treatment, and he died of cancer within the year. Although he had won on the battlefield, the victories were not enough. Ho and Giap learned their lesson and redoubled their efforts in guerrilla war. After de Lattre, the long French spiral toward defeat began.

ABOVE: Colonel Christian de Castries was the commander of the ill-fated French garrison at Dien Bien Phu. (US Army via Wikimedia Commons)

THE HEDGEHOG

In the spring of 1953, General Henri Navarre was appointed French military commander in Indochina. Navarre sought a new tactic and heeded the advice of Colonel Louis Berteil, commander of Mobile Group 7 and chief of planning. Berteil offered a 'hedgehog' strategy. Since the Viet Minh had ventured into Laos to protect their supply lines, the true vulnerability of the communists was in their rear areas. Berteil suggested the establishment of several forward military bases, or air-heads, defensible in themselves and capable of supporting offensive thrusts to sever the Viet Minh supply lines in Laos as well as deny them complete mastery of the countryside.

Navarre agreed and likened the proposed Operation Castor to an inkblot. French troops would establish these bases and then leach into the rural areas to fight the communists in their own backyard. The first of these bases would

ABOVE: This aerial view of the Nam Yum River Valley reveals some of the terrain that was difficult for the French to defend at Dien Bien Phu. (TTXVN via Wikimedia Commons)

ABOVE: Viet Minh labourers carry supplies on their backs to the battlefield at Dien Bien Phu. (TTXVN via Wikimedia Commons)

ABOVE: Viet Minh soldiers, willing to accept heavy casualties, charge a French strongpoint at Dien Bien Phu in the spring of 1954. (TTXVN via Wikimedia Commons)

be established in the extreme northwest of Indochina in Lai Chau Province at Dien Bien Phu, where an abandoned Japanese airstrip constructed during World War Two would facilitate operations.

The plan was daring, and Dien Bien Phu presented obvious defensive weaknesses. The distance would require the insertion of troops by air, parachute, and transport aircraft. Supply would be effected the same way. The position was located in the valley of the River Nam Yum, which stretched 10 miles and was surrounded by high ground. When Navarre revealed the location for Operation Castor, most of his officers were aghast. But Navarre was insistent, and on November 20, 1953, the first elite French airborne units, 9,000 strong, were inserted at Dien Bien Phu. Before the French ordeal was over, the defenders' numbers swelled to 16,000 airborne, Foreign Legion, Colonial, and loyal Vietnamese soldiers.

Meanwhile, Giap watched with interest. While the French improved the airstrip and built a series of strongpoints named Gabrielle, Beatrice, and Anne-Marie in the north, Claudine and Huguette to the west, Dominique and Eliane in the east, and Isabelle to the south, their commander, Colonel Christian de Castries, failed to occupy the surrounding heights, a mistake he came to rue. Giap later observed that Dien Bien Phu was a rice bowl with the French at the bottom and his Viet Minh around the rim.

Giap welcomed the gift of the high ground and patiently assembled five Viet Minh divisions, 50,000 men, whose early task was to dig trenches – ever closer and eventually encircling the French strongpoints. At the same time, Viet Minh fighters and civilian labourers painstakingly hauled 200 big guns, piece by piece, up the mountainsides. Some of these were 105mm howitzers capable of devastating plunging fire. Anti-aircraft guns were emplaced as well, intentioned to make the skies around the airstrip so hot that French planes could not land. Many of the guns were secreted in deep bunkers or revetments that made them virtually impervious to French counterbattery fire.

When the first Viet Minh artillery shells began to fall on Dien Bien Phu, it was readily apparent that the French had underestimated the resolve of the guerrillas. Soviet-made Katyusha rockets whined toward targets,

and flak peppered low-flying French aircraft causing a suspension of such flights and rendering the airstrip unusable. Soon enough, resupply efforts were made by planes flying so high that their drops were inaccurate and more French succour landed with the Viet Minh than with its intended recipients.

French casualties mounted steadily, outstripping the capacity of medical personnel to care for the wounded, and artillery commander Colonel Charles Piroth became distraught. "I am responsible! I am responsible!" he wailed before committing suicide with a hand grenade.

On March 13, Giap unleashed his ground troops on Beatrice. The 141st and 209th Regiments of the Viet Minh 132nd Division fought the 13th Battalion, 13th Foreign Legion Demi-Brigade for seven hours until Beatrice was in communist hands. The French suffered 350 casualties, while the attackers lost 600 killed and 1,200 wounded. But Viet Minh morale soared.

The next day, Viet Minh troops of the 308th Division hit Gabrielle, which was defended by an elite Algerian battalion. A counterattack by the French-led Vietnamese 5th Parachute Battalion was broken up by artillery fire, and the Algerians abandoned Gabrielle the following day. Ethnic Tai troops, some of whom deserted or changed sides in the midst of the siege, occupied Anne-Marie. The remaining defenders were evacuated on March 17.

For the next two weeks, the Viet Minh continued to pound the French with artillery fire and dig their trenches ever closer to the remaining strongpoints. By the end of March, Isabel was cut off. The French repelled assaults against Dominique, Eliane, and Huguette, but a mood of impending doom settled among Colonel de Castries and his staff officers. Giap knew that time was his ally. By May 7, 1954, all of Eliane and portions of the remaining strongpoints were overrun by the Viet Minh.

INEVITABLE

Outnumbered eight to one and with supplies dwindling and scores of wounded

languishing with inadequate medical care, de Castries contacted his commander, Major General René Cogny, in Hanoi. "The Viets are everywhere. The situation is very grave. The combat is confused and goes on all about. I feel the end is approaching, but we will fight to the finish." Cogny replied tersely, "…Of course, you have to finish the whole thing now. But what you have done until now is surely magnificent. Don't spoil it by hoisting the white flag…no surrender, no white flag."

However, the outcome at Dien Bien Phu was a fait accompli. As Viet Minh troops swarmed toward the French headquarters bunker, a soldier only 50ft away spotted a small white flag. The Viet Minh fighter stopped. He shouted, "You're not going to shoot anymore?" A French officer responded, "No. I'm not going to shoot anymore."

The humiliation of France was complete at Dien Bien Phu as 12,000 soldiers, 5,000 of them wounded, entered communist captivity, leaving 1,150 dead. The Viet Minh had suffered 8,000 killed and 15,000 wounded.

Giap had won a smashing victory.

After Dien Bien Phu, the Geneva Accords led to an agreement that was destined to fade away with years of war remaining. However, the French had no recourse but to withdraw from Vietnam, particularly after the United States declined to intervene militarily on their behalf. The last French soldier left Vietnam in 1956.

BELOW: French soldiers seek cover from devastating Viet Minh artillery fire at Dien Bien Phu. (US Army via Wikimedia Commons)

AMERICAN PERSPECTIVE

Once committed to an anti-colonial stance in the wake of World War Two, US foreign policy was altered with a burgeoning concern for consequences of a global spread of communism. Initially, the US government had been against the reestablishment of French rule in Indochina, supportive of an emerging 'Third World' movement, particularly in Africa and Asia.

In 1946, the United States granted independence to the Philippines, and in 1947 Great Britain relinquished control of India, once the proverbial 'Jewel in the Crown' of its empire. Ho Chi Minh had cooperated with the Allies during World War Two, rescuing downed pilots while working with the clandestine Office of Strategic Services in the fight against the Japanese. It seemed logical that the people of Vietnam should support a government of their own.

But then, the spectre of communism came front and centre. In China, the communists under Mao Tse-tung had won control of the vast country in 1949. In 1950, communist North Korea had invaded the democratic South. Three years later, a negotiated peace had ended the shooting during the Korean Conflict, but the tension on the peninsula was palpable. Meanwhile, the Soviet Union had detonated its first nuclear weapon in 1949; the Cold War was taking shape. And everywhere, the Soviets sponsored communist political movements that threatened the democracies of the world.

What about Southeast Asia? For all his earlier cooperation, Ho was still a communist. His nationalist movement was steeped in communist philosophy. Victory for the Viet Minh meant the establishment of another communist state, and quite probably other nations of Southeast Asia, including Laos, Cambodia, and perhaps Burma, Thailand and even India might fall to the communists as well.

COMMUNISTS!
By the mid-1950s, anti-communist rhetoric and even hysteria were gripping the United States. Senator Joseph McCarthy began a series of controversial hearings intended to identify and root communists out of the US government. Further, President Dwight D. Eisenhower delivered a speech on April 7, 1954, that described a departure from prior American foreign policy. He explained: "Finally, you have broader considerations that might follow what you would call the 'falling domino' principle. You have a row of dominoes set up, you knock over the first one, and what will happen to the last one is the certainty that it will go over very quickly. So, you could have a beginning of a disintegration that would have the most profound influences."

The so-called Domino Theory thus became a guiding principle of US foreign policy, one of containment of communism, through the 1980s as the Cold War waxed and waned. Although the Eisenhower

ABOVE: Senator Joseph McCarthy conducted controversial anti-communist hearings in the United States in the mid-1950s. (Library of Congress via Wikimedia Commons)

ABOVE: President Dwight D. Eisenhower and Secretary of State John Foster Dulles greet South Vietnamese President Ngo Dinh Diem in Washington, DC, in May 1957. (US Air Force via Wikimedia Commons)

administration had once supported independence for Vietnam, the about-face led to financial support for the French and supplies of military equipment and weapons. However, when the French faced a humiliating defeat at Dien Bien Phu, the US government declined to provide heavy air support or to introduce substantial ground troops on behalf of the beleaguered ally. In doing so, the Americans signed the death warrant of France in Indochina. The negotiated peace of the Geneva Accords allowed France to save a small measure of 'face' in the debacle.

After the French withdrew from Indochina, the United States remained as the only nation capable of contesting the global spread of communism. However, its options were limited. The government of South Vietnam was initially organised under Emperor Bao Dai and promised elections in 1956 would determine the future government of a unified Vietnam. In a short time, the virulent anti-communist Ngo Dinh Diem, was appointed minister of the interior in the South Vietnamese government. A notorious socialite and

ABOVE: Viet Minh guerrillas pose for a photograph in 1958. Many veterans of the war with France became members of the Viet Cong insurgency. (baophuyen.com via Wikimedia Commons)

ABOVE: Emperor Bao Dai was deposed by Ngo Dinh Diem, who became president of South Vietnam.
(Những bức ảnh chụp hoàng gia triều Nguyễn via Wikimedia Commons)

womaniser, Diem was Roman Catholic, educated in French schools, and committed to the defeat of Ho Chi Minh and the communists.

With US support, Diem deposed Bao Dai with a referendum and proclaimed himself President of the Republic of Vietnam on October 26, 1955. Diem refused to abide by the Geneva Accords, fearing that an election would result in a victory for the Viet Minh. He did so with US acquiescence and installed his brother, Ngo Dinh Nhu, as head of a secret police apparatus that used covert methods to repress opposition to the regime. Thousands of suspected communists were arrested in South Vietnam; opponents were silenced. Because of these brutal initiatives, Diem alienated many Vietnamese.

At the same time, Ho and the Viet Minh had hoped for a victory in the election that never took place. They were prepared to reignite hostilities if necessary. To solidify power in North Vietnam, Ho sanctioned a reign of terror against perceived enemies of the communist state. Many were executed, including landowners who were seen as capitalists, exploiting their tenant farmers. One in 20, Ho decreed, was such a villain. Death squads were sent to kill these landowners, and their land was then divided among the remaining farmers. Thousands were executed, some just on the suspicion of being disloyal.

Amid these terrible excesses both North and South, a de facto civil war erupted. The US government then found itself on the horns of a dilemma. Support for Diem carried the stigma of brutality, but there was little choice. Ho Chi Minh called his followers to action. The North Vietnamese Army was training and equipping with arms supplied by the Soviet Union and the People's Republic of China. Viet Minh veterans and young fighters loyal to Ho in the South took up arms and proclaimed themselves the National Liberation Front, better known as the Viet Cong, an insurgency dedicated to the overthrow of the Diem regime.

The Viet Cong were adept at guerrilla warfare. They came to villages across South Vietnam, sometimes in peace to assist with crops or building huts, but sometimes in ruthless rage, killing a local chief that had been appointed by Diem or terrorising the villagers into joining with them. The Diem government devised various attempts to safeguard villages from Viet Cong incursions. One of these, the Strategic Hamlet Programme, was intended to protect and separate the loyal Vietnamese from the Viet Cong. The programme received strong support from

ABOVE: Outer defences ring a South Vietnamese village which is part of the Strategic Hamlet Program in 1964.
(brotherreuse US Army via Wikimedia Commons)

the Eisenhower administration and that of his successor in 1960, President John F. Kennedy. However, the programme foundered as many villagers did not want to relocate from their existing homes. Leaders appointed by Diem were sometimes corrupt. At length, many villagers were simply not willing to cooperate, much less fight the Viet Cong.

ESCALATION

Although the true nature of the Kennedy administration's Vietnam policy will never be known – he was assassinated at age 46 on November 22, 1963 – the United States became further embroiled in Vietnam with each passing day. Kennedy's successor, Lyndon B. Johnson was eventually tasked with the decision to withdraw US support, which by that time included military advisors in country, or escalate American involvement in the conflict. Johnson chose escalation.

Days before Kennedy was assassinated, the Diem brothers had been murdered in a coup d'etat. The US government had informed South Vietnamese military leaders that no interference would occur in the event of the leaders' removal. Then, from late 1963 to mid-1965 at least seven governments rose and withered in the capital of Saigon. Nguyen Van Thieu, a participant in the coup against Diem, emerged as the leader of a military junta and then won election to the presidency of South Vietnam in 1967. He held the office until the end of the Vietnam War in 1975.

President Johnson was determined to win in Vietnam. Re-elected in 1964 amid opposition charges that he had not done enough to ensure victory, Johnson was also confronted by a growing domestic anti-war movement. Nevertheless, in order to commit more American military might, including young men to fight and die far from home, he needed a broad base of popular support. Favourable public opinion was critical to widening US involvement in Vietnam.

In early August 1964, an incident off the coast of Vietnam in the Gulf of Tonkin gave President Johnson the necessary casus belli.

ABOVE: While serving as South Vietnamese prime minister, Ngo Dinh Diem meets with army officers.
(Rufus Phillips US Army via Wikimedia Commons)

GULF OF TONKIN INCIDENT

ABOVE: In this photo taken from the deck of the destroyer USS *Maddox* on August 2, 1964, North Vietnamese torpedo boats press attacks in the Tonkin Gulf. (Official US Navy Photo via Wikimedia Commons)

By the spring of 1961, more than 500 American military advisors and special forces personnel were active in Vietnam, providing training and participating in actual combat against communist Viet Cong insurgents under the auspices of MACV-SOG (Military Assistance Command, Vietnam – Studies and Observations Group). By the end of 1962, there were 11,000 of them, and 53 American service personnel had been killed.

Both Presidents Kennedy and Johnson were keenly aware, however, that corruption and ineptitude within the South Vietnamese government, the ineffectiveness of the South Vietnamese Army, and growing support of the Viet Cong from their benefactors in the North and the peasantry across rural areas of the South were contributing to a toxic situation that might well end in defeat for the US and the fall of another country to a communist regime.

Following the coup d'etat that toppled the presidency of Ngo Dinh Diem and the assassination of Kennedy three weeks later, President Johnson inherited a vague policy toward Southeast Asia. The number of American military personnel in Vietnam had crept higher, but real commitment to victory had not materialised. Johnson and many of his political advisors saw Vietnam as a test of American resolve. Hawks in Congress favoured decisive action, and from November 1963 to the end of 1964, the number of American troops in Vietnam grew to 23,000.

Johnson watched the drifting South Vietnamese governments come and go while the communists gained the upper hand and pacification efforts in rural areas had obviously failed. Joint American and South Vietnamese military operations against the communists had thus far been conducted on a limited basis. Raids against coastal installations, bases, and infrastructure would never reach

a scope sufficient to turn the tide of the war. Soon enough, it became apparent that only a major escalation of hostilities, introducing US air power and greater numbers of ground troops to Southeast Asia, could reverse the deteriorating situation. American military

planners identified targets for air strikes, plans were readied for deployment of more ground forces. But the support of the American people was critical to such actions.

USS *MADDOX*

An unexpected development in the summer of 1964 provided the opportunity for the Johnson administration to execute its plans. American naval warships had been conducting surveillance operations off the coast of Vietnam for at least two years. Destroyers engaged in Operation DeSoto had utilised sensitive equipment to locate North Vietnamese radar sites and other installations. Often, these naval missions were in support of commando raids.

On August 2, 1964, the destroyer USS *Maddox* was engaged in such an operation in the Gulf of Tonkin. According to official reports, *Maddox* was in international waters, although it was inside the 12-mile offshore limit usually recognised. Radar indicated that three North Vietnamese P-4 torpedo boats

BELOW: The destroyer USS *Maddox* is shown underway in this photo contemporary with the Gulf of Tonkin Incident. (US Navy Photo via Wikimedia Commons)

BELOW: A North Vietnamese torpedo boat is shown under fire from the USS *Maddox* on August 2, 1964. (US Navy Photo via Wikimedia Commons)

were shadowing the destroyer with intent to attack. *Maddox* fired three warning shots, and the North Vietnamese replied with torpedoes and machine-gun fire. In the brief melee, *Maddox* was struck by a single bullet. All three torpedo boats sustained varying degrees of damage, driven off by fire from *Maddox* and planes launched from the aircraft carrier USS *Ticonderoga*. Three North Vietnamese sailors were killed and six wounded.

When President Johnson learned of the apparent attack, he responded with a public announcement that such patrols would continue and sent a second destroyer, USS *Turner Joy*, into the area. A second attack supposedly occurred on the evening of August 4, when radar aboard *Turner Joy* detected what appeared to be more North Vietnamese torpedo boats approaching. Both American destroyers opened fire, but no apparent damage was done to any vessel. Doubts as to the veracity of an actual attack quickly emerged, and years later analysis concluded that the events of August 4 had been due to American sailors mistaking the

ABOVE: A 5in main gun aboard the destroyer USS *Turner Joy* fires while at sea. (US Navy Photo via Wikimedia Commons)

ABOVE: Navy Captain John J. Herrick, commander of Destroyer Division 192, is shown aboard the USS *Maddox* on August 13, 1964. (PH3 White US Navy via Wikimedia Commons)

ABOVE: President Lyndon B. Johnson signs the Gulf of Tonkin Resolution on August 10, 1964.
(National Archives and Records Administration via Wikimedia Commons)

radar or sonar signatures of heavy waves in the Tonkin Gulf for attacking enemy craft. Radio intercepts that seemed to indicate an imminent attack were also later discounted.

Amid the confusion, the captain of the *Maddox* had sent a message reporting that his ship was "under continuous torpedo attack." However, he later clarified, "… freak weather effects on radar and overeager sonarmen may have accounted for many reports…."

In the immediate aftermath of the 'Gulf of Tonkin Incident', follow-up reports suggested that some of the US fire might indeed have been directed against a phantom enemy. Nevertheless, President Johnson seized the opportunity as a pretext to escalate American involvement in the war in Vietnam. Further evidence indicates that Secretary of Defense Robert McNamara may well have withheld the *Maddox* captain's subsequent communications from President Johnson. With the support of McNamara and National Security Advisor McGeorge Bundy, as well as other key cabinet members and military officers, Johnson ordered retaliatory airstrikes against specific targets in North Vietnam, an oil storage facility with 14 large tanks, and the 'aggressor' North Vietnamese Navy, which numbered about 50 patrol boats.

Within hours of these air strikes, Johnson delivered a televised address to the American people. "The North Vietnamese have decided to attack the US. This fact is plain for all the world to see. If we do not challenge these attacks, they will continue," he declared, presenting the incidents as unprovoked aggression. The president then went to Congress to request a joint resolution authorising the chief executive to take whatever action necessary to counter any additional threats to US forces or the country's allies in Southeast Asia.

The Gulf of Tonkin Resolution read in part: "Whereas ships from communist Vietnam broke international law and attacked US ships; Whereas these attacks are part of a plot of this communist country waging war against its neighbors; And whereas the US is helping the people of Southeast Asia to protect their freedom and live in peace… Resolve that Congress agrees with and supports the President to take all needed steps to repel any armed attack against US forces and to prevent further aggression by communist North Vietnam…."

RESOLUTION PASSED

The resolution passed the House of Representatives without a single dissenting vote, while the Senate approved overwhelmingly, by a vote of 89 to two. Interestingly, it is probable that few, if any, of the lawmakers voting in favour of the Gulf of Tonkin Resolution were aware that American military personnel were engaged in support of South Vietnamese troops in military raids against targets in the North, that there were serious doubts surrounding the accuracy of the events on August 4, or that the destroyers *Maddox* and *Turner Joy* were engaged in an intelligence-gathering mission on behalf of the South Vietnamese. Regardless, on August 7, 1964, President Johnson was handed sweeping authority to increase the American military commitment in Vietnam.

In the months that followed the Gulf of Tonkin Incident, the government of South Vietnam remained in disarray, while communist forces began to regularly attack installations where American military personnel were located. US bombing was stepped up, and by June 1965, it was apparent that more American ground troops would be needed to reverse an increasing tide of dismal battlefield performance by the South Vietnamese Army. At the request of General William Westmoreland, commander of US forces in Vietnam, President Johnson approved the deployment of 100,000 additional troops to Southeast Asia with 100,000 more to follow in 1966.

BATTLE OF IA DRANG

BELOW: American soldiers of the 1st Battalion, 7th Cavalry (Airmobile) leap from Huey helicopters at LZ X-Ray, November 14, 1965. (US Army via Wikimedia Commons)

The Battle of Ia Drang marked a new and dramatic escalation of combat operations in Vietnam. The first major clash between American troops and the soldiers of the North Vietnamese Army (People's Army of Vietnam or NVA), Ia Drang was a harbinger of heavy casualties to come and raised the curtain on strategy and tactics that characterised future battles.

Early action in the Vietnam War was limited to insurgency and counterinsurgency operations. Viet Cong guerrillas or sappers would typically use the cover of darkness to creep close to American bases and then lob mortar rounds, hand grenades, or rockets into these targets before slipping away. In response, the Americans and their South Vietnamese partners patrolled into areas surrounding bases and population centres, hunting for the guerrillas and their supporters by day.

The nip and tuck situation abruptly changed in the autumn of 1965, and the setting was the valley of the River Ia Drang in western Pleiku Province near the Cambodian border in Vietnam's Central

BELOW: Soldiers of the US 7th Cavalry Regiment (Airmobile) deploy at LZ X-Ray as Major Bruce Crandall pulls his Bell UH-1 helicopter away. (US Army via Wikimedia Commons)

Highlands. This was rough country, thick jungle occasionally broken by fields choked with elephant grass and scrub brush and dominated by the rugged Chu Pong Massif, hills and mountains strung along the Vietnam-Cambodia frontier.

North Vietnamese General Chu Huy Man ordered a bold offensive in October, aiming to overrun special forces bases at Duc Co, Dak Sut, and Plei Me and capture the city of Pleiku. In the process, the South Vietnamese district headquarters would be neutralised, and the territory of South Vietnam might eventually be cut in half.

When the North Vietnamese assault on Plei Me failed, the attacker became the pursued. The US 1st Brigade, 1st Cavalry Division hunted the NVA 32nd and 33rd

Regiments in the rural areas around Pleiku. The Americans staged from their base at An Khe, and the 1st Brigade was relieved by the 3rd Brigade in early November as efforts to bring the enemy to battle were frustrating.

When US senior officers feared that the NVA might slip away completely, Major General Harry Kinnard, commander of the 1st Cavalry Division (Airmobile), ordered a stepped up search and destroy mission. Colonel Thomas Brown of the 3rd Brigade was tasked with planning an operation south and southeast of Plei Me, where his 1st Battalion, 7th Cavalry (1/7), under Lieutenant Colonel Harold G. 'Hal' Moore, would use the recently developed airmobile tactics that defined future military operations in Vietnam.

ABOVE: Their M-16 assault rifles at the ready, American soldiers engage troops of the North Vietnamese Army at the Battle of Ia Drang. (US Army via Wikimedia Commons)

ABOVE: Lieutenant Colonel Harold G. 'Hal' Moore communicates during the battle at Ia Drang. Moore led the 1st Battalion, 7th Cavalry Regiment (Airmobile).
(US Army via Wikimedia Commons)

The North Vietnamese and Viet Cong, familiar with the countryside and its rough terrain, had not expected American and South Vietnamese forces to venture into remote areas due to a lack of roads that would facilitate mechanised ground transportation. They were surprised when Moore's 1st Battalion began arriving in the very area that had been chosen for a renewal of the offensive against the special forces base camps. The modern-day mounts of the US cavalrymen were Bell UH-1 Iroquois helicopters, nicknamed Hueys. These rotary aircraft would transport the combat troops into battle, supply them by air, and recover them along with casualties when the mission was completed.

Moore chose a series of landing zones (LZ) that could accommodate the helicopters, and the primary one was designated LZ X-Ray. Just before 11am on November 14, 1965, the first helicopters, carrying elements of Company B (Bravo), 1/7, and Moore's headquarters command group touched down at X-Ray, roughly the size of a football field, near the base of the Chu Pong Massif and with a dry creek bed running to the west. Supporting artillery of Batteries A and C, 1st Battalion, 21st Artillery was located at a point designated Falcon about five miles distant. Both accurate fire from these guns and close air support were critical in the battle that soon unfolded. In addition to tactical strikes using conventional bombs and napalm, heavy Boeing B-52 Stratofortress bombers flying from the island of Guam were employed for the first time in a tactical role.

The remainder of 1st Battalion arrived at LZ X-Ray in the afternoon after numerous 30-minute shuttle runs by the Hueys. Meanwhile, Moore sent patrols to locate enemy troops, resulting in contact during which 2nd Platoon, Bravo Company was cut off and surrounded on a low hill. Ultimately, at least three attempts were made to reach the 'lost' company before a linkup succeeded the following afternoon. Outnumbered roughly two to one, Moore decided to stand and defend LZ X-Ray. Throughout November 14, heavy fighting occurred along the creek bed and to the south of X-Ray. One NVA assault reached within 75 yards of the perimeter before it was driven back.

During the night, the communists probed the American perimeter but failed to break through. The lost platoon, its commander killed in action, fought off three attacks while led by Sergeant Ernie Savage. Reinforcements from Bravo Company, 2nd Battalion, 7th Regiment (2/7) arrived late in the afternoon, augmenting Moore's defensive positions as his command faced elements of three NVA regiments, the 32nd, 33rd, and 66th.

BROKEN ARROW

At daybreak on November 15, the NVA launched a strong attack against the sector held by Company C (Charlie), 1/7. The Americans took heavy casualties, but artillery fire decimated the attackers, and finally the NVA were driven back. Another coordinated assault, this time from three directions, was launched against LZ X-Ray just before 8am. While Charlie Company fought for survival, Moore sent available men from 2/7 to bolster their position. As enemy pressure reached a crescendo, the officer radioed "Broken Arrow," a message conveying that an American force was in danger of being overrun and asking every available aircraft over Vietnam to respond.

Air strikes killed and wounded scores of NVA troops and broke the back of the assault, but a pair of North American F-100 Super Sabre fighter-bombers were observed making runs with napalm dangerously close to the American perimeter. The first F-100 was warned away, but the second dropped its lethal cargo, inflicting some friendly-fire casualties. After the devastating air strikes, the NVA pulled back.

At approximately 4am on November 16, the first of four unsuccessful NVA assaults was repelled by the defenders of LZ X-Ray with effective artillery support. By noon the remainder of 2/7 and the 2nd Battalion, 5th Regiment (2/5) had reinforced LZ X-Ray. The NVA had observed the insertion of these troops, and a general withdrawal was ordered.

Moore's 1/7 was airlifted out of the area on the afternoon of November 16. The following day 2/5 marched to LZ Columbus, northeast of LZ X-Ray, and 2/7 was ordered to march to LZ Albany

ABOVE: Civilian reporter Joe Galloway received the Bronze Star for heroism during the Battle of Ia Drang. His is pictured in 2017 wearing the Bronze Star and 1st Cavalry Division (Airmobile) pins.
(Creative Commons Cmichel67 via Wikimedia Commons)

ABOVE: Platoon Leader Rick Rescorla, a veteran of both the British and US Armies, is shown in action at the Battle of Ia Drang. (US Army via Wikimedia Commons)

slightly further north. Although the trek of 2/5 was completed without major enemy contact, 2/7 was ambushed by elements of the 33rd and 66th NVA Regiments. In the vicious firefight that ensued, 155 US soldiers were killed and 124 wounded before reinforcements and air strikes compelled the communists to retire. The fighting ended on November 18 as the NVA disengaged.

Total casualty figures for the Ia Drang battle remain murky. American losses at LZ X-Ray are generally counted as 80 dead and 124 wounded. Total US casualties were approximately 235 killed and 250 wounded. North Vietnamese casualties were estimated at 1,200 dead and many more wounded.

Both sides claimed victory at Ia Drang, and while future US tactical operations would feature airmobile insertions along with strong artillery and air support, the NVA adapted. Communist officers would subsequently order their troops to maintain close contact with the Americans during battle, hoping to negate the superior firepower since their opponents would be concerned with inflicting casualties on their own troops.

Lieutenant Colonel Moore received the Distinguished Service Cross for his battlefield command at Ia Drang, while Joe Galloway, a journalist for United Press International, received the Bronze Star for assisting with the evacuation of wounded under fire. Galloway received the medal in 1998 and was the only civilian awarded the Bronze Star for combat gallantry in the Vietnam war. Moore and Galloway collaborated on the 1992 book *We Were Soldiers Once…and Young*, which became a major motion picture a decade later, starring Mel Gibson as Moore and Barry Pepper as Galloway.

Sergeant Savage also received the Distinguished Service Cross and Second Lieutenant Walter Marm received the Medal of Honor for courageously leading Company A, 1/7 while severely wounded. Huey pilots Major Bruce Crandall and Captain Ed Freeman also received the Medal of Honor for a combined 36 flights to extract casualties after medical evacuation helicopters had been driven off by enemy fire. Freeman received his medal in 2001, and Crandall in 2007.

THE VIET CONG

The tenuous terms of the Geneva Accords of 1954 proved fertile ground for a nascent armed opposition to the rule of the government of President Ngo Dinh Diem in South Vietnam, and logically its supporting superpower, the United States.

Embracing nationalist fervour and communist ideology, the self-proclaimed National Liberation Front of South Vietnam (NLF), took shape during the late 1950s and was formally organised in December 1960. Developed from a loose coalition of varied resistance groups into a highly trained military guerrilla force, the NLF proved a formidable adversary during the course of the Vietnam conflict. In keeping with the provisions of the Geneva Accords, Vietnamese military personnel were directed to return to their homes in either North or South Vietnam, then officially divided at the 17th parallel.

However, a relative few of these paramilitary personnel complied. Veterans of the Viet Minh who had fought the French, younger recruits, and communist-nationalist sympathisers often chose to remain underground in South Vietnam, either due to personal preference or at the behest of the North Vietnamese government. Their purpose was direct – to interfere with the establishment of a stable government in the South, conduct clandestine hit-and-run raids, build further allegiance to their cause among the people, and sow the threat of intimidation against any opposition.

The cohesion of multiple resistance groups in South Vietnam was engineered by Le Duan, a founding member of the Vietnamese Communist Party, veteran of the World War Two fight against the Japanese,

BELOW: South Vietnamese soldiers capture a Viet Cong guerrilla during operations in 1964. (US Army via Wikimedia Commons)

ABOVE: A Viet Cong guerrilla armed with a Soviet-made SKS assault rifle crouches in a tunnel prior to an offensive operation. (US Army via Wikimedia Commons)

and the defeat of the French. A native of Quang Tri Province in central Vietnam, he had been imprisoned in the 1930s but risen steadily in the party hierarchy. By the late 1950s, he was a member of the North Vietnamese Politburo and wielded considerable influence on the course of events. He authored a treatise titled *The Road to the South*, a blueprint for the unification of Vietnam under communist rule advocating

the overthrow of the Diem regime and the expulsion of foreign influence.

In 1956, Le was charged with directing the revolutionary activities in the South. However, his call for an immediate guerrilla war with the full support of the North Vietnamese Army (NVA) was postponed in favour of a limited insurgency while the communist government in Hanoi tended to economic reforms, military reorganisation, and its own consolidation of power. Instead, a restricted guerrilla campaign was authorised in anticipation of a concerted effort to overthrow the South Vietnamese government beginning in 1959.

Le Duan took the length of rope he was given and initiated limited violence in South Vietnam as early as mid-1957. A campaign of terror emerged with as many as 150 local leaders, teachers, and intelligentsia, branded as traitors to the cause, assassinated just in that year. In July, NLF guerrillas gunned down 17 people in a lightning attack on a bar at Chao Doc, and just weeks later the NLF murdered a local police chief and his entire family along a highway in broad daylight. When they ventured into the cities of South Vietnam, guerrillas spied, spread rumours of phantom attacks to come, and planted bombs in cafés and bars, killing and maiming many. Thirteen Americans were wounded in a series of bombings in Saigon, the South Vietnamese capital, in October.

The NLF insurgency soon became known as the Viet Cong, a shortened version of the phrase 'Vietnamese Communists'. The origin

ABOVE: A female Viet Cong guerrilla takes up a defensive position alongside her comrades. (Bộ Quốc phòng via Wikimedia Commons)

ABOVE: US Marines retrieve a Viet Cong signal drum in Quang Tri Province during operations in 1967. (Official USMC photo by Corporal A. C. Ferreira from the Jonathan F. Abel Collection (COLL/3611) at the Archives Branch, Marine Corps History Division via Wikimedia Commons)

BELOW: American soldiers stand with a blindfolded Viet Cong prisoner captured during Operation Abilene in April 1966. (Creative Commons NARA photo 111-CCV-441-CC34254 by SSgt Howard C. Breedlove via Wikimedia Commons)

of the new name is attributed to Diem initially as a derisive reference to the resistance and to newspapers in the South that began the widespread use of the term. During the course of the Vietnam war, the Viet Cong and their NVA comrades were known collectively to American troops as 'Charlie'.

The Viet Cong administration stretched across the provinces of the South and mirrored the larger communist structure in the north with its governing body and regional and district leaders, either individuals or groups of officials. Effective propaganda swayed many South Vietnamese, disillusioned with the corruption of the Diem government and later that of President Nguyen Van Thieu and the perceived interference of the United States, to join the ranks of the sophisticated insurgency. Those who refused to cooperate suffered consequences that were often extreme. The Viet Cong established both quasi-governmental structure and a military component, the Quan Doi Giai Phong, or Liberation Army.

The Viet Cong insurgency was characterised by clandestine activities. Its fighters hid in plain sight, virtually indistinguishable from the surrounding peasantry or common folk. When they were observed in action, they often wore dark, loose-fitting clothes and the

traditional Non la head covering. When they struck, they struck hard and then seemed to vanish into the surrounding jungle. The Viet Cong were adept at ambush. They constructed well-concealed booby traps that killed or wounded indiscriminately. They built elaborate networks of tunnels and dug individual 'spider holes' into which they quickly disappeared after emerging to fire automatic weapons. They were often well aware that a US or South Vietnamese Army operation was underway, tipped off by their spy network, the continual whirr of helicopter rotors, and the often deliberate pace of mechanised ground movements or foot patrols directed against them.

In 1962, the Viet Cong published an outline of their objectives. The preamble read: "…Overthrow the camouflaged colonial regime of the American imperialists and the dictatorial power of Ngo Dinh Diem, servant of the Americans, and institute a government of national democratic union. The present South Vietnamese regime is a camouflaged colonial regime dominated by the Yankees, and the South Vietnamese government is a servile government, implementing faithfully all the policies of the American imperialists. Therefore, this regime must be overthrown, and a government of national and democratic union put in its place…."

The growing military proficiency of the Viet Cong was demonstrated at the Battle of Ap Bac in Dinh Tuong Province in January 1963. A combined force of South Vietnamese troops and American advisors searching for a reported concentration of Viet Cong fighters stumbled into an ambush and sustained heavy casualties. Losing only 18 of their own killed and 38 wounded, the insurgents killed and wounded nearly 200 South Vietnamese Army (ARVN) soldiers. Three Americans died in the clash, and eight were wounded while five helicopters were shot down.

With increasing aid from North Vietnam, including arms and supplies along with NVA troops, the Viet Cong gained the grudging respect of their adversaries. In March 1966, the US Department of Defense (DOD) published a pamphlet titled *Know Your Enemy: The Viet Cong*. It read in part: "In little more than five years, the Viet Cong armed forces have grown from an essentially guerrilla army to one that includes regiments of uniformed, well-equipped, highly foot mobile regulars, capable of engaging in conventional operations of limited duration…Substantial quantities of portable war materials have been brought into South Vietnam by land and sea, as well as 8,000 to 10,000 North Vietnamese soldiers in the year 1964."

The DOD document concluded: "The Viet Cong is a tough enemy but no tougher than his opponents. He is not a superman, nor is he invincible. It is impossible to predict how long it will take but the Republic of Vietnam and the United States are committed to stopping his aggression. Our military effort in Vietnam is an essential element in achieving the objectives of freedom, peace, and progress in that war-torn country, which has fought so long and valiantly for these goals."

Directed at American military personnel, the communication is remarkable. The mere fact that the US military establishment felt it necessary to point out that the Viet Cong were not invincible is a testament to the insurgency's resourcefulness, combat prowess, and relentless will to win.

The DOD publication was released just 10 months after the US Army's 173rd Airborne Brigade, the first major American combat unit deployed to Vietnam, was established 'in country'. The 173rd arrived in May 1965, and in mid-June the Viet Cong summer offensive erupted. Twenty American soldiers along with dozens of

ABOVE: A US Marine corporal guards a Viet Cong prisoner captured during fighting in October 1965. (National Archives and Records Administration via Wikimedia Commons)

BELOW: Armed with an AK-47 assault rifle, a uniformed Viet Cong soldier stands beneath his movement's flag. (SSgt. Herman Kokojan via Wikimedia Commons)

American firepower, primarily artillery and air strikes. But more often, the communists dictated the time and the place at which they would engage, adhering to the phrase 'grab them by the belt buckle', fighting at close quarter and sometimes hand-to-hand to prevent US heavy ordnance from being employed for fear of casualties due to friendly fire.

The coordinated guerrilla effort during the Tet Offensive of 1968 ended in disaster for the Viet Cong, who suffered devastating losses. After the offensive, mass graves were discovered in the provincial capital of Hue, which had been temporarily occupied by the communists. Many local leaders and influential figures had been murdered, evidencing the terror tactics often employed by the Viet Cong. Subsequently, increased NVA support for guerrilla operations along with stepped-up infiltration of fighters from the North occurred.

Throughout the war in Vietnam, the Viet Cong displayed dedication, relentless drive, and ruthlessness. The number of casualties suffered by the guerrillas during the conflict is unknown, although in 1995 the Vietnamese government disclosed an estimate of 1.1 million combined Viet Cong and NVA deaths from 1955 to 1975. Other such estimates range from approximately 500,000 to nearly 1.5 million. In contrast, the Viet Cong are believed to have been responsible for roughly 33% of the civilian deaths during the war, executions and murders numbering as many as 600,000.

The Viet Cong established their 'provisional' government in South Vietnam in 1969 to function in areas under their control, but when the reunification of Vietnam occurred in the mid-1970s, its administrative authority was largely ceded to the government of North Vietnam in Hanoi.

South Vietnamese troops were killed when the communists overran a provincial capital city. Military advisors to President Lyndon Johnson then suggested that at least 500,000 troops would be required to defeat the Viet Cong within five years.

WILY AND AGGRESSIVE FOE

Meanwhile, the Central Intelligence Agency reported in July 1965: "The Viet Cong are well known as a wily and aggressive foe. Their so-called 'Summer Offensive' is a calculated effort to attack and destroy government forces in the provinces, under cover of the monsoon rains which hamper government reinforcement and resupply operations. Despite heavy casualties incurred in this effort, and in previous campaigns, the Viet Cong have managed over the years to increase their strength by means of infiltration and local recruitment of manpower in areas of South Vietnam under their control…."

By 1967, an estimated 280,000 Viet Cong guerrillas were active in South Vietnam, while the US military presence had grown steadily to nearly 400,000. Throughout the conflict, Viet Cong casualties were estimated to be substantially higher than their adversaries. However, the guerrillas relied on knowledge of the local terrain, the element of surprise, support from North Vietnam, and their ability to maintain lines of supply such as the famed Ho Chi Minh Trail, an extensive 900-mile network of dirt roads and cart paths from North Vietnam across eastern Laos and Cambodia and then into South Vietnam. Despite many American attempts to cut the Ho Chi Minh Trail, tons of supplies and thousands of reinforcements flowed to the Viet Cong through to the end of the conflict.

On those occasions when the Viet Cong fought in the open, they often sustained heavy casualties in the face of overwhelming

ABOVE: Viet Cong and civilian labourers carry supplies south along the Ho Chi Minh Trail. (US Army via Wikimedia Commons)

BELOW: Viet Cong soldiers carry a wounded American prisoner to an exchange of captives in 1973. (SSGT Herman Kokojan US Army via Wikimedia Commons)

STATE OF CONFLICT 1964-1965

Conceived in chaos, the government of South Vietnam foundered, unable to find a footing that would engender support from the people and steady leadership by army generals that might produce favourable results in the fight with the shadowy communist insurgency bent on the unification of the country.

In early 1964, it had become apparent that the options available to the US government for resolution of the turmoil in Vietnam were limited. There were calls for negotiation, for a shift of South Vietnamese perspective from anti-communist to neutral, and most vociferously for stepped up military aid for the South from the United States. Negotiation, it seemed, had been tried and failed with the unravelling of the Geneva Accords of 1954. Opponents of neutralisation argued that such a move would embolden the communists and lead to the rapid fall of South Vietnam.

Many senior military advisors to President Lyndon Johnson saw escalation of American involvement in Vietnam as the only viable option. Clearly, communist North Vietnam, as well as the Soviet Union and the People's Republic of China were providing military aid to the Viet Cong insurgency in the South. Secretly, the North Vietnamese government approved Resolution 9 on January 20, 1964, proclaiming that a total war against the South was underway and committing the country to military victory.

ABOVE: General William Westmoreland, a veteran of World War Two, took command of MACV in early 1964.
(US Department of Defense via Wikimedia Commons)

Just two days later, the US Joint Chiefs of Staff dispatched a classified memorandum to Secretary of Defense Robert McNamara urging an expansion of American military involvement in Vietnam, including bombing and the introduction of larger numbers of ground troops. Military Assistance Command, Vietnam

ABOVE: On the night of November 3, President Lyndon Johnson celebrates his victory in the election of 1964.
(LBJ Library photo by Cecil Stoughton via Wikimedia Commons)

(MACV) had been established in 1962, and in January 1964, MACV-SOG, its special operations group, was initiated as a subsidiary organisation to conduct covert missions and raids against the communist forces.

At the same time, Viet Cong terror attacks and strikes against both South Vietnamese and American targets were substantially increasing. On February 9, a communist bomb detonated during a softball game, killing two Americans, and seriously wounding 23. *Time Magazine* reported days later, "…Set off by two stolen, US-made fragmentation bombs buried in the soil, the sabotage was the gravest anti-American terrorist episode in South Vietnam's war against the Communist Viet Cong —and an unsettling commentary on the Saigon military regime's security apparatus, since the US stadium is next door to Vietnamese Joint General Staff headquarters…" Two weeks

ABOVE: One American was killed and another captured when a Cessna O-1 observation plane similar to this example was shot down by communist forces in 1964.
(US Army via Wikimedia Commons)

ABOVE: On Christmas Eve 1964, two Viet Cong sappers set off a bomb beneath the Brinks Hotel in Saigon, killing two American officers and wounding 60 people. (US Air Force via Wikimedia Commons)

ABOVE: A destroyed US helicopter lies in ashes at Camp Holloway in February 1965. (NARA photo 111-CCV-147-CC28794 by SP5 Allan Holm via Wikimedia Commons)

later, a Viet Cong bomb exploded aboard a train traveling from the South Vietnamese capital to the port of Da Nang on the East China Sea near the mouth of the River Han, killing 11 people.

On March 17, 1964, Secretary McNamara defined the overriding American policy linked to the Domino Theory, a significant step in the implementation of a strategy that included greater US military involvement in the war. "We seek an independent, non-communist South Vietnam…" the secretary remarked. "…Unless we can achieve that objective…almost all of Southeast Asia will probably fall under communist dominance…Thailand might hold for a period with our help but would be under grave pressure. Even the Philippines would become shaky and the threat to India to the west, Australia and New Zealand to the south, and Taiwan, Korea, and Japan to the north and east would be greatly increased."

Troops of the South Vietnamese Army (ARVN) were regularly accompanied by American advisors during combat operations against the Viet Cong, and inevitably there were casualties among them. On March 26, an American Cessna O-1 Bird Dog observation aircraft was shot down above Quang Tri Province. Its pilot, Captain Richard L. Whitesides, was killed. Listed officially as missing in action, his remains were not recovered until 2014. The observer, Captain Floyd Thompson, was captured and became one of the longest-held POWS in

American military history. He was released on March 16, 1973, after nine years in captivity.

Despite sustaining heavy losses to ARVN counterinsurgency missions, the Viet Cong were brazen in their attacks on the Americans and the South Vietnamese military infrastructure. On May 2, Viet Cong commandos slipped aboard the World War Two-vintage escort aircraft carrier USNS *Card* serving as a ferry in Saigon harbour and planted explosives. The resulting detonation sank the carrier, which was later repaired, and killed five US sailors. A Viet Cong ambush on May 14 killed 43 ARVN Rangers north of Saigon. During a press conference a month later, President Johnson reaffirmed that the US was "bound by solemn commitments" to support South Vietnam in its fight against the communists.

In the election year of 1964, Johnson campaigned as an advocate for peace, even after the Gulf of Tonkin Incident in August and the historic resolution that followed authorising the president to introduce further US military assets to Southeast Asia. Retaliatory air strikes were ongoing when Johnson told the American people in October that his administration was "…not about to send American boys 9 or 10,000 miles away from home to do what Asian boys ought to be doing for themselves."

But the die was cast. Johnson was elected to a four-year term as President by a landslide and considered the results of the polling an endorsement of his apparent Vietnam policy. By the end of 1964, US troop strength in Vietnam had grown to more than 23,000 with 26 killed, while the South Vietnamese had suffered nearly 7,500 dead. The Viet Cong and North Vietnamese Army (NVA) had lost 16,785 killed and many more wounded. However, they were already demonstrating a willingness to absorb tremendous casualties in pursuit of their long-term goal.

The coming of 1965 heralded a watershed year in the Vietnam war. The harsh reality

that the South Vietnamese were losing the war struck home, and the number of American troops in Vietnam increased rapidly. By the end of the year, roughly 185,000 US Marines and US Army soldiers were in country. Allied nations, including Australia, New Zealand, South Korea, and others sent contingents of their own to the struggle against the communists.

Still, the audacious Viet Cong and North Vietnamese regulars took a heavy toll. In January, the six-day Battle of Binh Gia left 201 ARVN soldiers and five Americans dead. On February 7, the Viet Cong attacked Camp Holloway along Route 19 near the city of Pleiku in the Central Highlands, killing eight Americans and wounding 128 while destroying 10 aircraft on the ground.

ARVN troops attacked the communists in an airmobile assault on January 21 in Kien Hoa Province, killing 46 Viet Cong and capturing 61 prisoners in an early operation, and Operation Flaming Dart, a series of 49 sorties by US aircraft in response to the assault on Camp Holloway hit numerous NVA troop concentrations, communications centres, and transport systems. Still, the Viet Cong were resilient. When insurgents detonated explosives at a hotel in Qui Nonh that was being used as a US barracks, 23 American soldiers and seven civilians were killed for the loss of two communist sappers. In response, Operation Flaming Dart II comprised 155 air missions against communist targets.

On March 8, the arrival of the 9th US Marine Expeditionary Force, 1,400 strong, at the port of Da Nang told the world that American ground forces were destined for sustained direct combat with the Viet Cong and NVA. In August, the Marines conducted Operation Starlight, the first large-scale Marine and thoroughly American ground operation of the war. The pre-emptive strike against 1,500 Viet Cong near Chu Lai left 614 Viet Cong dead and 42 captured with 45 Marines killed in action.

ABOVE: A US Marine Hawk missile battery comprises a portion of the defences at Da Nang air base. (Department of Defense (USMC) via Wikimedia Commons)

ROLLING THUNDER

On March 11, 1965 President Johnson initiated Operation Rolling Thunder, a lengthy bombing campaign against North Vietnamese infrastructure and interdiction of supply routes into South Vietnam and neighbouring Laos. Rolling Thunder had grown out of plans developed a year earlier for an eight-week aerial bombardment of selected targets in North Vietnam. The so-called '94 Target List' included roadways, bridges, oil and fuel depots, supply and storage facilities, harbour and dock installations, and troop barracks.

General William Westmoreland, appointed to succeed General Paul Harkins as MACV commander in January 1964, pursued a strategy that he believed would maximise the advantages of American firepower, technology, air superiority, and mobility. The tactic of search and destroy would bring US and ARVN ground troops swiftly into action via helicopter transport, and in pitched clashes with the Viet Cong and NVA wear down the enemy's combat efficiency and capability to continue the war through grinding attrition. Interestingly, the communist leaders were pursuing their own brand of attrition, hoping to exhaust the American will to wage a prolonged war as casualty lists grew, an anti-war movement took hold in the United States, and ordinary Americans began to question the rationale for continuing the fight.

General Westmoreland was acutely aware of the growing probability of Viet Cong hit-and-run attacks against American military bases, particularly large complexes such as Tan Sonh Nut Air Base outside Saigon and the air base and port facilities at Da Nang. He requested two battalions of Marines for Da Nang to guard against such infiltration. By the end of March, the Joint Chiefs of Staff had demonstrated their support for Westmoreland with a recommendation that half a million US fighting men be introduced to Vietnam so that

BELOW: The 9th Marine Expeditionary Force splashes ashore at Da Nang, a harbinger of increased US involvement in ground operations in Vietnam. (USMC Photo A183676 via Wikimedia Commons)

the mission in country would be transformed from one of "not simply withstanding the Viet Cong…but to gain effective operational superiority and assume the offensive…."

Westmoreland continued to signal his doubts about the combat effectiveness of the ARVN and its questionable leadership, while the bombing under Operation Rolling Thunder was stepped up with the spring. The involvement of the US Navy in the fighting increased as well, and the US introduced Operation Fact Sheet, the distribution of millions of propaganda leaflets across North Vietnam warning civilians to stay away from military installations that might be targeted by US aircraft and advocating that the people turn against the Hanoi government.

The ground war grew hotter as communist guerrillas continued their covert missions against military installations and cities in South Vietnam and larger battles were fought. At Dong Xoai just 60 miles northeast of Saigon, the Viet Cong overran a

ABOVE: A cache of Viet Cong weapons and ammunition was seized by US Navy and ARVN forces at Vung Ro Bay. (NARA photo 111-CCV-133-CC29932 via Wikimedia Commons)

district capital in Phuoc Long Province only to be driven out by counterattacking ARVN and US troops. While more than 350 Viet Cong were killed, ARVN losses were 416 dead, and seven Americans were killed while 12 were reported missing.

In November, the week before Thanksgiving, the first large engagement between American and NVA forces took place at Ia Drang. Although the NVA suffered greater losses according to the American standard of 'body count', the vicious fight convinced North Vietnamese leaders, including Ho Chi Minh, that their forces could indeed outlast the American military commitment to Vietnam.

By December 1965, more than 1,900 Americans had died in Vietnam along with over 11,000 ARVN troops. The North Vietnamese and Viet Cong had sustained a staggering 35,436 dead. The US armed forces had been augmented by 230,991 men through the continuing peacetime draft, more than twice the number called up for military service in 1964. The ranks of the NVA more than doubled year over year to 400,000.

BELOW: US Marines prepare for action with the support of airlift helicopters and armour during Operation Starlight. (USMC Photo A184966 via Wikimedia Commons)

AIR WAR VIETNAM

ABOVE: Two Boeing B-52 Stratofortress bombers fly over Cambodia during a mission in 1970. (US Army via Wikimedia Commons)

the North Vietnamese should be threatened to "…draw in their horns and stop their aggression, or we're going to bomb them back into the Stone Age." The general later denied making the statement, saying that he had only alluded to US capability to do so.

However, North Vietnamese and Viet Cong defences took a heavy toll on American aircraft through more than a decade of conflict. Further, strict rules of engagement – in the context of a so-called 'limited war' – often prevented US airmen from exercising the full advantage of superior weapons and firepower. US fighter pilots were prohibited from firing their AIM-7 Sparrow or AIM-9 Sidewinder air-to-air missiles against hostile targets until they could be visually identified, even though the ordnance was capable of target acquisition without such confirmation. US aircraft were prohibited from attacking some installations, shipping, or areas of the North for fear of provoking the Soviet Union or the People's Republic of China and widening the war.

ABOVE: A McDonnell Douglas F-4 Phantom fighter bomber plunges earthward during a bombing run in 1971. This Phantom is assigned to US Navy Fighter Squadron VF-111 aboard the aircraft carrier USS *Coral Sea*.
(US Navy via Wikimedia Commons)

One of the first notable indications of growing US involvement in Vietnam was the extension of air power to Southeast Asia. During the Vietnam era, the United States possessed one of the largest and most technologically advanced air forces in the world. Fixed wing and rotor-powered aircraft were deployed by every branch of the American military, the Air Force, Army, Navy, Marine Corps, and Coast Guard.

While the French fought their unsuccessful war to maintain control of Indochina in the early 1950s, American support came partially in the form of aircraft such as the Vought F4U Corsair and the Douglas A-1 Skyraider for tactical and ground support missions against the Viet Minh. By 1960, American instructors were training South Vietnamese pilots to fly the Skyraider and other attack aircraft, such as the Douglas A-4 Skyhawk, and various helicopter types. In addition, the Central Intelligence Agency (CIA) supported covert operations and delivered supplies to anti-communist forces as early as 1950 through the clandestine activities of Air America.

Concerted US air operations in Vietnam were undertaken in response to growing Viet Cong guerrilla attacks in the South to punish North Vietnam and its surrogates and cripple supply lines, infiltration routes, and infrastructure. Swiftly, the American air effort evolved both strategically and tactically to include bombing campaigns against selected targets North and South, airmobile insertion

of combat troops with accompanying supply and casualty evacuation, dogfights between opposing fighter aircraft, and other operations. American aircraft flew from bases in South Vietnam and neighbouring Thailand, from aircraft carriers off the Vietnamese coastline, and even from bases in the Marianas Islands of the Pacific and Okinawa with the introduction of the heavy Boeing B-52 Stratofortress bomber.

At the outset, some theorists believed overwhelming US air power might break the back of the communist insurgency in South Vietnam and force Ho Chi Minh and the leaders in the North to end their support for it. General Curtis LeMay, chief of staff of the air force, was famously quoted as saying

BELOW: A US Navy Grumman A-6 Intruder attack aircraft is laden with ordnance during a sortie over South Vietnam in November 1968. (US Navy via Wikimedia Common)

ABOVE: Napalm bombs explode among the buildings of a Viet Cong-controlled village in South Vietnam.
(National Archives and Records Administration)

ABOVE: A North Vietnamese SA-2 surface-to-air missile impacts an F-105 Thunderchief of the US Air Force over North Vietnam. (US Air Force via Wikimedia Commons)

Rolling Thunder encompassed more than 300,000 combat sorties and the delivery of 864,000 tons of bombs and missiles, more than the ordnance expended during the entire Korean War or World War Two in the Pacific theatre. A total of 922 American planes were shot down and 1,024 airmen killed, wounded, or captured. Estimates of North Vietnamese Army, Viet Cong, and civilian casualties range from 30,000 to 200,000.

During the first month of air operations, 26 bridges in North Vietnam were destroyed, but as Rolling Thunder wore on North Vietnamese air defence capability steadily improved. The Soviet Union and China supplied a variety of anti-aircraft weapons along with Mikoyan-Gurevich MiG-17, MiG-19, and Mig-21 fighters. The Soviets also provided the S-75 Desna air defence system, which mounted the SA-2 radar-guided surface-to-air missile, code named *Guideline* in NATO parlance. In time, the North Vietnamese capital of Hanoi was ringed by the heaviest concentration of sophisticated air defence weaponry in modern warfare. While American countermeasures were developed to jam communist radar, bombing of enemy airfields was prohibited. While the SA-2, popularly known as the SAM missile, was responsible for downing some US planes, its greatest effect was to compel American pilots to fly at lower altitudes, often into the teeth of North Vietnamese and Viet Cong anti-aircraft fire.

North Vietnamese fighter pilots conducted hit-and-run attacks against US F-105s on bombing missions, then broke off contact and headed back to their bases. Generally, the North Vietnamese avoided aerial dogfights with American Phantoms, but Phantom pilots discovered one distinct disadvantage early in the air war. The F-4 was originally deployed without a gun and armed with missiles only. While the AIM-7 and AIM-9 experienced excessive failure rates at times, dogfights that did take place were problematic for US pilots until the

ROLLING THUNDER

In March 1965, the air offensive codenamed Operation Rolling Thunder was authorised by President Lyndon Johnson as a means of bolstering South Vietnamese morale while stifling the communist takeover effort. From the outset, such goals would be difficult to quantify, and Rolling Thunder suffered from dysfunctional command. Targets, ordnance used, numbers of aircraft participating, and other details were regularly chosen by President Johnson and his civilian political advisors during Tuesday luncheons at the White House and dictated to the military. Initially, military officers were not part of the discourse.

Nevertheless, Rolling Thunder ebbed and flowed across Vietnamese skies for 44 months, and when it was halted in October 1968

its results had apparently fallen far short of expectations. Land-based US Air Force planes, including the North American F-100 Super Sabre, McDonnell Douglas F-4 Phantom II, Republic F-105 Thunderchief, and the mammoth B-52 Stratofortress flew thousands of missions along with naval aircraft, including the F-4, A-4, Grumman A-6 Intruder, Vought F-8 Crusader, Ling-Temco-Vought A-7 Corsair, and other types flying from the decks of Task Force 77 aircraft carriers off the coast of Vietnam in the Gulf of Tonkin at a geographic location dubbed 'Yankee Station'. A second navy location, 'Dixie Station' was established in the South China Sea at the same longitude as the South Vietnamese capital of Saigon to provide tactical air support to ground forces engaging the communists.

ABOVE: Colonel Robin Olds, leader of Operation Bolo, shot down four North Vietnamese MiG fighters over Vietnam. (US Air Force via Wikimedia Commons)

ABOVE: Smoke rises from oil facilities near Hanoi, the capital of North Vietnam, bombed during Operation Rolling Thunder. (US Army Heritage Education Center via Wikimedia Commons)

introduction of the F-4E, mounting a 20mm rapid-firing cannon. On January 2, 1967, US F-4s under the command of World War Two veteran and ace Colonel Robin Olds conducted Operation Bolo, luring North Vietnamese MiGs into a trap and shooting down as many as eight. In response, the North Vietnamese withdrew their fighters from active operations for the next 10 weeks and revised their air tactics.

Aerial kill ratios fluctuated during Rolling Thunder but usually favoured the Americans. Navy pilots were credited with shooting down 29 enemy fighters while losing only eight to MiGs. The majority of US aircraft losses during the Vietnam War were attributed to enemy light anti-aircraft weapons. A total of 170 US Navy airmen were shot down during Rolling Thunder, including future US Senator and presidential candidate John McCain, who was taken prisoner in 1967 and released nearly six years later.

Throughout the Vietnam War, both the versatility and vulnerability of the helicopter were demonstrated. The workhorse of US forces in country was the famed Bell UH-1 Iroquois, nicknamed Huey, which served as an airmobile transport vehicle for rapid insertion of combat troops, a stable fire-support platform when armed with machine guns or rockets, and a swift means of evacuating battlefield casualties. The lives of many wounded men were saved due to rapid extraction and transportation to medical facilities via the Huey. Other prominent rotor-wing types included the Bell AH-1 Cobra gunship, a highly effective attack helicopter, and the twin-rotor Boeing CH-47 Chinook, an essential heavy-lift transport aircraft. Hueys in service with the US Army logged an estimated 7.6 million flight hours, and losses were heavy. More than 2,700 personnel were killed in UH-1 operations, and more than 5,000 helicopters of all types were destroyed during the war. Tactical air support for ground operations continued throughout the conflict, sometimes tipping the outcome of an engagement in favour of the US and South Vietnamese.

By 1972, President Richard Nixon saw the implementation of strategic bombing as a means of diplomacy. US ground troops were being largely withdrawn from combat, but the major communist Easter Offensive required action to stem the tide. Nixon halted the Paris peace talks and approved Operation Linebacker, the first sustained bombing programme against North Vietnam since the end of Rolling Thunder in 1968. Linebacker raids hit targets of high value, including fuel and transportation stores, bridges and roads, supply lines, and electric power production.

LINEBACKER II

The raids were suspended in October 1972, and peace talks resumed. However, when the North Vietnamese abruptly broke off the negotiations in December, Nixon ordered a resumption of the bombing with Operation Linebacker II. B-52s participated in 11 days of heavy raids that came to be known as the 'Christmas Bombing' of North Vietnam. This time both Hanoi and the port city of Haiphong were targeted. The Soviets and Chinese denounced the raids, while the North Vietnamese government declared that thousands of civilians had been killed or injured in the flurry of 'carpet bombing'.

A public outcry against Linebacker II and continued raids against the North erupted across the United States, and one of the most famous images of the Vietnam era depicts Canadian-born Carol Feraci, a member of the Ray Coniff Singers set to perform at a White House dinner, surprising the President and the gathering by displaying a sign that read: "STOP THE KILLING." Feraci said boldly: "President Nixon, stop bombing human beings, animals, and vegetation. You go to church on Sundays and pray to Jesus Christ. If Jesus Christ were here tonight, you would not dare drop another bomb. Bless the Berrigans and bless Daniel Ellsberg." The Berrigan brothers, Philip, and Daniel were Roman Catholic priests committed to the anti-war movement, while Ellsberg was a military analyst and political activist who leaked the controversial Pentagon Papers, disclosing secret details of the US conduct of the war, to the public in 1971.

By the time US military involvement in Vietnam ended in 1973, American aircraft had conducted more than 5.25 million sorties against targets throughout Southeast Asia, including Vietnam, Cambodia, and Laos. From 1965 to 1975, American aircraft dropped approximately eight million tons of bombs, well over the tonnage delivered in Europe and the Pacific in World War Two. Nearly 10,000 US fixed-wing aircraft and helicopters were lost during the war, and casualties were heavy with more than 7,200 air personnel killed in action.

Controversy continues to surround the use of US air power in Vietnam, its veracity, and its perceived failures in the futile quest for victory.

Enemy Antiaircraft Weapons. North Vietnam used 57-mm (above), 85-mm (right), and 100-mm (below) weapons, as well as surface-to-air missiles (bottom) to combat U.S. aircraft in Laos.

ABOVE: The North Vietnamese and Viet Cong fielded a variety of Soviet-made antiaircraft guns and SA-2 surface-to-air missiles against American aircraft. (US Air Force via Wikimedia Commons)

BELOW: A US Air Force hunter-killer group, including a specialised radar-suppressing F-105 Wild Weasel, refuels in the air en route to targets during Operation Linebacker. (US Air Force Ken Hackman via Wikimedia Commons)

B-52 STRATOFORTRESS

ABOVE: A B-52 Stratofortress of the US Air Force drops its cargo of bombs over Vietnam. (US Air Force via Wikimedia Commons)

The Boeing B-52 Stratofortress heavy bomber was conceived as a strategic weapon in the US program of nuclear deterrence against war with the Soviet Union. An icon of the Cold War, the Stratofortress received the nickname 'Buff,' or Big Ugly Fat 'Fella'. While replacement designs have been considered and other bomber types have been constructed, the B-52 has remained in service with the US Air Force since its introduction in 1955. With upgrades and maintenance, it is expected to continue in service into the 2040s.

During the Vietnam war, the B-52 came to symbolise the might of American air power, both in the devastation it was capable of sowing and in the frustration that overwhelming firepower in a 'limited war' evidently could not in itself defeat the communists of North Vietnam and the Viet Cong guerrillas. The B-52 was employed primarily in a strategic bombing role and became well known for its sledgehammer attacks against Hanoi and Haiphong during Operation Linebacker II, the Christmas bombing of North Vietnam in 1972. The destructive B-52 raids are believed to have brought the communists back to the negotiating table in Paris.

The B-52 was initially used during the early stages of Operation Rolling Thunder in 1965 as 30 bombers of the 441st and 9th Bombardment Squadrons flew the first mission, Operation Arc Light, against enemy positions in the Ben Cat District north of Saigon. Although designed to carry nuclear weapons, the B-52 was modified to deliver a variety of conventional ordnance. During the conflict, the bombers hit targets in Vietnam, Cambodia, and Laos, including interdiction efforts against the Ho Chi Minh Trail. 'Big Belly' modifications to the massive aircraft in 1965 enhanced the payload capability of the B-52D to 54,000lb of bombs, a total of 108 individual bombs carried internally and externally. The bombload was roughly equal to that of nine World War Two-era Boeing B-17 Flying Fortress bombers.

The B-52 was used in tactical support for the first time during the Battle of Ia Drang in November 1965, bombing North Vietnamese Army troops engaged with US soldiers of the 7th Cavalry Regiment, 1st Cavalry Division (Airmobile). B-52s also flew tactical missions during the communist siege of the US combat base at Khe Sanh in the spring of 1968. During the same year, B-52s flew 3,377 missions over Laos.

The B-52s flew from Andersen Air Base on the island of Guam, U Tapao airfield in Thailand, and other locations. The mission from the Marianas was 13 hours long, requiring in-flight refuelling to extend the 6,000 mile range of the B-52D. The big bomber is notable for its service ceiling of approximately 50,000ft and its subsonic cruising speed of roughly 500mph powered by eight Pratt & Whitney J57-P-19W turbojet engines. The bomber is 156ft long with a wingspan of 185ft and height of 48ft. While a crew of six manned the B-52D, the number of crewmen has varied based on the particular variant. Due to its destructive capacity and diplomatic restraint, the use of the B-52 in Vietnam was often restricted.

During Linebacker II, B-52s hit targets in North Vietnam for 12 straight days, December 18-29, 1972, flying 729 sorties and dropping about 20,000 tons of bombs. A total of 16 B-52s and 43 crewmen were officially reported as lost during Linebacker II. Through the course of the war, 31 B-52s were lost, including 10 that were shot down over North Vietnam, while the crews of the big bombers flew 126,615 missions.

ABOVE: American heavy B-52 bombers deliver their payload over North Vietnam during Operation Linebacker II. (National Museum of the US Air Force via Wikimedia Commons)

BELOW: Soviet advisors examine the wreckage of a B-52 shot down over Hanoi in December 1972. (Creative Commons Photoarchive Sergey A. Varyukhina via Wikimedia Commons)

RANDY CUNNINGHAM AND WILLIE DRISCOLL

Air-to-air combat between opposing fighter pilots during the Vietnam war was a rather rare occurrence.

US Air Force and Navy pilots continually operated under strict rules of engagement, while the Vietnam People's Air Force (VPAF) was usually flying at a numerical disadvantage. The introduction of missiles contributed to engagements at greater distances than earlier wars, and the dogfighting of previous conflicts, with guns blazing, was seldom experienced.

Only two American pilots, Lieutenant Randy 'Duke' Cunningham of the US Navy, and Captain Steve Ritchie of the US Air Force, both flying McDonnell Douglas F-4 Phantom jets, became aces, each with five confirmed victories in the skies above Vietnam. Additionally, three officers, navy Lieutenant Willie 'Irish' Driscoll and US Air Force Captains Charles DeBellevue and Jeffrey Feinstein earned ace status, Driscoll as a radar intercept officer (RIO) flying with Cunningham, and DeBellevue and Feinstein as weapon systems officers (WSO). DeBellevue accompanied Ritchie during four missions in which kills were confirmed.

The VPAF pilots primarily flew Soviet-made MiG-17 and MiG-21 fighters, and at least 17 of them became aces. Nguyen Van Coc is believed to be the leading VPAF ace of the Vietnam conflict with nine aerial victories.

ABOVE: Lieutenants Randy Cunningham and Willie Driscoll meet with Secretary of the Navy John Warner (left) and Admiral Elmo Zumwalt, Chief of Naval Operations (right). (US Navy via Wikimedia Commons)

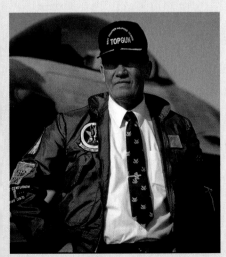

ABOVE: This photo of Duke Cunningham was taken in 1991, prior to the charges of corruption that sent him to jail. (Creative Commons DeanGarnerConsulting.com Wangtopgun via Wikimedia Commons)

Cunningham had earned his navy commission and pilot's wings in 1967, subsequently completing a tour of duty aboard the aircraft carrier USS *America*. In early 1972, Cunningham and Driscoll were assigned to Fighter Squadron VF-96, nicknamed the Fighting Falcons, aboard the carrier USS *Constellation*. They proved a proficient team flying the F-4J, callsign Showtime 112.

ESCORT MISSION

On January 19, assigned to escort photographic aircraft and attack planes on a mission over VPAF Quan Lang air base, near the town of Duc Son on the Vietnamese border with Laos, they dispatched a MiG-21 with a heat seeking AIM-9 Sidewinder missile. Driscoll had achieved a radar lock with a radar-guided AIM-7 Sparrow missile, but Cunningham knew that the Sparrow had reliability issues. Instead, the pilot opted for the Sidewinder. He called out, "Fox Two!" as the missile sped toward the enemy aircraft. The MiG-21 pilot broke hard and evaded the first missile. However, Cunningham quickly fired a second Sidewinder, which ripped into the MiG's tail section from 1,200 yards, sending it spiralling into the ground.

On May 8, Cunningham and Driscoll were flying escort for navy Grumman A-6 Intruder aircraft engaged in mining the harbour at Haiphong, North Vietnam,

during Operation Linebacker. Tangling with three VPAF MiG-17s, one of which had jumped his wingman, Lieutenant Brian Grant, Cunningham evaded an enemy Atoll air-to-air missile and maintained a firing position on one of the MiGs. A Sidewinder fired from long range missed the target, but a second struck home, destroying the enemy plane in mid-air. As the other two MiG-17s closed, Cunningham disengaged and headed back to the *Constellation*.

Two days later, on May 10, 1972, Cunningham and Driscoll flew the F-4J Showtime 100 and completed one of the epic fighter missions of the Vietnam war. While Ling-Temco-Vought A-7 Corsair attack planes hit the railyards at Hai Duong, as many as 20 North Vietnamese MiG-17s swarmed into

ABOVE: Lieutenants Randy 'Duke' Cunningham and Willie 'Irish' Driscoll flew this F-4J Phantom on May 10, 1972. (US Navy via Wikimedia Commons)

BELOW: Cunningham and Driscoll are shown in the cockpit of an F-4J Phantom fighter aboard the aircraft carrier USS *Constellation*. (US Navy via Wikimedia Commons)

the area. Cunningham and Driscoll dropped their cluster bomb munitions on a group of warehouses and turned to meet the enemy aircraft. Lieutenant Grant shouted a warning to break, and Cunningham responded, quickly acquiring one of the MiG-17s and engaging it with a Sidewinder. Immediately, Cunningham came to the aid of another Phantom with three MiG-17s on its tail. He shouted a warning to the American pilot and seconds later targeted one of the attacking MiGs, shooting it down with another Sidewinder.

During the aerial melee, Cunningham and Driscoll were separated from their wingman, but plenty of enemy fighters were still in the vicinity. Flying at 10,000ft, the Phantom duo headed straight for another MiG-17. The enemy pilot began firing his 23mm and 37mm cannon. As shells streaked toward his F-4, Cunningham went vertical and came out of the manoeuvre to find the MiG-17 close behind.

ABOVE: Captain Steve Ritchie and Captain Charles DeBellevue walk across an airfield in Vietnam.
(US Air Force via Wikimedia Commons)

"I looked back and there was the MiG, canopy to canopy with me!" Cunningham remembered. "He couldn't have been more than 30 feet away. I could see the pilot clearly, leather helmet, goggles, scarf… We were both going straight up, but I was out-zooming him. He fell behind, and as I came over the top, he started shooting. I had given him a predictable flight path, and he had taken advantage of it. The tracers were missing me, but not by much! I rolled out, and he pulled in right behind me."

The American airmen were impressed with the skill of their adversary, and a swirling dogfight continued. Twice the opposing pilots got into a rolling scissors manoeuvre, clawing for altitude and a narrow advantage.

"…Anyway, we're both going straight up and losing speed fast," Cunningham recalled. "I was down to 150 knots, and I knew I was going to have to go to full burner to hold it. I did, and we both pitched over the top. As he came over, I used rudder to get the airplane to turn to his belly side…He pitched over the top and started straight down. I went after him and, though I didn't think the Sidewinder would guide straight down with all the heat of the ground to look at, I squeezed one off anyway….There was just a little flash, and I thought, 'God, it missed him!' I started to fire my last Sidewinder and suddenly…a big flash of flame and black smoke erupted from his airplane. He didn't seem to go out of control, but he flew straight down into the ground. He didn't get out."

This air battle was later thought to have been an engagement with the esteemed Colonel Toomb, a VPAF ace who actually did not exist but may well have been inspired by the successes of Nguyen Van Coc. Regardless, the North Vietnamese pilot had fought gamely. Cunningham and

Driscoll had become the first US fighter aces of the Vietnam War, downing three MiG-17s in a single mission.

They turned seaward toward *Constellation*. However, the gruelling mission was not over. Flying above Nam Dinh, the F-4J was hit by a North Vietnamese SA-2 surface-to-air missile. Cunningham pulled the damaged Phantom out of a spin and flew on toward the South China Sea, realising that each second aloft improved the chance of rescue rather than spending the remainder of the war as a prisoner in North Vietnam.

"…I told Willie to stay with me just a few more seconds," said Cunningham. When the pilot shouted, "Eject!" Driscoll was gone. Cunningham followed. The downed airmen were soon rescued by US Marine Corps helicopters and transported to their carrier.

For the memorable day's action, both Cunningham and Driscoll received the Navy Cross. Cunningham also received two Silver Stars, the Purple Heart and 15 awards of the Air Medal during his Vietnam tours of duty. Driscoll also received two Silver Stars, the Purple Heart, and 10 awards of the Air Medal.

Driscoll went on the serve as an instructor at the US Navy Fighter Weapons School, popularly known as TOPGUN, and retired from active duty in 1982 with the rank of commander.

Cunningham was also a TOPGUN instructor and commanded Fighter Squadron VF-126 based at Naval Air Station Miramar, California. He retired from the navy with the rank of commander in 1987. Three years later, he was elected to the US House of Representatives; however, his career was tarnished when he was tried and convicted of corruption. He completed a lengthy prison term in 2013 and was pardoned by President Donald Trump in 2021.

BELOW: Captain Jeffrey Feinstein prepares to climb aboard a Phantom fighter in September 1972. (US Air Force via Wikimedia Commons)

THE DRAGON'S JAW

The steel through-truss Thanh Hoa Bridge was 540ft long, 56ft wide, and stood 50ft above the waters of the River Song Ma. A gigantic concrete pier in the centre and a pair of buttresses at either end supported the span. The Viet Minh had destroyed an earlier structure during their fight with the French, and the replacement had been constructed over seven years from 1957 to 1964.

The North Vietnamese went to great lengths to defend the bridge against US air attacks, while the Americans threw 871 aerial sorties in multiple attempts to drop the span into the river between 1965 and 1972. Numerous American airmen were killed in these raids, and 11 aircraft were lost.

The importance of the Thanh Hoa Bridge, nicknamed Ham Rog, or Dragon's Jaw, by the Vietnamese, lay in its link to the Ho Chi Minh Trail, the long supply line through neighbouring Laos that filtered supplies and equipment to communist forces in South Vietnam. Destroying the bridge meant severing the lifeline to the troops of the North Vietnamese Army and the Viet Cong guerrillas who depended on the trail for sustenance.

American efforts to destroy the Dragon's Jaw began on successive days in April 1965. Two raids by F-105 Thunderchief bombers carrying 750lb bombs and rocket-powered AGM-12 Bullpup guided missiles severely damaged the bridge, but the North Vietnamese proved adept at repairing it. The cost had been heavy with four American planes shot down. Acknowledging the importance of the Dragon's Jaw, the North Vietnamese had dedicated MiG-17 fighters and five air defence regiments, each

ABOVE: Heavy damage to the Dragon's Jaw is revealed in this aerial photo after a US raid with laser-guided weapons. (US Air Force via Wikimedia Commons)

comprising roughly 1,000 soldiers and 36 anti-aircraft guns, to fight off the American raids. Later Soviet-made surface-to-air missiles were also employed.

Through the spring of 1965, American air attacks destroyed 25 other bridges throughout North Vietnam, but the Dragon's Jaw was defiant. That autumn, the US Air Force removed the bridge from its route package, and the US Navy undertook the effort against the stubborn span. The results were much the same, and it appeared that the ordnance being employed was insufficient to inflict enough damage to render the bridge irreparable. Its heavy construction and the strength of the air defences had proven formidable.

The US Air Force had issued a report titled, *The Tale of Two Bridges and the Battle for the Skies over North Vietnam*, citing several reasons for the continuing effort to destroy the Dragon's Jaw. "The apparent invincibility of the bridge; its cost in men, aircraft, and ordnance; its potential strategic importance; its symbolic value to the North Vietnamese – all served as an incentive for US aviators to find different techniques to destroy it…."

In May 1966, Operation Carolina Moon, conceived to drop the Dragon's Jaw with the delivery of several massive 5,000lb explosive devices, ended in failure with the loss of a Lockheed C-130 transport plane modified to deliver the weapons as well as an escorting F-4 Phantom fighter. The remains of several of those airmen killed were not repatriated to the United States for many years, and others remain missing in action and presumed dead. Regular US Navy air strikes against the Dragon's Jaw continued for two more frustrating years. The bridge sustained damage from time to time, but the resourceful North Vietnamese were quite efficient in rebuilding and keeping it open. In 1968, the US government suspended air raids on North Vietnam.

The Dragon's Jaw was not targeted again until the commencement of Operation Linebacker in the spring of 1972. By this time, a new generation of precision munitions was being introduced, including the AGM-62 Walleye guided missile, the Paveway laser-guided bomb, and television-guided weapons. Phantom fighter bombers of the 8th Tactical Fighter Wing hit the Dragon's Jaw in late April and severely damaged the western section. Fourteen Phantoms returned on May 13, and their laser-guided bombs inflicted more damage.

On October 6, 1972, four Vought A-7 Corsairs at long last administered the coup de grace to the Dragon's Jaw. Flying from the aircraft carrier USS *America*, they hit the span with conventional bombs and Walleye missiles. The centre of the bridge collapsed into the Song Ma.

ABOVE: This aerial view of the Dragon's Jaw was taken by a US aircraft during Operation Linebacker in 1972. (US Navy via Wikimedia Commons)

ABOVE: US Navy Vought A-7 Corsair attack planes like this one struck the final blow against the Dragon's Jaw in October 1972. (Bbri4570 at en.wikipedia via Wikimedia Commons)

NAVAL WAR VIETNAM

Early naval support for South Vietnam began with Seventh Fleet and its offshore patrols, providing surveillance of North Vietnamese activities and leading to the Gulf of Tonkin Incident in 1964 that widened US involvement in the Vietnam conflict. By then, US Navy advisors had been in Southeast Asia since the 1950s, training and assisting with the organisation of the navy of the Republic of Vietnam. In 1969, a total of 564 such advisors were active and from their introduction the South Vietnamese Navy grew from 122 ships and 5,000 sailors to 42,000 personnel and 1,500 vessels of numerous types by 1972.

Through the course of the war, the navy transported roughly 95% of the supplies and equipment used by US and Vietnamese forces. The navy distribution system included small boats, shallow draft barges, and other watercraft that were active continually on inland waterways. These vessels staged from massive logistical and support facilities constructed by Seabees at the port of Da Nang, Saigon, and other points, while the recipients of materiel through the navy supply chain also

ABOVE: The aircraft carrier USS *Enterprise* sails in the Gulf of Tonkin, May 1966. (National Archives and Records Administration via Wikimedia Commons)

ABOVE: A US Navy Douglas A-4 Skyhawk attack aircraft flies over Vietnam in November 1967. (US Navy via Wikimedia Commons)

Approximately 1.9 million US Navy personnel served in Southeast Asia during the Vietnam conflict, and their contribution to the effort to defeat communist forces was truly diversified.

In addition to the thousands of carrier-based air strikes launched from Yankee Station in the north and Dixie Station in the South China Sea, Task Force 77 maintained a continuous presence off the coast of Vietnam. Additional US Navy operations included the interdiction of supplies along the waterways of Vietnam through the patrol and combat activities of the riverine, or 'brown water' navy, blockade duties to restrict the flow of supplies into North Vietnamese ports, mining of harbours, major construction projects completed by the famed Seabees (Construction Battalions), logistics and fire support, and amphibious transportation.

BELOW: The US Coast Guard cutter *Owasco* refuels during an Operation Market Time patrol off Vietnam. (US Coast Guard via Wikimedia Commons)

ABOVE: A Vought A-7 Corsair aircraft such as those used in Operation Pocket Money is shown in flight.
(US Navy via Wikimedia Commons)

BELOW: A UH-1E helicopter escorts PBRs along a river in Vietnam during anti-communist operations in 1968.
(US Navy via Wikimedia Commons)

included the Marine Corps, US Army, and US Air Force.

In contributing to the air war in Vietnam, Task Force 77 aircraft carriers conducted sustained strikes against North Vietnamese military and industrial infrastructure during the 44 months of Operation Rolling Thunder, hitting the communists in Vietnam, Laos, and Cambodia. In 1972, Operation Linebacker stemmed the tide of the communist Easter offensive, while Linebacker II, the Christmas bombing of North Vietnam, brought the North Vietnamese and Viet Cong back to the negotiating table after they had broken off peace discussions. The navy shouldered roughly 60% of the air effort during Linebacker, flying about 4,000 sorties per month. Tactical air support for major ground operations was often decisive as attack aircraft flying from Dixie Station delivered overwhelming firepower.

Naval artillery played a key role in suppressing communist offensive operations during the spring of 1972, and the guns of US warships fired 111,000 shells of varied calibres against littoral targets while countering the Easter offensive. At the same time, an estimated 85% of the imported materiel entering North Vietnam came through the major port of Haiphong. On May 9, 1972, the navy initiated Operation Pocket Money. Three US Marine A-6 Intruders and six US Navy Vought A-7 Corsair attack aircraft flying

from the aircraft carrier USS *Coral Sea* executed the first mining missions against Haiphong harbour. They were supported by the guided-missile cruiser USS *Chicago*, heavy cruiser USS *Newport News*, light cruisers *Providence* and *Oklahoma City*, and accompanying destroyers.

The mines were sown with 72-hour activation delays to allow neutral ships, most of which were flagged to communist countries, to evacuate Haiphong harbour. However, few did so. The escorting warships fired at North Vietnamese coastal SA-2 surface-to-air missile batteries and anti-aircraft gun emplacements, and *Chicago* shot down an enemy MiG fighter with a Talos anti-aircraft missile. Operation Pocket Money continued through the end of American involvement in the Vietnam war, and approximately 11,000 magnetic mines were sown.

OPERATION MARKET TIME

In February 1965, the navy instituted Operation Market Time to curtail the ability of the North Vietnamese to bring supplies into the country by clandestine

means. Task Force 115, also known as the Coastal Surveillance Force, employed three 'barrier' methods of interdiction in order to locate and seize North Vietnamese supply ships. After the capture of a 100-ton enemy trawler in secluded Vung Ro Bay, South Vietnam, the navy teamed with the US Coast Guard to identify, graph, and report the movements of vessels in the first barrier. The middle barrier included the establishment of a perimeter 40 miles off the Vietnamese coastline and the stopping and inspection of suspicious vessels by Coast Guard personnel stationed aboard cutters. The inner barrier consisted of coastal patrols by agile swift boats (Patrol Craft Fast) of the US and South Vietnamese navies.

The swift boats were shallow-draft, heavily armed patrol craft capable of a top speed of 32kts. Constructed with welded aluminium hulls, the boats were approximately 50ft long with a beam of 13ft, draft of three feet, and a crew of six. Two variants were built, and the specifications were similar. The swift boats were typically armed with a pair of .50-calibre machine guns, an 81mm mortar, and the 40mm Mk 19 grenade launcher. Evaluation of Operation Market Time in 1968 deemed the effort successful and resulted in the enemy's greater reliance on the Ho Chi Minh Trail, an overland route to the South via neighbouring Laos.

In December 1965, MACV (Military Assistance Command, Vietnam) authorised Task Force 116, also known as the River Patrol Force, and initiated Operation Game Warden, an effort to keep vital waterways free from communist magnetic mines and guerrilla attacks as troops, supplies, and equipment flowed to American and South Vietnamese forces from major cities such as Saigon and Hue to the interior of the country. Another dimension of Game Warden was the interdiction of waterborne

ABOVE: A heavily-armed PBR (Patrol Boat, Riverine) is shown on duty along a Vietnamese waterway.
(US Navy via Wikimedia Commons)

ABOVE: Several swift boats (Patrol Craft Fast) ply an inland waterway in Vietnam in search of communist infiltrators. (US Navy via Wikimedia Commons)

communist supply routes that fed the Ho Chi Minh Trail and supplies that infiltrated aboard small Viet Cong vessels through Cambodia.

The most commonly used patrol craft in Task Force 116 operations was the PBR (Patrol Boat, Riverine). Two models were constructed with slight variations on the 31ft length, 10½-foot beam, and shallow draft of two feet. Manned by a crew of four, the PBR was capable of a top speed of 28½kts, and its armament included twin .50-calibre machine guns forward in a rotating tub, a third .50-calibre machine gun mounted near the stern, and either a single .30-calibre (7.62mm) M60 machine gun or a pair of

these weapons mounted to the port and/or starboard sides.

Forces that included US Navy SEALs (Sea Air and Land Teams), small patrol craft, and minesweepers operated along many of the major rivers and tributaries of South Vietnam, particularly the great River Mekong and its extensive delta, alone encompassing 2,900 miles of inland waterway. Attack helicopters provided tactical air power as well. River Patrol Force missions impeded Viet Cong guerrilla operations, increased the flow of food and vital supplies to inland villages, and reduced communist terror campaigns against the civilian population. An active outreach to pacify local villages was enacted with humanitarian aid and propaganda messages sometimes broadcast via loudspeaker. According to official reports, the patrols of Task Force 116 subsequently played a key role in keeping the Rivers Perfume and Cua Viet navigable during the Tet Offensive of early 1968.

Market Time and Game Warden patrols were particularly hazardous. While conducting surveillance of sampan traffic on rivers and streams, American and South Vietnamese personnel inspected these craft for weapons caches and other evidence of Viet Cong activity. At any moment, a quiet situation might erupt in small-arms fire from both sides of a riverbank. Sailors aboard the patrol craft returned fire, but sometimes were unable to locate or identify a specific target before the close-quarter brawl ceased.

SEAL teams regularly deployed in 12-man platoons, and operations were generally conducted by six-man squads. Inserted either by boat or helicopter, these teams executed hit-and-run raids against enemy supply and troop concentrations, as well as ambushes, usually with heavy camouflage

ABOVE: A US Navy SEAL moves through deep mud as he comes ashore from a patrol boat along a waterway in Vietnam, 1970. (US Navy PHC A. Hill via Wikimedia Commons)

and under cover of night. During six years of such operations, the SEALs accounted for as many as 900 Viet Cong dead, while losing 46 of their own to hostile action. The last SEAL team was withdrawn from Vietnam in December 1971.

River Section 511 became the first American unit to patrol in the Mekong Delta as a fighting force and conducted some of the earliest brown water navy missions by the spring of 1966. Its 10 swift boats operated from Can Tho on the River Bassac to oppose the Viet Cong insurgency.

In late 1967, the Mobile Riverine Force, a joint navy and army force that also included the US Air Force Fifth Air Commando Squadron and Vietnamese components, initiated a programme of search and destroy that increased the effectiveness of Operation Game Warden. During one coordinated mission, elements of the US 9th Infantry Division worked in concert with Task Force 117 aboard riverine watercraft. In successive river assaults the army/navy offensive inflicted substantial casualties on the Viet Cong, and the kill ratio reported was 15 to one.

In late 1968, US Navy Task Forces 115, 116, and 117 joined with the South Vietnamese Navy in the Southeast Asia Lake, Ocean, River, and Delta Strategy, nicknamed SEALORDS, a concerted effort to stop the flow of communist troops and supplies into South Vietnam from Cambodia. The establishment of patrol barriers and increased interdiction efforts were combined with a greater South Vietnamese military and governmental presence in the Mekong Delta. The importance of SEALORDS was later underscored when the successful limitation of Viet Cong activity in the delta prevented the expansion of the North Vietnamese Easter Offensive in 1972.

ABOVE: US Navy patrol boats of Task Force 117 gather along a riverbank to rendezvous with South Vietnamese forces. (National Archives and Records Administration)

STATE OF CONFLICT 1966-1967

ABOVE: CH-47 Chinook helicopters deploy artillery pieces to forward positions in support of the 1st Cavalry Division (Airmobile) during Operation Masher. (National Archives and Records Administration via Wikimedia Commons)

ABOVE: A US Marine of Company F, 2nd Battalion, 7th Marines, fires an M79 grenade launcher at communist insurgents. (US Marine Corps via Wikimedia Commons)

As thousands of American troops were committed to Southeast Asia following the plea for more military strength on the ground, General William Westmoreland, commander of MACV (Military Assistance Command, Vietnam) was tasked with developing a comprehensive strategy that would lead to eventual victory over the communists.

American involvement in the war steadily increased in 1966 and 1967 on the premise that was later succinctly stated by Secretary of Defense Robert McNamara. "South Vietnam seemed to be crumbling with the only apparent antidote a massive injection of US troops."

After Westmoreland's call for additional American forces, his staff recognised the monumental task that lay before them, including the highest and best use of the military might at their disposal. Major General Phillip Davidson, MACV intelligence officer, described the situation. The Americans "had not one battle, but three to fight," he related. "First, to contain a growing enemy conventional threat; second, to develop the Republic of Vietnam's armed forces (RVNAF); and third, to pacify and protect the peasants in the South Vietnamese countryside. Each was a monumental task."

In response, a three-phase campaign that Westmoreland described as 'sustained'

ABOVE: Troops of the US 101st Airborne Division cross a rice field during a search and destroy mission in early 1966. (National Archives and Records Administration via Wikimedia Commons)

would be implemented. In phase one, US and allied forces would secure bases and defend population centres while training and upgrading the South Vietnamese military. This effort was begun in 1965. Phase two involved the stepped up effort to destroy the enemy while undertaking rural construction and infrastructure improvements. The US troops would "participate in clearing, securing, reserve reaction and offensive operations as required to support and sustain the resumption of pacification." In phase three, the allied command would lead the offensive that would culminate with the "defeat and destruction of the remaining enemy forces and base areas."

Westmoreland was under no illusions of a quick victory. A war of attrition, lengthy though it might be, would ultimately break the capacity of the communists to wage war and to supply the Viet Cong insurgency. The term 'body count' came into widespread use, as one measure of progress was in the number of enemy dead exacted during search and destroy campaigns and various battles. The body count statistics were immediately called into question due to the tendency of American officers to inflate their totals. Nevertheless, body count was used as an indicator that the allied forces were making progress.

On the ground, large areas were designated as free-fire zones after civilians had been relocated to safety and anyone remaining was presumed to be the enemy. American bombing and shelling made these areas quite hazardous. Meanwhile, the message that victory was in sight seemed contradictory to the images Americans viewed during nightly news reports that

ABOVE: US and South Vietnamese officials discuss strategy during the Honolulu Conference. President Lyndon Johnson is at right. (Yoichi Okamoto National Archives and Records Administration via Wikimedia Commons)

flashed images from the battlefield directly into their living rooms.

Amid an atmosphere of cautious optimism tinged with healthy scepticism, the Americans and South Vietnamese conducted a large number of search and destroy missions during 1966 and 1967, a total of 18 major offensive operations in 1966 alone. Generally, results of these were mixed at best. The allied units would complete their missions, often uncovering large caches of weapons and supplies and counting some Viet Cong and North Vietnamese Army casualties. However, the enemy was usually aware of a coming search and destroy operation and withdrew to safety prior to commencement. Then, when the Americans had withdrawn, they simply reoccupied the previously contested territory.

STRATEGIC OBJECTIVES

In February 1966, the leaders of the United States and South Vietnam met in Honolulu to define strategic objectives. The commitment to victory in battle however, seemed inherently contradictory to the strategy of rural pacification and nation building. Neither could take complete precedence, and an ominous polarity developed. In the United States, Staff

Sergeant Barry Sadler's recording of the rousing tune *The Ballad of the Green Berets* reached number one on the US charts in March 1966. Although the song struck a patriotic chord, American casualties mounted as operations intensified and the anti-war movement found its footing. In late March, demonstrations took place across the United States, a crowd of 20,000 marching down Fifth Avenue in New York City.

From January 4 to March 6, 1966, the US, and South Vietnamese (ARVN) armies launched Operation Masher/White Wing, their largest search and destroy mission to date. South Korean (ROK) troops also participated in the offensive in Binh Dinh Province, while US Marines embarked on Operation Double Eagle in nearby Quang Ngai Province. After nearly 10 weeks of fighting, Masher was concluded and deemed a victory as the tactic of air mobility proved capable of sustaining a prolonged effort in the field. Heavy air support, including 171 strikes by B-52 bombers and artillery fire that topped 130,000 shells, contributed to estimated communist losses topping 2,000 killed. A total of 288 Americans were killed, mostly from the 1st Cavalry Division (Airmobile) with 24 Marines lost during Double Eagle. Despite claims of success, reports in the

aftermath of Operation Masher indicated that the Viet Cong had reoccupied the zone of operations following the allied withdrawal.

In late February, the Battle of Suoi Bong Trang occurred during Operation Rolling Stone, an effort to protect engineers building a new road in Binh Duong Province. Troops of the US 1st Infantry Division and the Royal Australian Regiment fought off communist forces, inflicting 154 killed while losing 11 American dead. Typically, both sides claimed victory.

In April B-52 bombers struck North Vietnam for the first time, dropping nearly 600 tons of bombs in an attempt to disrupt the flow of supplies via the Ho Chi Minh Trail, and three battalions of US Marines fought alongside South Vietnamese troops in Operation Hot Springs/Lien Ket, killing more than 100 Viet Cong while eight ARVN soldiers died. In virtually every encounter, the number of casualties inflicted on the communists was substantially greater than the losses incurred by US and allied forces. However, in late May, a MACV report noted that US casualties for the week of May 15-21 were the highest of the war to date with 146 killed and 820 wounded.

During Operation Hawthorne in June, the position of Company C, 2nd Battalion, 502nd Parachute Infantry Regiment, was in danger of being overrun by North Vietnamese Army (NVA) regulars. Captain Bill Carpenter requested an air strike with napalm on his own position, as elements of the 101st Airborne Division sought to relieve ARVN troops under siege at Toumorong, near Dak To. The fight ended with more than 1,200 NVA dead.

In September, the US Department of Defense announced the largest call-up for the Selective Service draft of the entire war, projecting more than 49,000 men, the largest number since the Korean War, to be inducted by October. For the year, more than 280,000 men were drafted. On September 14, the US 196th Light Infantry Brigade and components of three infantry divisions, the 1st, 4th, and 25th, initiated Operation Attleboro. Five weeks of fighting northwest of Dau Tieng left 155 Americans dead and more than 1,000 NVA soldiers and Viet Cong killed along with 200 taken prisoner.

BELOW: US Marine amphibious craft come ashore in Vietnam while a Bell UH-1 helicopter approaches at right. (US Navy via Wikimedia Commons)

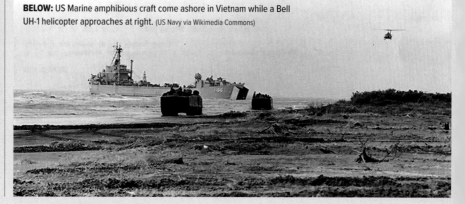

ABOVE: US soldiers advance along a jungle path in South Vietnam during search and destroy operations.
(US Army via Wikimedia Commons)

BELOW: American troops watch a US Marine Douglas A-4 Skyhawk streak across the sky after dropping bombs on Viet Cong positions.
(Defense Department Photo (Marine Corps) via Wikimedia Commons)

ABOVE: Soldiers of the 1st Cavalry Division (Airmobile) burn a hut previously occupied by Viet Cong insurgents in July 1967.
(National Archives and Records Administration via Wikimedia Commons)

As the year ended, frustration with quantifiable progress in the war effort was apparent within the US government. The US had dropped more bombs on North Vietnam than on Japan during World War Two and more than in the entire Korean War. A string of bases had been built from the Laotian border along the Demilitarized Zone (DMZ) separating North and South Vietnam to Quang Tri Province on the South China Sea to guard against enemy infiltration and supply.

Still, in October Secretary McNamara stated that the communists were losing an estimated 60,000 dead per year but "there is no sign of an impending break in enemy morale and it appears that he can more than replace his losses by infiltration from North Vietnam and recruitment in South Vietnam."

Indeed, the communists were never near the depletion of their available manpower despite heavy casualties. Controlling the pace of the ground war, the North Vietnamese military was always capable of withdrawing units from direct confrontation by pulling back across the frontiers of North Vietnam, Laos, or Cambodia.

SPRINGBOARD

General Westmoreland apparently viewed 1966 largely as a year of preparation and a springboard to increasing offensive operations in 1967. Ground fighting in Vietnam was most often short and sharp between opposing forces of fewer than 300-400 troops. An exception to this standard was Operation Cedar Falls and its follow-on Operation Junction City undertaken in January 1967 against the so-called Iron Triangle, a centre of enemy activity located northwest of Saigon.

Search and destroy operations sometimes extended over several months. Among these were Operation Prairie from August 1966 to January 1967, Operation Byrd from August 1966 to December 1967, and the combined Operations Thayer, Irving, and Thayer II from September 1966 to February 1967. During the five months of Operation Palm Beach, January 6 to May 31, 1967, the US Army 3rd Brigade, 9th Infantry Division in company with three additional infantry battalions killed 570 Viet Cong insurgents and lost 149 soldiers in action. Operation Pershing stretched from February 1967 to March 1968 as elements of four US, ARVN, and ROK divisions fought the 3rd NVA Division. An estimated 5,400 communist troops were killed; nearly 900 allied soldiers died.

In a letter written directly to Ho Chi Minh on February 8, 1967, President Lyndon Johnson made an offer. It read in part: "…I am prepared to order a cessation of bombing against your country and the stopping of further augmentation of US forces in South Viet-Nam as soon as I am assured that infiltration into South Viet-Nam by land and by sea has stopped. These acts of restraint on both sides would, I believe, make it possible for us to conduct serious and private discussions leading toward an early peace…."

Ho responded days later: "The Vietnamese people will never give way to force, it will never accept conversation under the clear threat of bombs."

The fighting continued.

Thirteen American helicopters were shot down in a single week during February 1967. From April to October, Operation Francis Marion was led by the US 4th Infantry Division and 173rd Airborne Brigade. In fighting at Darlac, Pleiku, and the Kon Tum Provinces, more than 1,500 NVA were killed in exchange for 300 American and 100 ARVN dead. In mid-April, General Westmoreland told the Joint Chiefs of Staff that another 201,000 American troops would be needed in country to maintain the combat initiative.

For three weeks in April and May, 1967 US Marines fought the NVA for control of three hills surrounding the combat base at Khe Sanh, leaving 940 communist dead and 155 Marines killed in action. The resurgent NVA ambushed the 4th Battalion, 503rd Airborne Infantry near Dak To on July 10, killing 26 Americans. At the end of the month, a Gallup poll revealed that 52% of the American people disapproved of the Johnson administration's handling of the war. Over half the respondents believed the US was actually losing.

As 1967 wore on, allied search and destroy missions and air sorties were countered by communist guerrilla and NVA ambushes, hit-and-run attacks, assaults on US bases, and terror strikes on population centres in South Vietnam. Two Viet Cong battalions massacred scores of civilians in the village of Dak Son in December.

At the end of 1967, American troop strength in Vietnam neared a half million with more than 15,000 killed and 109,000 wounded to date in the conflict. In that year alone, the South Vietnamese lost roughly 12,000 dead, and communist forces suffered a staggering 140,000 casualties.

Despite peace overtures, there appeared no end in sight to the war of attrition.

BELOW: Soldiers of the 6th Battalion, Royal Australian Regiment, rendezvous with helicopters for extraction from the field. (Ward, Barrie Collection Database of the Australian War Memorial via Wikimedia Commons)

OPERATIONS CEDAR FALLS AND JUNCTION CITY

For years, the Viet Cong had operated freely in an area of nearly 120 square miles and scarcely 30 miles from the heart of Saigon, the South Vietnamese capital city. By the mid-1960s, the territory was such a communist stronghold that it had come to be known as the Iron Triangle.

Stretching from the River Saigon in the southwest to the Than Dien Forest in the north and River Thi Tinh to the east, the Iron Triangle was therefore perceived as a 'dagger pointed at Saigon'. Considering the results of Operation Attleboro encouraging, General William Westmoreland, MACV commander, sought to build on the search and destroy concept with the largest ground operation of the Vietnam War.

Operation Cedar Falls involved 30,000 US and South Vietnamese soldiers in an effort to clear the Iron Triangle. Westmoreland took advantage of the dry season and ordered the offensive to begin on January 8, 1967, while a follow-up offensive dubbed Operation Junction City was slated to follow with a sweep of the area designated as War Zone C.

Cedar Falls was conceived as a classic hammer and anvil offensive under the direct control of Major General Jonathan Seaman, commander of the II Field Force. The hammer would consist of the 2nd and 3rd Brigades, 1st Cavalry Division (Airmobile) to the north and northwest of the Iron Triangle along with the 173rd Airborne Brigade to the east. The anvil included the 2nd Brigade, 25th Infantry Division and the

ABOVE: Vietnamese villagers evacuated during Operation Cedar Falls occupied this makeshift shelter at Phu Loi in January 1967. (Office of History, Headquarters US Army Corps of Engineers via Wikimedia Commons)

196th Infantry Brigade south of the River Saigon. The 35th ARVN Ranger Battalion, US 1st Battalion, 503rd Infantry Regiment, and the 1st Squadron, 4th Cavalry Regiment were positioned north of the river. The hammer would strike the enemy while the anvil cut off its route of retreat. Intelligence reports indicated that the headquarters of the communist Military Region IV were located in the Iron Triangle, along with a troop concentration that included the Viet Cong 272nd Regiment, elements of the 165th Regiment, and the Phu Loi Local Force Battalion, a strength estimated at several thousand guerrillas.

With the blocking forces deployed, the offensive began on the morning of January 9 with the helicopter insertion of troops into a landing zone near the edge of the Than Dien Forest. The 2nd Battalion, 16th Infantry Regiment began a search and destroy sweep south of the River Saigon and covered heavy equipment that cleared large areas of jungle foliage to expose enemy positions. This work accompanied the continuing aerial spraying of a defoliant known popularly as Agent Orange, effective in the task but later proven to have substantial environmental impact and cause long-term health problems for individuals who were exposed.

A major objective of Cedar Falls was the occupation of the village of Ben Suc,

where an elaborate network of tunnels was located, and the 1st Battalion, 26th Infantry secured Ben Suc in a textbook airmobile assault on the first day of Cedar Falls.

American forces took control of the west side of the Iron Triangle and moved rapidly into the enemy territory from the north. Operating through January 26, the allied forces – with the Americans bearing the brunt of the fighting – killed 700 Viet Cong and captured a like number. They eliminated at least 1,100 bunkers

ABOVE: An American M113 personnel carrier and M48 Patton tank negotiate a road between the jungle and a rubber plantation during Operation Cedar Falls.
(US Army via Wikimedia Commons)

ABOVE: American soldiers of the 173rd Airborne Brigade guard Viet Cong prisoners in the Thanh Dien Forest during Operation Cedar Falls. (National Archives and Records Administration via Wikimedia Commons)

and fortified positions, 400 tunnels and another 500 strongpoints, while capturing 3,700 tons of rice, nearly 500,000 enemy documents, over 600 small-arms and crew-served weapons, and thousands of rounds of ammunition. Tunnel rats cleared many subterranean passages, while the Viet Cong largely avoided direct combat. Fewer than 100 American and South Vietnamese troops were killed.

'HEARTS AND MINDS'

One problematic aspect of Cedar Falls was the evacuation of nearly 6,000 civilians at Ben Suc. These villagers were to be relocated to Phu Loi, their huts razed, and the area subsequently declared a free-fire zone, where any adult inhabitant would be considered a communist guerrilla. Although the intent was to evacuate the villagers as humanely as possible, the execution was gruelling and ultimately inhumane. Many of those who observed it described the pitiful state of the civilians as they moved out with their livestock and whatever they could carry. Some later said that they were not allowed to take anything from their homes, and the South Vietnamese tasked with establishing an adequate refugee camp were given little advance notice of the pending operation. Therefore, the relocation produced far more suffering than anticipated and generated substantial animosity among the villagers for the Americans. In the end, when the Viet Cong returned to the Iron Triangle after Cedar Falls, many of these civilians provided support for the communists.

Through the course of Operation Cedar Falls, allied troops thrust deep into the Iron Triangle, cutting it in half and completing search and destroy missions while engaging in occasional firefights with the few Viet Cong guerrillas that had remained to offer resistance. One veteran communist fighter later told the *New York Times*: "Our policy was to avoid the enemy and protect our force. Only our local guerrilla units coped with the enemies, mainly by hit-and-run tactics. They also concealed their fighters during the day while moving and ambushing the American soldiers at night."

ABOVE: This Vietnamese village was burned to the ground during search and destroy operations in 1967.
(Office of History, Headquarters US Army Corps of Engineers via Wikimedia Commons)

Another fighter remarked: "We knew when, where and how many days they would carry out their operation. We had a lot of agents who worked at the Dong Du base of the 25th Division and in Saigon, who collected information and sent it to us." Still, Cedar Falls took its toll. The combat losses and the confiscation of foodstuffs and other supplies created a lengthy but temporary hardship. In time, the Viet Cong did return to the Iron Triangle.

Perceiving that Cedar Falls had secured the Iron Triangle, US commanders initiated Operation Junction City on February 22, 1967. For the next 82 days, the assault on the Viet Cong infrastructure continued. Junction City involved 22 US Army and four ARVN infantry battalions, 17 artillery battalions, 4,000 aircraft sorties that heavily bombed areas under communist control, and the airmobile capabilities and gunfire support of 249 helicopters. American and South Vietnamese airborne troops also executed the largest parachute combat deployment of the war.

Supplies, weapons, and equipment were seized and destroyed in the systematic clearing of War Zone C. Bases were established and garrisoned by CIDG (Civilian Irregular Defense Group) units, which consisted of irregular anti-communist paramilitary personnel of indigenous minorities such as the Montagnards, inhabitants of the mountainous country of Vietnam's Central Highlands.

Although the Viet Cong avoided heavy engagements, there were several intense firefights during the allied search and destroy sweep through Tay Ninh Province. At Ap Bau Bang, Ap Gau, and Prek Klok, communist counterattacks were repulsed with heavy losses, and with the conclusion of Junction City, the Viet Cong 9th Division

had been seriously weakened. Estimates of communist casualties included 2,728 killed and 34 captured. A total of 282 Americans were killed in action.

Although both Cedar Falls and Junction City were declared successful, the majority of Viet Cong units avoided overwhelming American and ARVN ground strength, air, and artillery support. Many slipped away to safety in neighbouring Cambodia to fight another day. In time, they were afforded the opportunity.

Cedar Falls and Junction City ultimately achieved mixed results. The tactical military gains were largely temporary, and in a strategic sense the painful evacuation of innocent civilians obviously damaged the American effort to win the hearts and minds of the Vietnamese people.

ABOVE: US armoured vehicles and infantry push forward against light Viet Cong resistance during Operation Junction City. (US Army via Wikimedia Commons)

ABOVE: A US soldier watches planes drop supplies to troops engaged in Operation Junction City.
(US Army via Wikimedia Commons)

THE CU CHI TUNNELS

The resourcefulness of the communist guerrillas in Vietnam is well known, and perhaps the best example of the insurgents' ingenuity is the elaborate network of underground tunnels utilised first by the Viet Minh to fight the French in the 1940s and then expanded considerably by the Viet Cong in the war against the South Vietnamese and their American benefactors.

During more than three decades of warfare, the communists constructed thousands of miles of underground tunnels, digging by hand and with rudimentary tools in an arduous task that raised the combat arts of concealment, mobility, and surprise to incredible levels of performance. Built with adequate ventilation, sometimes on three levels from depths of 10ft to 40ft below the surface, the tunnels served as storage spaces for weapons and supplies, as hospitals, kitchens, staging centres for ambushes and rapid movement, shelters, and headquarters. The tunnel complex in the Cu Chi district of the communist stronghold nicknamed the Iron Triangle, less than 50 miles from Saigon, was one of the most elaborate, linking 155 miles of underground labyrinth from the outskirts of the South Vietnamese capital to the Cambodian frontier.

Entrances were camouflaged so effectively that they were often undiscovered until opposing ground forces had passed them by, while the Viet Cong could quickly emerge from one or more of these small entryways,

ABOVE: The camouflaged entrance to a tunnel at Cu Chi is shown in the open position.

(Kevyn Jacobs via Wikimedia Commons)

ABOVE: Tunnel rat Sergeant Ronald H. Payne, armed with a Colt .45-calibre pistol and flashlight prepares to clear a Viet Cong tunnel during Operation Cedar Falls, 1967.

(US Army via Wikimedia Commons)

clash with the enemy, and then seemingly vanish. They were often located near small villages and ringed with booby traps that might trigger explosives, trap doors with sharpened stakes named 'punji sticks' that could penetrate a soldier's boot, or even dump boxes of scorpions from above on passing troops.

Eliminating tunnels wherever and whenever possible became an objective of several US and allied search and destroy missions. When a tunnel entrance was discovered, it might be blasted, or 'crimped', with explosives or inundated with water

or noxious gas. However, these methods proved ineffective as the tunnels had been constructed to thwart such tactics.

During Operation Crimp, a search and destroy mission involving 8,000 American and Australian soldiers in January 1966, a network of tunnels was discovered near Cu Chi in Binh Duong Province. Completing a four-day exploration, Australian engineers of 3 Field Troop discovered the complexity of the Viet Cong system and earned the nickname 'Tunnel Rats'. Soon enough, a training programme was developed for volunteers in the dangerous business of searching the tunnels. These intrepid men would enter a tunnel armed usually with only a knife, .45-calibre pistol, and flashlight, moving cautiously to avoid booby traps or guerrillas who might be waiting just a few feet away.

In January 1967, Operation Cedar Falls also targeted the tunnels in the vicinity of Cu Chi and the Iron Triangle. Tunnel rats of the US 1st Battalion, 5th Infantry Regiment, 25th 'Tropic Lightning' Division seized more than 500,000 communist documents in an intelligence coup, while caches of weapons and supplies were destroyed, creating logistical difficulties for the enemy.

Such operations did succeed in clearing some Viet Cong tunnels, but the sheer scale of the communist underground network made complete neutralisation virtually impossible. Throughout the war, the tunnels were a continuing problem, facilitating guerrilla operations during the Tet Offensive of early 1968 and beyond.

After the war, the government of Vietnam preserved 75 miles of the Cu Chi tunnel network, and the area is now visited by thousands of tourists each year.

ABOVE: A section of the Viet Cong tunnel network at Cu Chi is open to visitors today. (Kevyn Jacobs via Wikimedia Commons)

BATTLE OF DAK TO

American and South Vietnamese victories in early 1967 had driven Viet Cong units and command apparatus out of some areas in South Vietnam as well as to sanctuaries in neighbouring Cambodia and Laos. Within weeks, however, the communists had regrouped and resolved to strike back.

In the summer, intelligence reports indicated that the Viet Cong and North Vietnamese Army (NVA) were in the midst of a build-up of forces in the border areas. Operation Greeley was launched to force the enemy out of the mountainous region, and by August the belief that the communists were building strength in Cambodia and

Laos was confirmed. One development that intrigued US commanders was the appearance of a Viet Cong engineering company constructing a hospital on the banks of the River Song Be in western Kontum Province, near the convergence of the Vietnamese, Cambodian, and Laotian borders, and west of the American special forces camp at Loc Ninh. Lieutenant General Frederick C. Weyand, commander of II Field Force, was prompted to order contingency plans for the defence of the provincial capitals of Loc Ninh and Song Be.

On October 29, the Viet Cong hit the Loc Ninh special forces camp with an artillery barrage, and the defenders responded with counterbattery fire and air strikes. For the next week, fighting raged. The defenders were hard pressed, and the timely arrival of reinforcements helped to break the momentum of the communist thrust. When the fighting at Loc Ninh subsided, an estimated 852 Viet Cong were dead and 50 US and South Vietnamese soldiers had been killed. Loc Ninh signalled the beginning of a series of bloody clashes called the Border Battles.

While the guerrillas attacked Loc Ninh, the NVA and other Viet Cong units totalling about 12,000 troops, including the NVA 24th, 32nd, 66th, and 174th Regiments, were observed moving from Pleiku into Kantum Province, assuming positions to attack the Dak To special forces camp. A series of sharp engagements ensued, and these are often collectively referred to as the Battle of Dak To. Tactically, the objective of North Vietnamese General Nguyen Chi Thanh was to destroy a battalion-sized concentration of American forces in the field surrounding Dak To and also to draw large numbers of allied troops out of population centres and into the countryside. Strategically, such US and ARVN troop movements would weaken the response to guerrilla operations in major cities

ABOVE: A squad leader of the 173rd Airborne Brigade mans an M60 machine gun in preparation for the final assault on Hill 875 during the Battle of Dak To. (National Archives and Records Administration via Wikimedia Commons)

BELOW: This aerial view of the special forces camp at Dak To looks toward the Laotian frontier and reveals the ruggedness of the surrounding terrain. (US Army via Wikimedia Commons)

BELOW: Soldiers of the 173rd Airborne Brigade meet helicopters to evacuate wounded during the Battle of Dak To, November 1967. (US Army via Wikimedia Commons)

during the communist Tet Offensive planned for early 1968.

In early November, General William Peers, commander of the US 4th Infantry Division, was notified that a defecting NVA soldier was willing to talk. Sergeant Vu Hong of the 66th Infantry Regiment had deserted from a 50-man reconnaissance party that was identifying firing positions for mortars and 122mm rockets on the night of November 2 and surrendered at the village of Bak Ri. During interrogation, the defector revealed that four NVA regiments were headed for the base at Dak To and a CIDG (Civilian Irregular Defense Group) base at nearby Ben Het.

OPERATION MACARTHUR

Peers put the intelligence to good use and countered with the launching of Operation MacArthur on November 3, precipitating the Dak To engagements. Based on information received, Peers ordered the 3rd Battalion, 12th Infantry Regiment and the 3rd Battalion, 8th Infantry Regiment to attack, pre-emptively hitting known NVA positions. Aware of the intended attack against Dak To, the Americans committed further troop strength, including the 173rd Airborne Brigade and the 1st Brigade, 1st Cavalry Division (Airmobile), in the effort to push the communists out of an extensive series of fortified positions on the high ground surrounding the special forces camp.

In preparation for ground assaults, heavy air bombardment and artillery fire were laid on communist positions. Still, heavy fighting lay ahead. Elements of the 4th Division battled the NVA for the high ground during an agonizing three weeks. From November 6 to 14, the 3rd Battalion, 12th Infantry took serious casualties along Ngok Kon Kring Ridge

ABOVE: Troops of the 8th Infantry Regiment, 4th Division descend Hill 742 during the Battle of Dak To.
(US Army via Wikimedia Commons)

ABOVE: In the heat of combat during the Battle of Dak To, an American soldier gestures with his M-16 assault rifle on Hill 882. (US Army via Wikimedia Commons)

and at Hills 1124, 1089, and 1021, where enemy 60mm mortar and shoulder-fired RPG (rocket-propelled grenade) fire was intense. Companies A and C of the 12th Infantry took Hill 1338 on November 17 after two days of vicious combat. By the third week of fighting, American troops occupied Dogbone Hill, at that time one of their most forward positions. Although subjected to continual enemy mortar and rocket barrages, the US troops were supplied by CH-47 Chinook and UH-1 helicopters that flew in supplies, artillery pieces, ammunition, and reinforcements.

Into late November, battles for control of tactically vital hills and ridges continued. The 173rd Airborne Brigade, coming off its key participation in Operation Junction City, fought the communists for control of Hill 875, just outside the town of Dak To. The terrain was rugged, dotted with elephant grass, thick shrubs, and tall stands of bamboo, and some of the most savage, see-saw fighting of the Vietnam conflict took place there. Throughout the struggle, effective air support was limited due to the

dense foliage and the close proximity of the opposing forces, but the 4th Battalion, 173rd was able to establish Fire Support Base 15 on Hill 823 in early fighting.

On November 23, the 4th Battalion reached the summit of Hill 875 and discovered that the enemy had withdrawn. Although Hill 875 was in American hands, one of the worst friendly fire incidents of the conflict had occurred on the initial day of the final assaults against this important high ground. On November 19, a Marine Corps attack aircraft dropped a 500lb bomb on 173rd Airborne positions, killing 42 Americans and wounding 45.

Throughout the fighting, the NVA kept the airstrip at Dak To under constant mortar, rocket, and small-arms fire. On November 12, accurate enemy fire destroyed several large C-130 Hercules transport aircraft on the ground and set off ammunition and fuel dumps at the special forces' base. A huge blast detonated 1,100 tons of shells and rifle rounds. Despite the setback, the flow of critical supplies was maintained, and when the Battle of Dak To had finally ended in late November, 2,096 tactical air sorties had been flown in support of the ground troops, including 257 strikes by heavy B-52 bombers. American artillery fired 151,000 rounds against enemy positions.

A total of 376 US soldiers were killed and 1,441 wounded in the Battle of Dak To, while ARVN losses were 79 killed in action. Estimates of NVA and Viet Cong casualties included 1,000 to 1,445 dead.

The tactical result of the Battle of Dak To was a clear victory for the Americans and South Vietnamese forces. The communist enemy was cleared from Kontum Province, and the 1st NVA Division had been rendered virtually ineffective as a fighting force. Roughly 75% of its pre-Dak To strength was eliminated prior to the coming Tet Offensive. The flow of reinforcements and supplies through Cambodia to the Viet Cong was impeded at least temporarily.

Strategically, the communists had succeeded in drawing roughly one-half of the American combat troops in South Vietnam away from the cities. Therefore, the response to the guerrilla assaults in population centres during the Tet Offensive would be seriously handicapped.

ABOVE: US soldiers are shown destroying bunkers following the capture of Hill 875 after savage fighting at Dak To.
(US Army Heritage and Education Center via Wikimedia Commons)

GENERAL VO NGUYEN GIAP

Second only to Ho Chi Minh, General Vo Nguyen Giap stands out among the early leaders of communist Vietnam. Giap played the foremost role in the development of military strategy and tactics that defeated the French in Indochina and eventually compelled the United States to withdraw its armed forces after more than a decade of futile support for the insecure government of South Vietnam.

Unlike many communist leaders, Giap appeared to revel in the limelight and adulation he received when the conflict was over. Particularly, the French praised his military prowess, and his own writings reflect an unusual self-aggrandizement. Giap was not a trained military man, and his critics have sometimes pointed to heavy losses sustained in the few pitched battles against overwhelming French and US military might. Nevertheless, he remains the iconic figure of a military movement that eventually outlasted its adversaries and provided the support for the establishment of the communist government in Hanoi during decades of strife.

ABOVE: In 1942, Giap posed with communist leader Ho Chi Minh. (遼東半島 via Wikimedia Commons)

Giap was a superb organiser and led the growth of an embryonic communist insurgency from a rabble of armed peasants into an effective army, both in the conventional sense and in the shadowy implementation of Viet Minh and Viet Cong guerrilla tactics. He commanded the Viet Minh in the decisive Battle of Dien Bien Phu, which sounded the death knell of French involvement in Indochina in 1954, seizing the advantages offered to him by the ineptitude of his enemies and leveraging the nationalist/communist fervour of the troops under his

ABOVE: General Vo Nguyen Giap was a national hero when this photo was taken in 1957.

(Unknown author (in Vietnam) via Wikimedia Commons)

command. He is seen as the architect of victory and the leader of communist forces in the decisive Tet Offensive of early 1968 and the Easter Offensive of 1972, and then the culminating collapse of the South Vietnamese Army in 1975.

Despite the fact that some historians have later asserted that real control of major military activities was heavily influenced by the communist method of collective decision making, the participation of Chinese strategists, and the notion that subordinate commanders may have wielded real tactical and strategic authority, Giap remains as the principal figure who moulded the communist masses into an effective fighting force.

Born on August 25, 1911, at Le Thuy in Quang Binh Province, Giap was the son of a committed anti-colonial educator. The family was poor, but the boy studied at the French Lycee Nationale in Hue, the same secondary school that Ho Chi Minh attended. He received a law degree from Hanoi University. While still a student he developed his own ardent belief in

ABOVE: Shortly after the defeat of Japan in World War Two, Vo Nguyen Giap reviews communist troops.

(Unknown author (in Vietnam) via Wikimedia Commons)

an autonomous Vietnam. He joined the communist party in 1926 and was arrested by the French for fomenting unrest. As a teacher of history at the Lycee Thanh Long, he persuaded a number of colleagues to embrace revolutionary political theory.

When the communist party was outlawed in Indochina, Giap fled to China. His wife was arrested and died in prison three years later, and his sister-in-law was put death by guillotine. Meanwhile, Giap was emerging as a military leader. During World War Two, he committed to the formation of the Viet Minh, receiving support from the Nationalist government in China during the fight against the occupying Japanese in exchange for intelligence gathered via his network of spies across northern Vietnam. Ho Chi Minh sanctioned the formation of propaganda teams that became the nucleus of the communist armed forces. By the spring of 1945, Ho had named Giap the commander of the Viet Minh insurgents, and the guerillas were organised well enough for Giap to march his peasant army into Hanoi.

RUTHLESS

Without formal military background, Giap was a student of history, and his theories of organisation and strategy were based largely on the Chinese pattern under Mao Tse-tung. Three stages of conflict guided his actions. These were the inception of a revolutionary movement, the escalation of guerrilla war to an equal footing with the enemy, and finally the overwhelming of that enemy by the communist forces. While contemporaries remember Giap as an arrogant, driven, ambitious, and sometimes impulsive leader who was inculcated with communist doctrine, he was also at times ruthless.

Giap was known to have approved of brutal purges, including the executions of political opponents during the formative years of the communist revolution. After Ho proclaimed an independent Vietnam,

ABOVE: This photo of an aging Vo Nguyen Giap was taken in 2008 when he was 97 years old.
(Creative Commons Ricardo Stuckert via Wikimedia Commons)

ABOVE: General Giap is shown greeting Cuban communist dictator Fidel Castro.
(Creative Commons Clay Gilliland via Wikimedia Commons)

Giap was given charge of all security and police forces and retained command of the military while strictly enforcing censorship of the media to support the communist regime. He did not spare the ranks of the Viet Minh. In 1946, a total of 360 representatives were elected to the national assembly. Before the assembly convened, their number was curtailed to 291 and 37 representatives were officially recognised as leaders of the opposition. Giap ordered the arrest of 200 people during the opening session, and when it concluded only 20 opposition members retained their seats. A large number of those taken into custody were imprisoned for lengthy periods or executed.

The communist victory in China was a turning point for Giap and the Viet Minh. After Mao took power, the revolutionaries were supplied with heavy weapons and adequate equipment for the first time, while Chinese advisors trained the militia. However, Giap was somewhat impetuous, sending his guerrillas against the French in a pitched battle in the Red River delta in 1950. The defeat cost the communists 20,000 casualties.

But the French provided an opportunity for redemption when they established a forward base at Dien Bien Phu. Giap recognised the weaknesses in the French position, moving artillery into the surrounding mountains while troops dug a series of trenches ever closer to enemy strongpoints. Viet Minh guns pounded the French, while several defensive positions fell to heavy assault. Despite severe casualties, Giap was relentless. The French surrender in the spring of 1954 gained him lasting fame.

During the subsequent fight against the US and South Vietnamese, Giap was at his best in the movement of forces, conventional and guerrilla, and in the supply and logistics aspects that were critical to sustained operations in the South. His fame and reputation provided inspiration to the ranks of the North Vietnamese Army (NVA) and the Viet Cong guerrilla movement, while his organisational prowess was evident in the coordinated attacks on 35 major cities across South Vietnam during the Tet Offensive. In his book *Big Victory,*

Great Task, Giap described his strategy to counter American military superiority as one which involved matching its strength where possible. However, when the odds were against the NVA or Viet Cong they were to avoid a major battle.

Giap was a national hero by the time the South Vietnamese regime collapsed, and total victory was achieved in 1975. The political rift between the Soviet Union and the People's Republic of China also divided the leadership of a unified Vietnam. Giap was a confirmed ally of the Soviets, and his stance led to friction with other top communists. Despite such political wrangling that some historians conclude had led to his marginalisation in the communist government, he served as minister of national defence and became a deputy prime minister during the late 1970s. He was a full member of the North Vietnamese politburo until 1982.

During his later years, Giap refused to assert political influence during periods of economic decline and concerns related to military involvement in Cambodia. He preferred to burnish his reputation as the Napoleon of Southeast Asia. He relinquished the office of deputy prime minister in 1991 and received few public accolades until the 40th anniversary of the Dien Bien Phu victory in 1994. He died on October 4, 2013, at the age of 102, and following a state funeral he was buried in Quang Binh Province.

VÕ NGUYÊN GIÁP
ĐẠI TƯỚNG TỔNG TƯ LỆNH

ABOVE: This display honouring the career of General Vo Nguyen Giap is located in the Vietnam Military History Museum in Hanoi.
(Creative Commons Clay Gilliland via Wikimedia Commons)

GENERAL WILLIAM C. WESTMORELAND

ABOVE: General William C. Westmoreland commanded US forces in Vietnam 1964-1968.
(Defense Visual Information Center via Wikimedia Commons)

"Militarily, we succeeded in Vietnam. We won every engagement we were involved in out there," said General William C. Westmoreland, commander of US military forces in Vietnam from 1964 to 1968. From that purely military perspective there is truth in the statement. American forces were victorious virtually every time the communist North Vietnamese Army or Viet Cong insurgency was confronted in a major battle of the Vietnam War.

In fact, Westmoreland got what he wanted on more than one occasion. He chose to wage a war of attrition, wearing the communists down by inflicting heavy casualties with a 'body count' of enemy dead to back up his reports to the White House, Congress, and the American people that the US and its South Vietnamese allies were winning the war. When he asked for more resources, particularly greater numbers of American combat troops, he received them. From the time he took command in 1964 until he was kicked upstairs to the post of US Army Chief of Staff, the number of American service personnel under his command rose exponentially from 16,000 to 535,000.

In the fall of 1967, Westmoreland wrote in a telegram to General Creighton Abrams, his deputy commander and successor in Saigon, that there was "some light at the end of the tunnel," but he told a CBS News reporter years later that Senator Henry Cabot Lodge had actually coined the phrase. "I was optimistic, but I did not forecast the end of the war, as I have been accused," he commented. He then clarified later that he did not imply through his statements that the Americans were "grinding down the enemy" that the "war was about to be over."

After the Vietnam experience, Westmoreland spent the rest of his life defending his actions while in command. He firmly believed that American firepower and mobility would win the war of attrition, and he applied the airmobile tactic along with the search and destroy operational precept throughout. Perhaps his greatest miscalculation was his underestimation of the ability of the communists to make good their losses in men and materiel. In the end, it was the Americans who were exhausted with the cost of the conflict. In the autumn of 1967, the resilient communists took advantage of Westmoreland's commitment of large numbers of troops to rural areas across the countryside and away from Vietnamese population centres.

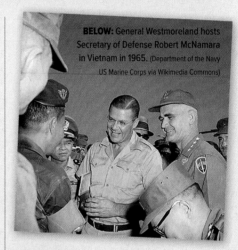

BELOW: General Westmoreland hosts Secretary of Defense Robert McNamara in Vietnam in 1965. (Department of the Navy US Marine Corps via Wikimedia Commons)

REPLACED

Although search and destroy operations such as Cedar Falls and Junction City were tactically successful, the resourceful NVA and Viet Cong were nevertheless able to launch the Tet Offensive, a coordinated attack across 35 cities in South Vietnam, in January 1968. Despite the fact that Tet was a military defeat for the communists, the widespread chaos, scenes of buildings afire in the heart of Saigon, and the sight of guerrillas in city streets undermined Westmoreland's assurances

ABOVE: General Westmoreland meets President Lyndon Johnson at Cam Ranh Air Base in Vietnam, December 1967.
(US Air Force via Wikimedia Commons)

BELOW: General Westmoreland accompanies President Johnson while presenting medals to troops of the US 82nd Airborne Division. (National Archives and Records Administration via Wikimedia Commons)

BELOW: General Westmoreland stands with President Johnson and South Vietnamese officials in 1966. (National Archives and Records Administration via Wikimedia Commons)

to chief of staff of the 82nd Airborne Division and served as an instructor at the Command and General Staff College.

When the Korean War broke out, Westmoreland commanded the 187th Regimental Combat Team for a year before returning to the Pentagon for five years, serving as deputy assistant chief of staff for manpower. With the rank of major general, he led the 101st Airborne Division from 1958-1960, and was then appointed superintendent of West Point. In the summer of 1963, he was promoted to lieutenant general in command of the XVIII Airborne Corps.

A year later, Westmoreland was in command in Vietnam, turning his growing strength into an offensive weapon and his own role from one of advising the South Vietnamese military to commanding an offensive against the communists in the war of attrition he had anticipated.

Controversy swirled around the concept of 'body count', while he manipulated the estimates of enemy troop strength that were reported to the US Congress. He made three trips to the United States in 1967 and during public speaking engagements reported that the situation in Vietnam was moving in a positive direction. Then, the shock of the Tet Offensive not only discredited those reports but also undermined public confidence in the administration of President Lyndon Johnson.

In 1982, nine years after US military operations in Vietnam ended, the retired general filed suit against CBS, investigative reporter Mike Wallace, and other related parties for libel, alleging that a documentary titled *The Uncounted Enemy: A Vietnam Deception*, had been produced and released in a deliberate effort to damage his reputation while exposing the intentionally under-reported strength of the enemy. The suit was settled out of court.

When his term as Army Chief of Staff ended in 1972, Westmoreland was offered the post of Supreme Allied Commander in Europe but opted to retire. He ran unsuccessfully for the governorship of South Carolina, and in 1974 his book *A Solder Reports* presented the case for his conduct of the war in Vietnam. Westmoreland suffered from Alzheimer's disease for many years and died at age 91 on July 18, 2005. He is interred in the West Point cemetery.

BELOW: General Westmoreland is sworn in as Army Chief of Staff, July 3, 1968. (Creative Commons Army Archive Lewis Sorley via Wikimedia Commons)

that the US was in fact winning in Vietnam. In the subsequent loss of confidence, he was replaced by General Abrams.

In hindsight, Westmoreland said: "I've made this statement many times: If I would have to do it over again, I would have made known the forthcoming Tet Offensive." In the end, William Westmoreland has come to be known as 'the general who won every battle until he lost the war'.

When he was chosen for the top post in Vietnam, General Westmoreland appeared to be the right military man for the job. He had served as deputy to MACV (Military Assistance Command, Vietnam) commander General Paul Harkins for six months when he was elevated in June 1964. During the next four years, he led the allied forces against the NVA and Viet Cong insurgency, and though tactical operations were often deemed victories, the campaign to win the hearts and minds of the Vietnamese people, engage the enemy in a decisive battle, and destroy the will of the communists to continue the struggle remained elusive.

Westmoreland was born in Spartanburg, South Carolina, on March 26, 1914, the son of a local textile manufacturer. He attended military school at The Citadel in Charleston, and then transferred to the US Military Academy at West Point, graduating in 1936 as first captain, the top cadet in his class, and recipient of the Pershing Sword.

During World War Two, Westmoreland served as an officer with the 34th Field Artillery Battalion, 9th Infantry Division. He performed with great efficiency, directing his guns in a critical stand against the Germans following the disastrous defeat of American forces at Kasserine Pass, Tunisia, in February 1942, and later in Sicily during Operation Husky in support of the 82nd Airborne Division. He earned the praise of airborne commanding generals Maxwell Taylor and James M. Gavin. In February 1944, he was elevated to executive officer of the 9th Division artillery, and in October to division chief of staff. Immediately after World War Two, he commanded the 60th Infantry Regiment during the occupation of Germany and continued his rise through the US Army command structure. Numerous postings were followed by command of the 504th Parachute Infantry Regiment on the recommendation of General Gavin. He rose

THE TET OFFENSIVE

ABOVE: Black smoke billows through Saigon after explosions rock the capital city during the opening hours of the Tet Offensive. (National Archives Still Picture Records Section, Special Media Archives Services Division (NWCS-S) via Wikimedia Commons)

ABOVE: Viet Cong guerrillas armed with AK-47 assault rifles and carrying American-made radios pose prior to the Tet Offensive. (US Army Center of Military History via Wikimedia Commons)

Tet, the observance of the lunar new year, is a major holiday across Vietnam. For several years, the communist North Vietnamese and Viet Cong and the South Vietnamese and their American sponsors had agreed to a truce of 36 hours. There would be no fighting as families gathered for the festive occasion.

However, on January 30, 1968, everything changed. Viet Cong insurgents struck in 13 cities across Vietnam, setting off bombs, firing rifles and machine guns at government facilities, and terrorising the urban residents. The communist offensive spread like a brushfire. Within hours, 35 major population centres were wracked with violence and soon 100 cities and villages were embroiled in the fighting.

ABOVE: Prior to the Tet Offensive, Viet Cong infiltrators study a map of District 7 and the vicinity of Saigon. (PD-Vietnam via Wikimedia Commons)

The North Vietnamese command headed by General Vo Nguyen Giap had conceived the Tet Offensive in an effort to destabilise the corrupt government of South Vietnam and set off a general uprising against the regime of President Nguyen Van Thieu. Further, Giap was aware of media reports from American military commanders, particularly General William Westmoreland, commander of US forces in Vietnam, who implied that the war effort was moving steadily toward victory. The North Vietnamese wanted to demonstrate that in reality the conclusion of hostilities was quite distant.

Therefore, Giap reasoned, with the support of the American public for the war already waning, a successful offensive marked by the ability of the Viet Cong to strike in the South at the time and place of their own choosing would further sway public opinion in the United States. Perhaps the administration of President

Lyndon Johnson would be obliged to decrease the US military commitment to South Vietnam or even withdraw American forces completely.

Preliminary communist operations to facilitate the Tet Offensive had begun in the autumn of 1967 with a build-up of forces and occasional attacks on the US forward base at Khe Sanh near South Vietnam's border with Laos as well as other locations in Vietnam's central highlands. The subsequent siege of Khe Sanh began on January 21, 1968 and lasted 77 days. The garrison of US Marines and South Vietnamese Rangers, at times under intense pressure, held out as General Westmoreland and President Johnson both believed in the early stages of the action that Khe Sanh would be the focus of an anticipated communist offensive.

Meanwhile, multiple search and destroy missions had pulled many allied troops out of South Vietnamese cities and into the countryside. Two of the largest such operations, Cedar Falls and Junction City were deemed tactical victories, but there was little concerted response to some rather ominous signs, including increased insurgent presence in urban areas, which signalled the coming of the Tet operation.

DAMAGED CREDIBILITY

As the Tet Offensive progressed, it became clear that the first communist objective was a failure. The US and South Vietnamese responded rapidly. Taking advantage of the military situation in which both Viet Cong and North Vietnamese Army (NVA) troops were in the open and exposed, they inflicted more than 175,000 casualties on

BELOW: US Marines armed with M-14 rifles encounter Viet Cong guerrillas near Da Nang during the Tet Offensive. (Department of Defense Department of the Navy US Marine Corps via Wikimedia Commons)

ABOVE: South Vietnamese National Police Chief Nguyen Ngoc Loan prepares to execute Viet Cong insurgent captive Nguyen Van Lem in a Saigon street. (Eddie Adams Associated Press via Wikimedia Common)

the communist forces. Militarily, Tet was a costly failure. However, the second objective was achieved. The US Military propaganda machine's reports asserting that victory was near were exposed as overly optimistic or even deliberately deceptive disinformation. During the nine months of the Tet Offensive, the credibility of the American military establishment was destroyed at home.

When General Westmoreland requested an additional 200,000 combat troops for Vietnam, President Johnson refused. By the summer of 1968, Westmoreland was recalled to Washington and appointed Army Chief of Staff, replaced in Vietnam by General Creighton Abrams. Johnson suggested peace negotiations and restrained American bombers from attacking targets north of the 20th parallel. Still, the damage to his presidency was done. In March 1968, he addressed a television audience across the United States and announced: "I shall not seek, and I will not accept, the nomination of my party for another term as your President."

With the Johnson administration a casualty of Tet, President Richard Nixon took office determined to pursue policies of 'Vietnamisation', turning the war effort fully over to South Vietnam, and a euphemistic 'peace with honour' exit for the United States. By the time the Tet Offensive had ebbed in September 1968, more than 50,000 casualties had been absorbed by American, South Vietnamese, and allied forces. All the while, Americans watched the street fighting on their televisions during dinner hour news broadcasts.

In itself, the offensive was shocking. The Viet Cong and NVA acted brutally. The most vicious fighting took place in the provincial capital of Hue, the ancient seat of power for a line of emperors and a centre of learning

situated on the shore of the Perfume River. The communists swept into Hue on the opening day of Tet, rounding up members of the intelligentsia, local government, and average citizens suspected of assisting the Americans and South Vietnamese. Many were shot on the spot and buried in mass graves. At least 2,800 people were murdered while another 3,000 simply vanished.

When the US Marines entered Hue, they found the communists ensconced within the walls of its old citadel. The historic buildings of the citadel were pummelled by American artillery fire and airstrikes. Marine squads supported by tanks fought street to

street and structure to structure against the stubborn enemy. More than 200 Marines died in the month-long fight for Hue, and more than 5,000 Viet Cong and NVA soldiers were killed or wounded.

Atrocities occurred on both sides. In the heart of Saigon, the South Vietnamese capital city, television cameras whirred as Nguyen Ngoc Loan, chief of the country's national police, pointed a revolver at the head of a captured Viet Cong guerrilla and executed the man in the street.

Nowhere was the chaos during the early hours of the Tet Offensive more fully revealed than in Saigon. Preliminary reports of the Viet Cong and NVA attacks had been filtering into the US embassy there for some time when the war came dramatically home to the nexus of the American presence in Southeast Asia. In the predawn hours of January 31, members of the elite Viet Cong C-10 Sapper Battalion climbed into a taxi and a small truck and departed their safe house at an auto repair facility in the city.

The 19 guerrillas sped toward the US embassy, relocated recently from its original site to a three-acre tract near the British and French embassies and the Presidential Palace after a communist car bomb had exploded in March 1965, destroying the original building, and killing 22 people. The construction of the new embassy's main chancery building had concluded just four months earlier.

The communists had trained extensively for their mission to breach the compound wall, occupy the main building, and take hostages. They had been bolstered by assurances from the commander at Viet Cong Sub-Region 6 headquarters that a large group of anti-government students would converge on the embassy after daylight, followed rapidly by substantial Viet Cong forces that would provide relief by afternoon.

ABOVE: South Vietnamese Rangers crouch along a Saigon street as they search for Viet Cong insurgents. (Department of Defense via Wikimedia Commons)

The two vehicles stopped in the street adjacent to the compound wall. The insurgents quickly exited and set explosives that blasted a hole through the concrete and marble just large enough for a man to squeeze through. At 2:47am, the blast alerted two American guards, Specialist Charles Daniel, and Private First Class William Sebast, on duty at the nearby night gate. Daniel shouted into his radio: "They're coming in! They're coming in!" The two Viet Cong leaders, Ut Nho and Bay Tuyen, squeezed through the hole first and were promptly shot dead by the guards but seconds later, two Vietnamese men employed as drivers by the US State Department but actually Viet Cong operatives, shot the guards to death from behind.

At the time of the attack only three US Marines, six American civilians, and two Vietnamese employees were inside the chancery. Marine Sergeant Ronald Harper responded to the radio warning and reached the chancery entrance just in time to close the heavy teakwood doors, which stood firm against blasts from rocket-propelled grenades and small arms. Unable to gain entry to the building, the remaining insurgents were soon trapped by a detachment of Marines that rushed through the main gate. They took up positions behind six large concrete planters in the embassy courtyard.

Army Military Police (MP) Sergeant Johnnie Thomas and Specialist Owen Mebust headed toward the sounds of fighting in their Jeep but were killed by Viet Cong fire at the main gate. Meanwhile, Marine Sergeant Rudy Soto, Jr., watched the unfolding attack from the roof of the chancery. He fired a 12-gauge shotgun at the intruders, and when that weapon jammed, he pulled a .38-calibre revolver and emptied it in their direction. Marine Corporal James Marshall fired at the enemy from the roof of an outbuilding but was killed within minutes.

BELOW: Damage to the US Embassy chancery building and compound wall is shown after the fight with Viet Cong insurgents on January 31, 1968. (US Army Military History Institute via Wikimedia Commons)

ABOVE: US Marines walk through the ruins of the village of Dai Do, Vietnam, after communist insurgents have been forced out of the area during the Tet Offensive. (Schulimson US Federal Government via Wikimedia Commons)

ABOVE: US Military Police take up a firing position behind a tree just across the street from the embassy in Saigon. (US Army Military History Institute via Wikimedia Commons)

101ST AIRBORNE

At 4:20am, General Westmoreland ordered the 716th MP Battalion to eliminate the insurgents. Headquarters of the 101st Airborne Division received orders to send troops to the embassy while elements of the division were already engaged with the Viet Cong at the Bien Hoa Army Base east of Saigon. At roughly 5am, a helicopter carrying troopers of the 101st flew low toward the chancery, drawing heavy fire from the surviving insurgents but the Marines and MPs had already killed most of them. The helicopter veered away but soon returned to discharge its human cargo.

After six hours, the embassy compound was secured. Five Americans and 18 Viet Cong had been killed; their bodies strewn about the courtyard. One guerrilla was captured alive and General Westmoreland arrived to survey the scene, while Ellsworth Bunker, US Ambassador to South Vietnam, ordered the embassy to open for business later in the day. The attempt to present a normal atmosphere to reporters and onlookers failed. Everyone knew the situation in Vietnam had changed dramatically.

The Tet Offensive was the turning point of American involvement in the Vietnam war. Although a significant tactical defeat for the communist forces, Tet was a strategic victory for them. In its wake, Americans at home were shaken and many of those who had at least moderately supported the war now concluded that the US was mired in an unwinnable stalemate.

KHE SANH

ABOVE: A fuel dump blazes at the Khe Sanh Marine combat base after a communist artillery barrage.
(US Department of Defense via Wikimedia Commons)

The buildup of communist forces seemed to indicate that a pitched battle was coming. Since 1962, the US Army had maintained a small camp at Khe Sanh along Route 9 just six miles from the South Vietnamese border with Laos and near the Demilitarized Zone (DMZ) in the northwest of the country. In 1966, the US Marines established a forward base near the village as well.

A year later, intelligence reports raised concerns. The communist movement toward Khe Sanh coincided with a strategic marshalling of forces in urban centres prior to the launching of the Tet Offensive the following January, and it remains unclear to this day whether the North Vietnamese command intended to fight a major battle at Khe Sanh or to create a diversion. In response, the Americans occupied outposts on the hills surrounding the base while General William Westmoreland, commander of US forces in Vietnam, with the support of President Lyndon Johnson, made the tactical decision to defend Khe Sanh.

Some American officers disagreed with that decision, citing the base's lack of tactical importance and the resemblance to the French commitment at Dien Bien Phu that had ended in disastrous defeat 13 years earlier. However, the defenders of Khe Sanh did hold advantages that the French did not. Overwhelming air power could be brought to bear on the enemy if necessary, while airlift capabilities could keep the base supplied in the event that overland approaches were cut.

The defence of Khe Sanh was code named Operation Scotland, and reinforcements were ordered to the area. The arrival of elements of the 26th Marines and the later introduction of the South Vietnamese Army (ARVN) 37th Ranger Battalion raised the number of defenders to about 6,000. The airstrip and defensive perimeter were refurbished and strengthened while large stores of ammunition were delivered in anticipation of a siege. Skirmishes broke out in the autumn of 1967, and when the communists ambushed a supply column on Route 9, ground replenishment operations were suspended. In December, elements of three North Vietnamese Army (NVA) divisions, the 320th, 324th, and 325th, were detected in the Khe Sanh area, and another, the 304th, was identified soon afterward, indicating communist strength had increased to about 17,000.

Shortly after midnight on January 21, 1968, the North Vietnamese Army (NVA) unleashed a heavy artillery barrage on the main Marine base. A shell detonated the ammunition dump, destroying nearly the entire stock of artillery rounds and setting off tear gas canisters, small-arms rounds, and hand grenades in a spectacular explosion. Three hundred NVA regulars surged toward the outpost at Hill 861. The ferocious assault was beaten back by Company K, 3rd Battalion, 26th Marines, but the NVA battalion-strength attack had temporarily penetrated the northwest perimeter.

A gruelling 77-day siege followed. The defenders at Khe Sanh were subjected to incessant artillery and mortar fire, and in response Gen Westmoreland initiated Operation Niagara, a combined artillery and aerial bombardment involving the use of advanced technology to detect the presence of enemy troops. Between January 22 and the end of March, US aircraft conducted 24,000 tactical sorties, while B-52 heavy bombers flew 2,700 missions as 14,223 tons of bombs rained down on the NVA. Still, enemy artillery, rockets, and mortars made the landing strip a shooting gallery.

LOST HERCULES

In early February, a Lockheed KC-130 tanker/transport plane was hit by enemy ground fire on approach to the airstrip. The plane erupted in a ball of fire, killing eight men. Resupply of the main base at Khe Sanh was then mainly accomplished by quick arrivals and departures of smaller Fairchild C-123 Provider transports and airdrops

ABOVE: In February 1968, President Lyndon Johnson views a scale model of the Marine base at Khe Sanh.
(US Department of Defense via Wikimedia Commons)

BELOW: A Lockheed C-130 Hercules transport flies low to deliver supplies at Khe Sanh. (US Air Force via Wikimedia Commons)

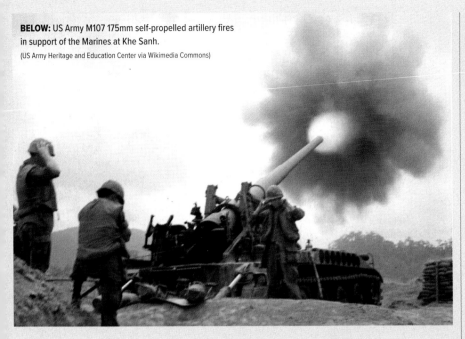

BELOW: US Army M107 175mm self-propelled artillery fires in support of the Marines at Khe Sanh.

(US Army Heritage and Education Center via Wikimedia Commons)

BELOW: A US Marine stands outside a bunker at Khe Sanh prior to the siege of early 1968. (Creative Commons Archives Branch USMC History Division via Wikimedia Commons)

arrived just in time to stem the NVA tide. Twenty-seven Americans and 150 enemy troops were killed.

The situation at Khe Sanh was in doubt for a time, and President Johnson became obsessed with the unfolding siege. He gazed at a scale model of the base, and General Earle Wheeler, chairman of the Joint Chiefs of Staff, contemplated the use of tactical nuclear weapons to fight off the communists. Westmoreland discounted such drastic measures but might well have agreed if required to save the base from annihilation. Indeed, the NVA had dug trenches only 30 yards away from the base's southeastern perimeter.

Heavy fighting continued through the end of February, and the tragedy of the 'Ghost Patrol' underscored the strength of the communist forces that surrounded Khe Sanh. On February 25, a 40-man patrol from Company B, 3rd Platoon, 1st Battalion, 26th Marines dashed into an ambush while pursuing three NVA soldiers skirting a treeline. Fewer than half the Marines returned to base after the debacle.

On the night of March 1, enemy forces were discovered massing for a decisive attack. Colonel David E. Lownds of the 26th Marines called for air support and artillery bombardment of the assembly areas. Massive firepower rained down on the communists, and two assaults on ARVN Ranger positions were repulsed. Sporadic NVA attacks continued through mid-March, and at the end of the month a Marine counterattack southeast of the perimeter killed 115 NVA soldiers for the loss of 10 Marines.

North Vietnamese troops were soon being withdrawn, and Gen Westmoreland authorised Operation Pegasus, a joint mission of Marine, US Army, and ARVN forces, to make contact with the Khe Sanh garrison and end the siege. American and ARVN forces lost 703 killed and more than 2,600 wounded at Khe Sanh. Estimates of NVA casualties approach 15,000.

American forces occupied Khe Sanh until Westmoreland was relieved of command in June 1968. Ironically, his successor, General Creighton Abrams, ordered the base closed days later. Bulldozers razed the fortifications, and questions emerged as to how such ground had been so important to defend for months and then summarily abandoned.

from Lockheed C-130 Hercules transports at higher altitudes and flying low to eject pallets fitted with drag parachutes, while Douglas A-4 Skyhawk attack aircraft worked in tandem with helicopters to resupply the outposts. In Operation Sierra a tactic dubbed 'super gaggle' was employed as the Skyhawks suppressed NVA anti-aircraft fire while Boeing Vertol CH-46 Sea Knight helicopters dashed in to deliver nets full of food, ammunition, and medical supplies.

With the inception of the Tet Offensive on January 30, 1968, a brief lull fell across Khe Sanh. But during the first week of February, the NVA launched savage ground assaults against the base and its outposts with renewed vigour. In the predawn darkness of February 5, Hill 861 was hit again. Marines

of Company E, 2nd Battalion, 26th Marines fought desperately to plug a gap in the northern sector of their line. After two hours of brutal fighting, the enemy was repulsed. Company E suffered 33 dead, and 100 communist soldiers were killed in the melee.

On February 7, communist troops overran the special forces camp at Lang Vei in the northwest corner of Quang Tri Province. The survivors filtered back to Khe Sanh. At the same time, the heavy bombardment of the Marine camp had taken its toll. One rocket tore into a bunker occupied by Marines of Company B, 3rd Recon Battalion, killing four and wounding 16. About a mile from Khe Sanh, a platoon from Company A, 1st Battalion, 9th Marines fought for their lives at Hill 64 on February 8. A relief force

ABOVE: Smoke rises during a firefight along the perimeter of the US Marine forward base at Khe Sanh.

(US Government via Wikimedia Commons)

THE BATTLE OF HUE

During the opening hours of the Tet Offensive, communist troops of the North Vietnamese Army (NVA) and Viet Cong guerrillas attacked 36 of 44 provincial capitals across South Vietnam. One of these was Hue, capital of Thura Thien Hue Province and the third largest city of South Vietnam.

Hue was an ancient city, once the seat of power of the Nguyen dynasty of emperors, and an important religious and cultural centre renowned for its beautiful temples and courtyards. Situated along the Perfume River, the city was 31 miles south of the Demilitarized Zone (DMZ) and 50 miles south of the 17th parallel that divided North and South Vietnam.

The heart of Hue was the Citadel, a fortress with surrounding walls nearly 30ft high and three feet thick. When communist forces stormed into Hue on January 31, 1968, they swiftly took control of most of the city, including the Citadel. The Viet Cong immediately began rounding up local officials, teachers, religious leaders, and those identified as counter-revolutionaries. Many of these captives were summarily executed and buried in mass graves that were discovered

ABOVE: Marines of Company A, 1st Battalion, 1st Marines engage in house-to-house fighting in Hue.
(USMC Archives via Wikimedia Commons)

ABOVE: US Marines accompanied by an M48 Patton tank clear streets and houses in southern Hue, 1968.
(Creative Commons WO W. A. Parks, USMC official photographer via Wikimedia Commons)

ABOVE: A Marine M50 Ontos vehicle mounting six 106mm recoilless rifles leads a convoy near Hue on January 31, 1968.
(Creative Commons USMC Archives via Wikimedia Commons)

just over a month later when US and South Vietnamese troops regained control of the city. Approximately 2,800 bodies were found, and roughly 3,000 other individuals were missing.

At least 8,000 Viet Cong and NVA regulars initially attacked Hue, and the communist strength surged to roughly 12,000 during the course of the 32-day battle. At the Citadel, only the headquarters and elements of the crack 1st Army of the Republic of Vietnam (ARVN) Division in the northeast corner held out. In the south, the MACV (Military Assistance Command, Vietnam) compound, where 200 US and Australian military advisors to the 1st ARVN Division were located, remained in allied hands as well. The closest US combat units were located at the Marine base at Phu Bai, a forward command

post of the 1st Marine Division, eight miles south on Highway 1. As reports of the attack on Hue filtered into Phu Bai, steps were taken to counter the enemy thrust.

REINFORCEMENTS

Initially, Marine officers believed that the communist attack was only a small-scale affair, and a single Marine company was sent up Highway 1 to support the occupants of the MACV compound. Company A, 1st Battalion, 1st Marines and four M48 Patton tanks of the 3rd Tank Battalion reached the Phu Cam Canal on the southern edge of Hue before a fusillade of enemy fire stopped their progress. The intensity of this encounter made it abundantly clear that more than a small-unit nuisance attack was taking place. The communists had secured government buildings in the 'New City' to the south, the walled Imperial Palace inside the Citadel, and the densely populated Gia Hoa District to the east.

The Marines at Phu Bai were hit by enemy rockets and artillery fire, and reports of communist attacks along the length of Highway 1 were received. Nevertheless, a relief column was formed to come to the aid of Company A, which was pinned down by enemy fire. This force, which included some officers of the 1st Battalion, 1st Marines and Company G, 2nd Battalion, 5th Marines under the command of Lieutenant Colonel Marcus Gravel, lost 10 killed and 30 wounded but managed to rescue Company A and slug its way to the MACV compound. Gravel was ordered to link up with the 1st ARVN Division headquarters in the Citadel but was forced back by heavy machine-gun and B40 rocket-propelled grenade fire. Ten more Marines became casualties while attempting to cross the Nguyen Hoang Bridge that linked the New City to the Citadel. After two hours of fighting more than 30% of Company G 2/5 had been killed or wounded.

The following day, Marines, US Army, and ARVN forces began the arduous task of rooting the communists out of their strong positions. The Marines bore the brunt of the fighting at the Citadel and in other urban locations, their first such action since the house-to-house encounter with North Korean troops in Seoul during the Korean War in 1950. As the Marines fought their way into Hue, elements of the US Army's 101st Airborne Division and 1st Cavalry Division (Airmobile) blocked the roads northwest and southwest of the city, shutting off the previously steady flow of supplies and reinforcements to the communists and cutting their lines of communication.

The 2/5 Marines fought against tenacious NVA and Viet Cong resistance in the south, and one Marine officer declared: "It's going to be like this for every house, every block. One man can keep a whole unit pinned down. We need air and artillery. We'll get no place without it." Reluctantly, American forces did unleash heavy firepower against many structures in Hue that were considered sacred or held historical significance. By February 14, after a rugged fight to secure 11 city blocks, most of Hue south of the Perfume River, was cleared with 38 Marines killed and more than 320 wounded. The NVA and Viet Cong lost about 1,000 dead in their dogged fight.

The 1/5 Marines manoeuvred to attack enemy positions in Hue from the north. During nine days of harrowing combat, they moved south to oust the communists from the Citadel while the 2/5 Marines pushed north. At least three NVA battalions occupied

ABOVE: US Marines attack the Dong Ba tower in the Citadel at Hue during the Tet Offensive of early 1968.
(US Army via Wikimedia Commons)

ABOVE: A group of US Marines, one of them wounded, shelters behind a wall during the fighting at Hue.
(National Archives and Records Administration via Wikimedia Commons)

BELOW: US Marines move down a war-torn street in the provincial capital of Hue during mopping up operations.
(USMC Archives via Wikimedia Commons)

the Citadel, and the Dong Ba bell tower, where the Viet Cong flag fluttered, was an immediate objective. US aircraft and artillery pounded the tower, which soon became a jumble of debris. The Viet Cong unleashed a torrent of automatic weapons fire from above, and six Marines were killed in the climactic assault that retook the vantage point on February 15.

The battle for control of the Citadel continued as the Marine tanks' 90mm guns and Ontos tracked vehicles mounting six 106mm recoilless rifles blasted buildings to rubble. Many Viet Cong and NVA defenders died in the collapsing heaps of stone. Casualties were heavy, and in five days of fighting from February 12-17, the 1/5 Marines lost 47 killed and 240 wounded. By the 22nd, the NVA clung only to the southwestern section of the Citadel. Company L, 1/5 Marines attempted to retake the Imperial Palace, but intense enemy fire forced a temporary withdrawal. As the Marines regrouped, they received orders handing over

the task of reclaiming the structure to the ARVN 32nd Battalion, 3rd Regiment.

Two days later the beleaguered 1st ARVN Division fought its way to the outer wall of the Citadel and joined up with the 1st Cavalry Division (Airmobile), but another week of fighting remained until the last remnants of the communist forces were killed, captured, or withdrew across the border into neighbouring Laos. Hue was finally declared secure on March 2. Once a glittering jewel of Southeast Asia, the city was laid waste.

The Battle of Hue involved some of the heaviest combat of the Vietnam war. After nearly a month of fighting, 211 US Marines and US Army troops had been killed and more than 1,300 wounded, while ARVN casualties included 384 dead and 1,800 wounded. Estimates of communist casualties topped 5,000 killed and 3,000 wounded. The defeat at Hue was the most significant tactical setback communist forces experienced during the Tet Offensive.

THE MY LAI MASSACRE

ABOVE: A Vietnamese woman recoils in terror as US soldiers commit atrocities at My Lai.

(Ronald L. Haeberle Department of Defense via Wikimedia Commons)

When 2nd Lieutenant William Calley led the 1st Platoon, Company C, 1st Battalion, 20th Regiment, 11th Infantry Brigade, 23rd (America) Division of the US Army into the small hamlet of My Lai in Quang Ngai province on the morning of March 16, 1968, the soldiers were edgy.

The Americans had been searching the countryside for the elusive Viet Cong 48th Battalion for weeks. They had taken casualties during brisk firefights and from booby traps carefully concealed by the enemy along jungle trails. Finally, they had been told that morning that their opportunity to engage the Viet Cong in a decisive battle had come. Captain Ernest Medina told Calley that anyone encountered in the vicinity should be considered Viet Cong or at least a Viet Cong sympathiser. The civilian population was supposedly evacuated.

Medina was apparently unaware that an artillery barrage ordered early that morning to clear a landing zone for the helicopters to insert Charlie Company had actually frightened the civilians, prompting many of them to return to My Lai to seek shelter from the bombardment. The situation soon became a disaster. When the American soldiers began to scour the countryside, the reports of M-16 rifles, M-60 machine guns, and grenades reverberated across the area. Charlie Company had gone berserk, shooting civilians on sight, rounding up

others to await orders for their execution, and raping young women.

Calley evidently sanctioned the atrocities that unfolded across the village and into the surrounding jungle. In one instance, he ordered a soldier to eliminate a group of captives, mostly women, children, and the elderly. His cold comment was: "You know what to do with them." When the soldier misinterpreted the order, thinking he was to continue to guard them, Calley returned a few minutes later and flew

ABOVE: An American soldier sets fire to a hut on March 16, 1969, during the massacre at My Lai.

(Ronald L. Haeberle Department of Defense via Wikimedia Commons)

into a rage, shooting some of the civilians himself and ordering the soldier to join in – which he did.

The soldiers of Charlie Company killed indiscriminately, and at least 150 innocent people were murdered in an irrigation ditch. The rampage began around 8am and by 11am at least 500 villagers lay dead.

As the murderous spree unfolded, Sergeant Ron Haeberle, a photographer for the US Army attached to Company C, took photographs of the mayhem. He used one camera with black and white film to record images of soldiers rounding up and questioning civilians, blazing huts, and searches for Viet Cong supply stores. Haeberle also carried a personal camera with colour film. He took photos of bodies strewn in heaps – dead women and children lying lifeless along a trail. He retained the colour film and did not provide it to the army.

Flying overhead in a helicopter, Warrant Officer Hugh Thompson realised what was happening. He spotted wounded and radioed for medical personnel. Then, he saw US soldiers closing in on a group of civilians. Thompson descended quickly, landing his helicopter between the soldiers and the frightened villagers, preventing their execution.

When he returned to his base that morning, Thompson reported what he had seen. Only a superficial investigation was conducted, and on April 24, 1971, Colonel Oran Henderson, commander of the 11th Infantry Brigade, judged that 20 civilians

ABOVE: An American soldier feeds the flames of a Vietnamese home at My Lai.

(Ronald L. Haeberle Department of Defense via Wikimedia Commons)

ABOVE: After shooting himself in the foot while trying to clear a jammed weapon, a soldier is carried out of My Lai.
(Ronald L. Haeberle Department of Defense via Wikimedia Commons)

ABOVE: A memorial to the victims of the My Lai massacre stands near the site of the atrocity.
(Creative Commons JvL via Wikimedia Commons)

had been killed during a skirmish with the Viet Cong or in the artillery barrage at My Lai that had preceded the insertion of Charlie Company, discounting Thompson's eyewitness account of the murders.

The subsequent coverup soon came under the scrutiny of others who had seen the massacre in progress or heard of it from individuals who were present at My Lai. Among the sceptics was Ronald Ridenhour, a helicopter gunner who launched a personal investigation into what had happened at My Lai. After a year of research and interviewing participants, Ridenhour sent letters to 30 members of the US Congress, Admiral Thomas Moorer, then chairman of the Joint Chiefs of Staff, Secretary of Defense Melvin Laird, and President Richard Nixon. In the inquiry that followed, the conduct of Medina, Henderson, Thompson, and Calley, along

with others, was examined. On September 5, 1969, Calley was charged with six specifications of premeditated murder in the deaths of 109 villagers. Medina, nine enlisted men, and one other officer were also charged.

On November 13, a story on the massacre at My Lai written by freelance journalist Seymour Hersh was published in newspapers across the United States. A second article was internationally syndicated a week later, sparking outrage in the US and abroad. On the same day, several of Haeberle's colour photos were published in the Cleveland Plain Dealer newspaper. Ordinary Americans were appalled, and the anti-war movement decried the horrific incident. Regardless, the impact of the My Lai massacre tarnished the reputation of the American military and contributed substantially to the burgeoning

disillusionment of the people with the war in Vietnam.

Calley's trial began on November 17, 1970, and on March 29, 1971, a jury of six officers convicted him of the premeditated murder of 22 Vietnamese civilians. The other defendants were acquitted. Sentenced to life in prison, Calley was taken into custody. However, a series of reviews and appeals resulted in substantial reductions. He was released in September 1974.

American public opinion was sharply divided during the disposition of Calley's case. Many believed that the conviction was unjustified and considered the disgraced officer a scapegoat. At the White House, the Nixon administration received more than 5,000 letters and telegrams in support of Calley. Nevertheless, some observers pointed to My Lai as indicative of the US involvement in Vietnam, the lack of discipline among the rank and file of the American military, and the ineptitude of the US Army's command and control.

In the midst of the Calley trial, Lieutenant General William Peers led a commission to investigate the army coverup. His final report was a scathing indictment of the local command and condemned the events of March 16, 1968, as well as the attempt to hide it from the world. The report stated: "…at every command level from company to division actions were taken or omitted which together effectively concealed from higher headquarters the events which transpired…." In the wake of the Peers Commission findings, 14 officers were charged, but 13 cases were dismissed due to lack of evidence. Colonel Henderson, the ranking officer implicated, was acquitted of dereliction of duty in December 1971.

Many other atrocities committed by American and South Vietnamese military personnel occurred during the war. One of these was the so-called Green Beret Affair. The elite special forces component of the US Army, the Green Berets were

ABOVE: An unidentified Vietnamese man sits dejected amid the chaos of the My Lai massacre.
(Ronald L. Haeberle Department of Defense via Wikimedia Commons)

ABOVE: Family members search for the bodies of victims in the aftermath of the Viet Cong massacre at Hue.
(Douglas Pike Collection via Wikimedia Commons)

legendary. They engaged in both covert and overt operations in Vietnam. One of their clandestine assignments was dubbed Project GAMMA, an intelligence gathering effort centred on communist activity in Cambodia.

When Thai Khac Chuyen, a South Vietnamese GAMMA operative, was discovered to be a double agent, a discussion arose as to his fate. Apparently, Green Beret officers contacted the CIA (Central Intelligence Agency), which suggested the 'elimination' of the suspect. In response, Green Berets drugged Chuyen on June 20, 1969, carried him to a boat, shot him twice in the head, and threw his body, weighed down with chains, into the waters of Nha Trang Bay.

Sergeant Alvin Smith, Chuyen's handler, contact the CIA, which referred the matter to the Army Criminal Investigative Division. Smith identified the Green Berets involved in the murder in exchange for immunity from prosecution. Colonel Robert Rheault, a 43-year-old West Point graduate, was arrested along with two majors, three captains, a chief warrant officer, and a sergeant first class.

The ensuing prosecution never gained momentum. The CIA issued a statement denying any knowledge of Chuyen and soon refused to make its personnel available for testimony. General Creighton Abrams, commander of US forces in Vietnam, also refused on the grounds of national security. In September 1969, Secretary of the Army Stanley Resor announced that all charges were being dropped. Project GAMMA was discontinued six months later.

TERROR

The communist North Vietnamese Army (NVA) and Viet Cong guerrillas used murder

ABOVE: Lieutenant William Calley was convicted of murder during the perpetration of the My Lai massacre.
(US Army via Wikimedia Commons)

as a terror weapon to gain and keep control of much of rural South Vietnam. In addition to the executions of at least 2,800 people during their occupation of the provincial capital of Hue during the Tet Offensive, communist troops and insurgents slaughtered thousands of civilians, abducted thousands more, assassinated local leaders and political figures, and planted bombs that killed indiscriminately in crowded urban areas.

In December 1960, a Viet Cong bomb killed one man and injured two more at the Saigon Golf Club. The following year, the guerrillas blew up a truck carrying 20 schoolgirls and then shot several survivors. Two were killed and 10 wounded. Later in 1961, insurgents sacked the government buildings in the city of Phuroc Vinh and beheaded the administrative staff. They killed a Roman Catholic priest in December.

In 1962, Viet Cong guerrillas captured two wounded American soldiers and shot both of them execution style when they were unable to keep up with the marching column. They bombed a Saigon restaurant and a hotel inflicting numerous casualties and kidnapped several Christian missionaries who were never heard from again. Communist infiltrators continued their campaign of terror in Saigon throughout the war, tossing grenades into public gatherings, bombing movie theatres, and even abducting a teacher who was later found with her throat cut.

Fifteen Vietnamese civilians were killed and four injured in the explosion of a Viet Cong mine on a rural dirt road on March 18, 1966, and in September an attempt to disrupt elections precipitated 166 terror incidents. Nineteen people were killed and 120 wounded in attacks on polling places. In March 1967, a dozen South Vietnamese captives were shot or stabbed before guerrillas fled an advancing unit of the South Vietnamese Army (ARVN). In December, the Viet Cong massacred as many as 250 Montagnard villagers at Dak Son.

Communist atrocities were widespread during the Tet Offensive of early 1968, and on March 21, NVA regulars attacked a refugee centre in Kontum Province, killing 17 and wounding 36, mostly women and children. Attacks on villages in Quang Nam Province killed 74 civilians in June 1970, and NVA and Viet Cong forces both participated in the Duc Duc massacre on March 29, 1971, killing 103 civilians, and kidnapping 37.

The litany of communist atrocities committed during the Vietnam War lengthened until hostilities ceased in 1975 in sobering adherence to the old phrase that the end justifies the means. Thus, the Vietnam war starkly plumbed the terrible depths of man's inhumanity to man.

ABOVE: Freelance journalist Seymour Hersh broke the story of the My Lai massacre in newspapers around the world. (Creative Commons Giorgio Montersino via Wikimedia Commons)

THE UBIQUITOUS HUEY

Its official name was the Bell UH-1 Iroquois, but to everyone it was simply known as the 'Huey'. A series of multi-role helicopters that has become an iconic symbol of the Vietnam War, the Huey carved its place in history during the long involvement of the US military in Southeast Asia.

The UH-1 prototype, designated XH-40, first flew in October 1956, and during a production run that spanned four decades over 16,000 were built in more than two dozen variants. Originally identified as the HU-1, the first of these helicopters arrived in Vietnam during the late 1950s and earned the famous nickname of 'Huey'. However, after the Defense Department standardised aircraft nomenclature to the US Air Force style in 1962 and the helicopter became the UH-1, the nickname stuck.

The Huey was instantly recognisable with its wide body, specifically designed for the roles it would play in wartime. The helicopter proved versatile, first in the evacuation of battlefield wounded. During such medevac missions, called dustoffs, the Hueys could accommodate six stretchers. They transported more than two million wounded troops through the course of the conflict. Their speed and efficiency alongside the courage of the combat pilots and crewmen that flew them became legendary. Although the medevac flights were among the most dangerous missions, a wounded soldier in Vietnam was usually evacuated to a medical facility within an hour. More than 99% of those wounded who were alive 24 hours later survived the war.

The Huey also became the modern-day iron horse of the US Army's new doctrine of airmobile warfare, the swift insertion

ABOVE: Troops of the US 9th Cavalry Regiment exit a Huey during combat operations in Vietnam.
(US Army via Wikimedia Commons)

and retrieval of ground troops by helicopter during combat missions. The tactics rendered former large-scale parachute operations virtually obsolete and ushered in the new era of air assault. The US Marines also participated in air assault missions, as the Hueys made hazardous troop-carrying runs into landing zones (LZ) followed by quick departures. Dubbed 'slicks', the helicopters that functioned primarily as transports carried a crew of four, including the pilot, co-pilot, crew chief, and door gunner. Slicks were armed with only a pair of .30-caliber M-60 machine guns mounted at the doors.

ABOVE: A Huey takes off with a 4th Infantry Division combat team aboard in 1969.
(National Archives and Records Administration via Wikimedia Commons)

ABOVE: The Bell UH-1 Iroquois, or Huey, was a mainstay of American military operations in Vietnam.
(Creative Commons Airwolfhound via Wikimedia Commons)

Used by the US Army, Navy, and Air Force in Vietnam, the Huey also proved adept in the airlift supply, search and rescue, electronic warfare, and fire support roles. The US Navy deployed armed Hueys in support of its riverine forces operating in the Mekong Delta and the extensive waterways of South Vietnam. Among other tasks, the US Air Force deployed Hueys with the 20th Special Operations Squadron to conduct covert reconnaissance missions and psychological warfare operations in Laos and Cambodia.

Continuous modifications were made to the UH-1 during the Vietnam era, and one of the most significant was the addition of substantial armament. The slicks were particularly vulnerable to enemy fire as they approached a 'hot' LZ, and as early as 1962, field modifications were introduced. Hueys were armed with external M-60 machine guns and rocket pods to fly escort

BELOW: A heavily armed Bell AH-1 Huey Cobra gunship flies over the Vietnamese countryside.
(US Army Heritage and Education Center)

and provide suppressing fire against ground targets. Hueys fitted with external armament were called 'gunships'. By 1963, gunships were being purpose built, and the UH-1C variant could also carry a 40mm grenade launcher mounted forward in the chin.

In 1967, the US Army introduced the AH-1 Huey Cobra gunship, designed for escort missions and as a devastating fire support platform with a top speed of 140mph. One veteran Cobra pilot recalled: "The adrenaline rush that goes with flying those missions is incredible. You've got so many things going on in the cockpit and there are so many things going on around you."

Literally armed to the teeth, the Cobra carried up to 3,000lb of ordnance. Weaponry included a pair of .30-calibre multi-barrel miniguns, 40mm grenade launchers, 2.75-inch rockets, and a 20mm cannon. The highly manoeuvrable Cobra was retired from US service in 2001 but remains active with the armed forces of several nations.

The Huey was distinguishable not only by its distinctive profile, but also due to the hum of its main rotor blade that was powered by a turboshaft engine rather than other contemporary helicopter types that were driven by piston engines. The turbine engine was rugged and reliable, providing a significant improvement in performance over earlier powerplants. Initially, the UH-1 was equipped

with the Lycoming YT53-L-1 engine that generated 700hp, and in 1966 the Lycoming T53-L-13, capable of 1,400hp and a top speed of 127 miles per hour was introduced with the UH-1H variant. The UH-1H operated at a service ceiling of 12,600ft with a range of 318 miles and a capacity of up to 14 fully equipped combat troops.

During the course of the Vietnam conflict, more than 12,000 helicopters of various types were in service with US and South Vietnamese forces, and roughly 5,000 of them were lost to enemy fire or accidents. Records indicate that for every 7.9 sorties flown between 1966 and 1971, one US Army helicopter was lost. Approximately 5,000 Hueys were in service during the war, and half of these were shot down. More Hueys were lost than any other aircraft type in Vietnam, and pilots logged well over 7.5 million flight hours.

The remarkable service life of the UH-1 series has extended beyond half a century,

and the Huey remains in service today in more than 40 countries.

OTHER TYPES

Among other significant helicopter types deployed to Vietnam, the Boeing Vertol CH-47 Chinook stands out as a twin-rotor troop, equipment, and supply transport capable of carrying a gross payload of 46,000lb. In its combat configuration, the CH-47 could transport 55 fully equipped soldiers along with heavy weapons and substantial provisions. Men and equipment are rapidly offloaded via its power-operated rear cargo door and loading ramp. During the evacuation of Saigon in 1975, a lone Chinook carried 147 Vietnamese refugees to safety. The type remains in service today.

The Hughes OH-6 Cayuse, nicknamed 'Loach' (light observation helicopter), performed scouting duties, and its pilots regularly came under enemy fire as they flew above the dense jungles of Vietnam. The Loach was often paired with the Cobra in so-called 'hunter-killer' missions with the Loach pilot pinpointing enemy positions on the ground and the Cobra unleashing a torrent of fire.

The Sikorsky S-64 Skycrane, a twin-engine heavy airlift helicopter, remains in service today. Easily identified with its 'stick' fuselage, the S-64 uses six rotor blades of 72ft diameter and a hoist capable of transporting up to 10 tons. In Vietnam, the Skycrane was primarily used in the recovery of damaged aircraft.

The Sikorsky HH-3E, nicknamed 'Jolly Green Giant', was a welcome sight to many downed pilots in need of rescue on the ground or at sea. The HH-3E was designed for the search and rescue role. The first helicopter capable of mid-air refuelling, the Jolly Green Giant deployed a hoist, which was lowered to retrieve personnel. Flying the big chopper was particularly hazardous as it hovered during a rescue and was quite vulnerable to enemy fire.

ABOVE: The Hughes OH-6 Cayuse, or Loach, was a familiar sight in the skies over Vietnam.
(US Army via Wikimedia Commons)

ABOVE: A Sikorsky Jolly Green Giant refuels in mid-air while on a mission over North Vietnam. (US Air Force via Wikimedia Commons)

WALTER CRONKITE AND THE MEDIA

ABOVE: Walter Cronkite and a CBS News crew interview the commanding officer of the 1st Battalion, 1st Marines during the Battle for Hue, Tet Offensive, 1968. (National Archives and Records Administration)

The news media brought coverage of the Vietnam war home to the United States and the rest of the world with unprecedented immediacy and intensity. From 1950 to 1966, the percentage of American households that owned a television set soared from 9% to 93%. Well over half the ordinary citizens surveyed in a contemporary poll indicated that the broadcast medium was their primary source of news.

In homes across the United States, the dinner hour was punctuated with reports of the fighting in Vietnam. Both colour and black and white film footage of the fighting and the destruction and devastation of combat were standard fare. While it has become somewhat cliché to describe Vietnam as the first 'television war', the undeniable fact remains that the near real time images of men in combat, bloodied, muddied, crawling, and crouching while bullets whizzed around them, the heart rending scenes of women and children huddled in frightened clusters, and the moments of apparent madness were unsettling and repugnant to many Americans.

From 1964 to 1968 as American involvement in the war increased, the number of journalists in Southeast Asia was in lock step, growing from a mere dozen or so to more than 600. While raw camera footage was flashed around the world via satellite, reporters also wrote compelling narratives of their experiences embedded with combat units or interviews with officers and ordinary soldiers who bore the brunt of the fighting. Photojournalists brought still images of sheer terror and suffering to the pages of popular magazines and newspapers. Unlike prior wars, there was little censorship on the part of the US government. Even as Washington officials and senior military leaders proffered the narrative that America and South Vietnam were winning the war, the reality seemed to contradict such assurances.

Therefore, the news media played an active, and some would say decisive, role in determining the destiny of American involvement in Southeast Asia – even to the extent that some historians aver that the Vietnam war was lost in the living rooms and the streets of American cities rather than on the battlefield.

Days after the communists launched the Tet Offensive on January 30, 1968, and American homes were flooded with images of chaos and carnage, respected veteran journalist Walter Cronkite ventured to Vietnam. Cronkite had covered World War Two for United Press International and actually flew on bombing raids over Nazi Germany. In 1962, he became the anchor of CBS Evening News. The programme was expanded from 15 minutes to a half hour, and his steady,

ABOVE: Walter Cronkite interviews a South Vietnamese professor at Hue University on February 20, 1968. (National Archives and Records Administration via Wikimedia Commons)

ABOVE: CBS News correspondent Morton Dean sits in the door of a helicopter in Vietnam, 1971.

(Creative Commons Morton Dean via Wikimedia Commons)

that fuelled disillusionment with the conflict at home. Casualty lists lengthened substantially year over year. Families had sons and daughters in service far away, and their futures were uncertain. Social change was sweeping the country as the civil rights movement, an awakening of women's rights, economic issues, and a widening of the 'generation gap', combined to cause a palpable angst among Americans. Further, the erosion of trust in the very government that symbolised truth and justice raised cynicism and anti-war sentiment to new heights.

The media did play a critical role in exposing the duplicity of the Johnson

ABOVE: French correspondent Bernard Fall sits with US soldiers in Vietnam. He was killed by a land mine on patrol with American soldiers in 1967.

(US Army Bernard B Fall, Vietnam author via Wikimedia Commons)

analytical voice, stage presence, and acknowledged objectivity made Cronkite the 'most trusted man in America'.

After two weeks in Vietnam, Cronkite presented his experience and perspective on the war to the American people during a 10pm broadcast on February 27, 1968. The programme aired for just 30 minutes, but its impact on the American psyche was profound.

Cronkite's grim, matter-of-fact assessment most surely altered the course of US involvement in the conflict. He commented: "We've been too often disappointed by the optimism of the American leaders…both in Vietnam and Washington to have faith any longer in the silver linings they find in the darkest clouds. For it seems now more certain than ever, that the bloody experience of Vietnam is to end in a stalemate. To say that we are closer to victory today is to believe in the face of the evidence, the optimists who have been wrong in the past…To say that we are mired in stalemate seems the only realistic, if unsatisfactory conclusion. But it is increasingly clear to this reporter that the only rational way out then will be to negotiate, not as victors, but as an honorable people who lived up to their pledge to defend democracy, and did the best they could."

President Lyndon Johnson was then confronted with the realisation that ordinary Americans were fatigued with the war and no longer supported his policies. According to his press secretary George Christian, Johnson later lamented: "If I've lost Cronkite, I've lost middle America." A month afterward, the President announced to a television audience that he would not seek re-election in 1968.

Indeed, though the communists suffered a serious tactical defeat during the Tet

Offensive, their strategic victory lay in the galvanizing of American public opinion against continuing to contribute lives and treasure to a war of attrition with no end in sight. As the war dragged on, early media support for the apparent effort to stem the tide of communism in Southeast Asia eroded to the extent that some observers accused reporters of attempting to undermine the war effort. Others contend that the coverage of the war was accurate and appropriate in its stark and compelling delivery, images that continue to haunt those who remember amid the words of those who fought, who led, who deceived, and who died.

In truth, the media coverage of the Vietnam war was one factor in many

ABOVE: A US Marine covers the landing of a helicopter in Vietnam in this photo by Dirck Halstead.

(US Department of Defense Dirck Halstead via Wikimedia Commons)

ABOVE: US Marine combat photographer Byron G. Highland was killed in the same blast that claimed the life of Bernard Fall in Vietnam.
(National Archives and Records Administration via Wikimedia Commons)

administration. Secretary of Defense Robert McNamara, General William Westmoreland, and other American leaders had continually tried to reassure the public as to the 'light at the end of the tunnel'. The United States and South Vietnam, a bulwark against the spread of communism in Southeast Asia, were winning the war. McNamara touted the commitment of growing numbers of American troops to the widening conflict, but at the same time he authorised a lengthy history of the American involvement in the conflict from the end of World War Two to the 1960s.

McNamara and other proponents of increased American involvement in Vietnam issued positive assessments of

ABOVE: Daniel Ellsberg, who leaked excerpts of the Pentagon Papers to the New York Times, holds a press conference in 1972.
(Gotfryd, Bernard, photographer via Wikimedia Commons)

progress, while the 7,000 pages of the classified *Report of the Office of the Secretary of Defense Vietnam Task Force*, popularly known as the 'Pentagon Papers', told quite a different story. In 1971, Daniel Ellsberg, an analyst who had worked on the report, was personally disillusioned. Ellsberg leaked excerpts of the Pentagon Papers to the *New York Times*, which published the first in a series of articles that laid bare the government's deception. When the administration of President Richard Nixon sued to suppress further reporting, the US Supreme Court ruled in favour of the newspaper, which published further prima facie evidence. The media, therefore, played a pivotal role in the unravelling of the tangled government web.

ABOVE: Cameras draped around his neck, *Life* magazine photojournalist Larry Burrows readies for a mission in 1967. (US Marine Photo National Archives and Records Administration via Wikimedia Commons)

Meanwhile, the news media continued to report on the human catastrophe that was the Vietnam war. A terrifying image of a young Vietnamese girl, seriously burned in a napalm attack by American aircraft and running naked down a country road, was seared into the collective American consciousness. Photos of the twisted bodies of victims of the My Lai Massacre were published in newspapers, and ordinary people around the world were horrified. Cameras whirred, and reporters shoved microphones into the faces of haggard GIs, one of whom moaned, "I just want to go home."

Early in the escalation of America's military involvement, a young reporter/ photographer for *Life* magazine recorded a harrowing experience in combat. In its April 16, 1965, edition, *Life* presented the experience of British-born Larry Burrows, who had boarded a US Marine helicopter for

a flight into the maelstrom just days earlier. His story and photos in *One Ride With Yankee Papa 13* resonate across the decades as one of the most vivid and compelling reports of Vietnam. Burrows wrote of 21-year-old crew chief Corporal James Farley, 20-year-old gunner PFC Wayne Hoilien, pilot Captain Peter Vogel, and co-pilot 1st Lieutenant James Magel, living and dying.

"The Viet Cong, dug in along a tree line, were just waiting for us to come into the landing zone," Burrows recounted in the pages of *Life*. "We were all like sitting ducks and their raking crossfire was murderous… Hoilien was pouring machine-gun fire at a second V.C. gun position at the tree line to our left. Bullet holes had ripped both left and right of his seat. The plexiglass had been shot out of the cockpit and one V.C. bullet had nicked our pilot's neck. We climbed and climbed fast the hell out of there. Hoilien was still firing gunbursts at the tree line."

When Yankee Papa 13 was clear, Farley and Hoilien tried to care for the mortally wounded Magel. "He looked pale, and I wondered how long he could hold on," Burrows wrote. "Farley began bandaging Magel's wound. The wind from the doorway kept whipping the bandages across his face. Then the blood started to come from his nose and mouth and a glazed look came into his eyes. Farley tried mouth-to-mouth resuscitation, but Magel was dead. Nobody said a word."

Burrows' series of accompanying photos concludes with an anguished Farley, head bowed in exhaustion and grief, trying to cope.

On February 10, 1971, Larry Burrows died with three other reporters when the helicopter they were aboard was shot down over Laos. He was 44 years old. From 1955 to 1975, a total of 63 journalists died while covering the war in Vietnam.

ABOVE: News correspondent Wallace Terry interviews an American soldier in Vietnam in 1969.
(Creative Commons Alconte via Wikimedia Commons)

OPPOSITION AT HOME

ABOVE: Anti-war demonstrators make their way through the streets of Chicago during the Democratic National Convention in August 1968. (Creative Commons David Wilson via Wikimedia Commons)

For artist Lorraine Schneider, it was her "own personal picket sign," a social commentary on the Vietnam war in a small two-inch by two-inch work produced for a show at New York's Pratt Institute in 1965. It featured a sunflower drawn in black and white and in childlike print the slogan "war is not healthy for children and other living things."

Although created in response to the growing tragedy of the Vietnam war, the work of art still sends a relevant message today, nearly 60 years later. Opposition to the war in Vietnam took on many forms – art, literature, music, demonstrations, rhetoric and response, and violence – and these gained momentum, increasing steadily along with American involvement in the conflict.

The common thread of 1960s counterculture wove its way through the anti-war movement and became energised with the immediacy of information, the images produced and flashed across the globe, the lengthening casualty lists, and the uncertainty of future loss when it became apparent that there was no end in sight. Early anti-war activities were often organised on college campuses, where a group called Students for Democratic Society (SDS) staged teach-ins to familiarise people with the situation in Vietnam.

Just three months before his assassination on November 22, 1963, President John F. Kennedy told CBS News anchor Walter Cronkite: "In the final analysis, it is their war. They are the ones who have to win it or lose it. We can help them, we can give them equipment, we can send our men out there as advisors, but they have to win it, the people of Vietnam, against the communists."

While the course of Kennedy's policy toward Vietnam remains shrouded in theory and conjecture, his successor, President Lyndon Johnson, committed to a widening US involvement in the war. Johnson's authorisation of Operation Rolling Thunder, the bombing of North Vietnam, and deployment of US Marines to Southeast Asia in March 1965, served as catalysts for the burgeoning anti-war movement. Three days after the first Marine came ashore in Southeast Asia, a protester entered the White House on a public tour and spilled pig's blood across the carpet in the state dining room.

Six weeks later, SDS brought 15,000 protesters into the streets of Washington, D.C. Anti-war activities attracted a variety of people, students, artists, sports figures, Hollywood stars, advocates of the civil rights movement, and more. In the summer of 1965, civil rights leader Dr Martin Luther King, Jr, and Dr Benjamin Spock, renowned for his books on raising children, were featured speakers before a crowd of 17,000 at Madison Square Garden in New York. Prior to his assassination in April 1968, Dr King decried the disparity among Black casualties compared to overall numbers of those killed. He had called the war "a blasphemy against all that America stands for."

While most of the American people understood the premise for American involvement in the war and favoured the containment of communism in the midst of the Cold War, the small but vocal nucleus of anti-war protesters asked relevant questions as to the importance of Vietnam in the context of US national security. Some averred that the conflict was an internal Vietnamese civil war that should be settled by the Vietnamese themselves. Others were confirmed peace activists or young people opposed to the prospect of compulsory military service.

Three days of demonstrations took place in major cities in March 1966, and protesters voiced their displeasure not only with President Johnson, but also with Congress and the US military establishment. By early 1967, the protests had grown in size and

ABOVE: Students at the University of San Diego march against the Vietnam War in 1971.
(*Alcalá* yearbook, 1971, University of San Diego via Wikimedia Commons)

ABOVE: One of many protests against the Vietnam War, this march in Washington, DC, took place in the spring of 1971.
(Creative Commons Leena A. Krohn via Wikimedia Commons)

ABOVE: With the Lincoln Memorial in the background, demonstrators march toward the Pentagon on October 21, 1967. (Photo by Frank Wolfe via Wikimedia Commons)

scope. On April 15, a crowd of more than 100,000 marched through the streets of New York City and rallied at the United Nations building. When 400 buses brought 30,000 people from New York to Washington, D.C., on June 8, the protesters gathered outside the White House, and the Johnson family heard the chant 'Hey, hey LBJ, how many kids did you kill today'?

On October 21, with public opinion polls reflecting for the first time less than 50% approval for the conduct of the war, roughly 100,000 protesters gathered at the Lincoln Memorial in Washington, D.C., and among them were veterans recently returned from Vietnam. Many of them were members of the organisation Vietnam Veterans Against the War who threw away their medals and denounced the violence they had participated in and witnessed. About half the protesters pushed through police cordons and barricades, marching to the Pentagon where scores of people were arrested, and troops were called in to restore order. Author Norman Mailer was among those hauled to jail, and his book on the incident, *Armies of the Night*, won a 1969 Pulitzer Prize.

When singer/actress Eartha Kitt attended a White House luncheon on January 18,

1968, she scolded President Johnson and reduced the First Lady, Lady Bird Johnson, to tears with her defence of the protesters. Kitt declared: "They feel like they are going to raise sons – and I know what it's like, and you have children of your own, Mrs. Johnson – we raise children and send them to war."

By early 1968, the number of American service personnel in Vietnam was approximately a half million with more than 15,000 dead and nearly 110,000 wounded. Opposition to the draft grew exponentially,

and one of its most prominent opponents was world heavyweight boxing champion Muhammad Ali, who refused to comply when drafted and declared himself a conscientious objector. Ali was stripped of his heavyweight title, handed a prison sentence that was later reversed by the US Supreme Court, and subjected to a three-year ban from boxing.

The anti-war movement and counter-culture phenomenon became pervasive during the Vietnam era, and the work of artists and entertainers often reflected strong emotions. Such songs as *Fortunate Son* by Creedence Clearwater Revival, *What's Going On?* by Marvin Gaye, *Give Peace a Chance* and *Imagine* by John Lennon, *Blowin' in the Wind* by Bob Dylan, and many others became anthems of the peace movement. At the famed Woodstock Music and Art Fair in August 1969, the group Country Joe and the Fish performed their hit song *Feel Like I'm Fixin' to Die Rag*, released two years earlier with its famous lyric: "Well come on all of you big strong men, Uncle Sam needs your help again./ He got himself in a terrible jam, way down yonder in Vietnam,/ Put down your books and pick up a gun, we're gonna have a whole lotta fun/ And its 1,2,3…what are we fighting for?/ Don't ask me I don't give a damn, the next stop is Vietnam…"

DISILLUSIONMENT

The shock of the Tet Offensive in early 1968, though a military defeat for communist forces, impressed on the American public that

ABOVE: A demonstrator offers a flower to a soldier of the Military Police guarding an entrance to the Pentagon.
(Creative Commons S.Sgt. Albert R. Simpson National Archives and Records Administration via Wikimedia Commons)

ABOVE: Dr Martin Luther King, Jr, denounces the Vietnam war on the St. Paul campus of the University of Minnesota in 1967. (Creative Commons Minnesota Historical Society via Wikimedia Commons)

ABOVE: An anti-war protester hangs a banner prior to a rally attended by thousands of demonstrators in 1971. (*Alcalá* yearbook, 1971, University of San Diego via Wikimedia Commons)

there was no real end in sight for the Vietnam War. Widespread disillusionment followed as polls reflected only a 35% approval of the Johnson administration's conduct of the war. A full 50% solidly disapproved. That summer, violence erupted in the streets of Chicago during the Democratic National Convention. Johnson had decided not to run for re-election, and while Minnesota Senator Hubert Humphrey secured his party's nomination for president, police battled at least 10,000 rioters and many across the county stared at television screens in disbelief.

The violence spawned the famed trial of the Chicago Seven, arrested for conspiracy,

inciting a riot, and other crimes. The trial was a spectacle, and the defendants, including Jerry Rubin and Abbie Hoffman, founders of the Yippie movement (Youth International Party), Black Panther leader Bobby Seale, Tom Hayden, a founder of SDS, Dave Dellinger and Rennie Davis of the National Mobilization Committee to End the War in Vietnam, and others, were convicted on certain charges, some of which were later reversed on appeal.

During the administration of President Richard Nixon, the anti-war movement remained vigorous. Nixon was convinced that the anti-war faction was a vocal minority and spoke of the significant number of Americans who actually constituted a great 'silent majority' that supported the efforts of his administration to obtain 'peace with honor' for the United States while withdrawing American troops from Vietnam and instituting his policy of 'Vietnamisation'. Even while American military involvement was being curtailed, anti-war activities continued.

Activists broke into local draft board offices, carried files into the streets of cities large and small, and set them on fire. Some young men burned their draft cards in open defiance of the law, and others, perhaps as many as 100,000, fled to Canada to avoid being called up for military service. More than 1.9 million personnel were drafted into the US military during the Vietnam conflict, and the first draft lottery since 1942, during World War Two, was conducted on December 1, 1969. Standards for draft deferments, such as attending college, marital status, and other criteria, were altered several times during the war, and these were often criticised as favouring the well-to-do or wealthy. The draft was ended in 1973.

ABOVE: Actress and singer Eartha Kitt confronted President Lyndon Johnson on the Vietnam war during a White House luncheon. (Van Vechten Collection Library of Congress via Wikimedia Commons)

A national .moratorium day' featuring rallies and demonstrations occurred on October 15, 1969, and when Nixon announced the incursion of US troops into Vietnam's neighbour Cambodia on April 30, 1970, violence erupted on college campuses across the country. The tragic deaths of four students at Kent State University in Ohio occurred on May 4, and another tragic shooting of students took place at Jackson State University in Mississippi days later. On May 8, the so-called 'Hard Hat Riot' occurred in lower Manhattan when student protesters on Wall Street were confronted by angry construction workers and a massive street brawl broke out.

In early 1971, Daniel Ellsberg, a military analyst, leaked excerpts of the classified Pentagon Papers, revealing quite a different perspective on the course of the war than government and military leaders had proffered to the American people. Public distrust of the government reached a new high, fuelling more demonstrations. In May 1971, more than 25,000 demonstrators attempted to disrupt traffic in Washington, D.C., and more than 7,000 were arrested when 12,000 law enforcement personnel cleared the city streets.

Anti-war protests continued through the remainder of American military involvement in Vietnam, and their influence on the course of events was profound. Although peace negotiations had been lurching forward since the spring of 1968, terms were not concluded until early 1973.

ABOVE: A group of young American men who have fled the draft gather for counselling in Canada. (Creative Commons Laura Jones via Wikimedia Commons)

NIXON EMERGENT

When he addressed a meeting of the National Security Council in the Cabinet Room of the White House on the morning of February 2, 1972 President Richard Nixon was emphatic.

"…The main thing we all have to understand here is that the greatest miscalculation the North Vietnamese can make is that we will pay, on our part, an exorbitant price because of the political situation in the United States," the President declared in frustration. "That's not true. Because there's one determination I've made. We're not going to lose out there. I determined that long ago.

"We wouldn't have gone into Cambodia; we wouldn't have gone into Laos, if we had not made that determination," Nixon continued. "If politics is what was motivating what we were doing, I would have declared immediately after I took office in January of 1969, that the whole damn thing was the fault of Johnson and Kennedy, it was the 'Democrats' war,' and we're ending it like Eisenhower ended Korea, and we're getting the hell out, and let it go down the tube. We didn't do that. We didn't do it, because politically, whatever, it would have been wrong for the country, wrong for the world, and so forth and so on, but having come this long way and come to this point, the United States is not going to lose. And that means we will do what is necessary…."

President Nixon was a pragmatic politician, and a survivor. A former member of the US

ABOVE: Richard Nixon (right) stands with John F. Kennedy prior to their historic television debate in 1960.
(Associated Press via Wikimedia Commons)

House of Representatives and the Senate from California, he had served as vice president in the Eisenhower administration and then lost the presidential election of 1960 to Democrat John F. Kennedy. Two years later he lost his bid for the governorship of California. Eight years afterward, he was elected to the highest office in the land. He had campaigned on

a pledge to restore order at home, to quell the spasms of unrest and violence that had persisted, and to end the war in Vietnam. And he expected the American people to allow him a year or so to accomplish both. Some historians and news reporters have cited evidence that Nixon interfered with the progress of peace negotiations during the election of 1968 to keep the issue before the American people and help assure his victory.

The President reasoned that he could leverage improving relations with the Soviet Union and the People's Republic of China to pressure the North Vietnamese government to negotiate in earnest. He also believed that the North Vietnamese respected the possibility of intensified US military operations. Rapidly, however, he realised that ending the war would be a much more arduous process than originally thought.

Nixon ordered the secret bombing of communist bases in 'neutral' Cambodia in March 1969 and met with South Vietnamese President Nguyen Van Thieu at Midway Atoll in the Pacific in June, announcing

ABOVE: President Richard Nixon assumed responsibility for the conduct of the Vietnam war with his election in 1968. (Department of Defense Department of the Army via Wikimedia Commons)

ABOVE: The Nixon family posed for this portrait in December 1971 while the Vietnam war raged.
(White House Photo Office Collection (Nixon Administration), 1/20/1969 - 8/9/1974 via Wikimedia Commons)

ABOVE: President Richard Nixon campaigns in Pennsylvania in 1968, promising to restore order and end the war in Vietnam. (Executive Office of the President of the United States Ollie Atkins, White House photographer via Wikimedia Commons)

his programme of Vietnamisation, the staged withdrawal of American troops from Vietnam in conjunction with training and support that would enable ARVN forces to fight and win on their own. The following month, the first of 25,000 US troops were pulling out of Southeast Asia.

These steps were taken to demonstrate to the American people that progress was being made in the process of US disengagement. However, the ability of the South Vietnamese to take on more responsibility for military operations against the communist forces remained an open question. Early indications were that the South Vietnamese Army (ARVN) would require American expertise for an extended period before it could fight on its own. At the same time, National Security Advisor Henry Kissinger began secret peace negotiations with North Vietnamese politburo representative Le Duc Tho, as it had become apparent that the public negotiations in Paris were more show than substance.

PUBLIC DISAPPROVAL

With the anti-war movement more energised than ever, Nixon began to fear the erosion of public support for his policies. In September 1969, a nationwide poll revealed that only 35% of Americans approved of his conduct of the war. On November 3, he went directly to the people, essentially asking for more time for the peace process to produce tangible results. In later years, he remembered the televised speech as the most important of his political career. He referred to a 'Great Silent Majority' of Americans who supported a continued strategy of Vietnamisation and peace talks. He asserted that the anti-war movement would never dictate American foreign policy.

"Now let me begin by describing the situation I found when I was inaugurated on

ABOVE: President Nixon shakes the hand of Mao Tse-tung during his state visit to Peking in 1972. (White House Photo Office Collection (Nixon Administration), 1/20/1969 - 8/9/1974 via Wikimedia Commons)

January 20," he offered. "The war had been going on for four years. Thirty-one thousand Americans had been killed in action. The training programme for the South Vietnamese was behind schedule. Five hundred and forty-thousand Americans were in Vietnam with no plans to reduce the number. No progress had been made at the negotiations in Paris and the United States had not put forth a comprehensive peace proposal…"

The President went on to describe the situation in Vietnam and his concerted effort to gain peace with honour. He added, "Let us be united for peace. Let us also be united against defeat. Because let us understand – North Vietnam cannot defeat or humiliate the United States. Only Americans can do that…."

In the aftermath of the broadcast, polling indicated that 75% of Americans considered themselves part of that 'silent majority'. Still, progress was agonisingly slow. Heartened by the apparent upswing of support, the President boldly stated during a December news conference that the war was nearing a "conclusion as a result of the plan that we have instituted."

The pronouncement, however, was premature. By 1970, US troop strength in Vietnam had decreased by 200,000, but in the spring, Nixon ordered the Cambodia incursion, responding to increasing North Vietnamese operations in support of the communist Khmer Rouge insurgency that threatened the new government of Lon Nol and to reduce infiltration of supplies and troops into South Vietnam. The public disclosure of the incursion produced a surge of protests across the country, reaching a crescendo with the shooting deaths of four students at Kent State University.

Some Americans did, in fact, see the Cambodia incursion as an escalation of the war and Nixon as duplicitous. The incursion did succeed in slowing down communist operations and provided some additional time for Vietnamisation to mature, but the staggering failure of Operation Lam Son 719, an ARVN offensive into Cambodia and Laos launched in February 1971, indicated that the South Vietnamese were far from being militarily self-sufficient.

When the North Vietnamese launched the Easter Offensive across South Vietnam in the spring of 1972, Nixon was determined to quell the threat of communist victory and unleashed heavy air attacks that turned the tide, allowing US and ARVN forces to halt the enemy. In a successful effort to compel the North Vietnamese and Viet Cong to commit to real progress at the negotiating table, the President ordered the mining of the North Vietnamese port of Haiphong and other harbours. He authorised Operation Linebacker, a sustained bombing campaign against North Vietnam, in May 1972.

Nixon's willingness to step up the pressure militarily sent a clear signal to the North

ABOVE: President Nixon greets US soldiers during a visit to South Vietnam in the summer of 1969. (Executive Office of the President of the United States the Nixon Library via Wikimedia Commons)

ABOVE: President Nixon discusses issues with National Security Advisor Henry Kissinger (left), Vice President Gerald Ford (third from left), and White House Chief of Staff Alexander Haig, Jr. (White House Photo Office Collection (Nixon Administration), 1/20/1969 - 8/9/1974 via Wikimedia Commons)

Vietnamese, and peace talks between Kissinger and Le Du Tho resumed later in the year. By mid-October, the diplomats had reached a tentative peace agreement. South Vietnamese President Thieu, however, refused to agree to the terms for two primary reasons: North Vietnamese troops already in South Vietnam were not to be withdrawn, and the Provisional Revolutionary Government, an independent shadow government of South Vietnam proclaimed by the North Vietnamese in June 1969, would be legitimised.

IMPASSE

Renewed negotiations between Kissinger and Le Duc Tho reached an impasse, twice failing to make any progress. President Nixon ordered Operation Lineback II, the

so-called 'Christmas Bombing' of North Vietnam, in late 1972. He essentially delivered an ultimatum to Thieu as well, threatening to cut off all US aid to South Vietnam if cooperation was not forthcoming.

Despite these apparent headwinds regarding the peace process, Nixon was re-elected for a second term as President in November, defeating Democratic opponent Senator George McGovern in a landslide with an electoral college vote of 520-17. Nixon carried 49 states, while McGovern won only Massachusetts and the District of Columbia. Nixon also received nearly 61% of the popular vote.

Although the Christmas bombing of North Vietnam was condemned by many countries, it apparently had the desired effect. Peace

negotiations resumed on January 8, 1973, and terms were concluded 15 days later. The Paris Peace Accords were signed on January 27. Amid the flurry of signatures and the flash of cameras, Nixon had assured Thieu that any North Vietnamese breach of the terms of the peace agreement would bring American military might back into play.

ABOVE: President Nixon leaves the White House after resigning the presidency in August 1974. (White House Photo Office Collection (Nixon Administration), 1/20/1969 - 8/9/1974 via Wikimedia Commons)

The endgame in Vietnam, however, was quite different. The fighting continued even as the Americans withdrew and their prisoners of war were repatriated. The South Vietnamese military proved incapable of standing alone, and communist forces were ultimately victorious in April 1975.

Meanwhile, the Nixon administration turned its attention to economic issues such as curbing a domestic rate of inflation that exceeded 6% in 1973, continuing détente with the Soviets following the Moscow Summit of 1972, and improving relations with China after the President's historic visit there, which ended a quarter century of non-engagement between the two countries.

Soon, however, the Watergate Scandal overshadowed everything else, and the Nixon administration crumbled under its weight. The President resigned from office on August 8, 1974, and was succeeded by Vice President Gerald Ford. A month later, Ford issued a controversial pardon of Nixon for any wrongdoing he may have committed while serving as President.

Perhaps the most controversial President in US history, Richard Nixon died on April 22, 1994, at the age of 81. During his long years of retirement, his legacy in tatters due to Watergate, the former President wrote several books. One of them was wistfully titled *No More Vietnams*.

ABOVE: President Nixon bids farewell to South Vietnamese President Nguyen Van Thieu following a conference in the spring of 1973. (White House Photo Office Collection (Nixon Administration), 1/20/1969 - 8/9/1974 via Wikimedia Commons)

STATE OF CONFLICT 1968

ABOVE: Dr Martin Luther King, Jr, addresses an anti-war rally in Minnesota. King was assassinated on April 4, 1968.
(Creative Commons Minnesota Historical Society via Wikimedia Commons)

ABOVE: Wearing combat gear, US Navy personnel stand watch on a balcony in Saigon during the Tet Offensive.
(US Navy via Wikimedia Commons)

The Tet Offensive shattered the calm of the Vietnamese lunar new year holiday, and with it the resolve of the American people to see the bloody conflict in Southeast Asia through to its end – if ever there could be an end.

The year 1968 was a watershed in the history of the Vietnam war. While Tet rocked cities and villages across Vietnam, the political landscape across America was altered by a pair of tragic events. On April 4, Dr Martin Luther King, Jr, the most influential leader of the civil rights movement in America, was gunned down on the balcony of the Lorraine Motel in Memphis, Tennessee. A wave of violence – 54 days of rioting – shook American cities in the aftermath of King's assassination.

On June 5, Senator Robert F. Kennedy of New York, campaigning for the Democratic nomination for President of the United States, was fatally wounded in the kitchen of the Ambassador Hotel in Los Angeles, California. Kennedy, the younger brother of President John F. Kennedy and former attorney general of the United States, had just won the California Democratic primary, gaining strong momentum toward the nomination. Campaigning on a platform of social reform, racial and economic equality, and accommodative foreign policy, he had called the Vietnam war the "gravest kind of error."

Meanwhile, President Lyndon Johnson's conduct of the Vietnam conflict had cost him substantial support among the electorate. He had authorised increases of American combat troops in Vietnam to nearly 550,000, while the US spent almost $80bn on the war during the year. The 12 months of 1968 would prove the costliest of the entire war in American lives with 16,899 killed. Total American deaths edged above 36,000. The heaviest single-day death toll for American troops during the fighting was January 31, as 246 US personnel were killed in the opening hours of the Tet Offensive.

March was a hard month for Johnson. A request from General Westmoreland for 205,000 additional troops was turned down after being roundly criticised in Congress and its details published in the *New York Times*. On the presidential primary ballot in New Hampshire, he had barely won over anti-war candidate Eugene McCarthy on March 12. On March 26, his so-called 'Wise Men', led by Secretary of State Dean Rusk and Secretary of Defense Clark Clifford advised that "…an American military solution in Vietnam was no longer attainable." And on March 30, a Gallup poll revealed that 63% of Americans disapproved of Johnson's conduct of the war effort.

The unpopularity of the Johnson administration had only been exacerbated by the apparent lack of control of the situation on the ground in South Vietnam as revealed by the Tet Offensive, and 60% of Americans told a Harris poll that they considered the offensive a defeat of US goals and objectives

BELOW: Ordnance delivered during close air support operations hits Viet Cong positions at Khe Sanh.
(US Marine Corps Archives via Wikimedia Commons)

ABOVE: Senator Robert F. Kennedy concludes a speech at the Ambassador Hotel in Los Angeles moments before he was shot by an assassin on June 5, 1968. (Creative Commons Sven Walnum via Wikimedia Commons)

ABOVE: General Creighton Abrams greets officers in South Vietnam. Abrams replaced General William Westmoreland as commander of MACV in June 1968. (US Department of Defense Admiral Elmo Zumwalt Jr. via Wikimedia Commons)

in Vietnam. Johnson's presidency was a casualty of Tet, and on March 31, he shocked a nationwide television audience with the blunt statement: "I shall not seek, and I will not accept, the nomination of my party for another term as your President."

Shortly after Johnson withdrew from the presidential race, General William Westmoreland, MACV (Military Assistance Command, Vietnam) commander, was recalled to the United States to assume the post of Chief of Staff of the Army after four years of fitful and frustrating fighting on his watch. Westmoreland was replaced by General Creighton Abrams in June. On January 27, 1968, four days before Tet, Westmoreland had stated in an annual report to the White House on the state of the war: "…In many areas the enemy has been driven away from the population centers; in others he has been compelled to disperse and evade contact, thus nullifying much of his potential. The year [1967] ended with the enemy increasingly resorting to desperation tactics in attempting to achieve military/psychological victory; and he has experienced only failure in these attempts."

Minnesota Senator Hubert Humphrey secured the Democratic nomination for President at the party's convention in Chicago in late August 1968. The violence that occurred in the city's streets during the

ABOVE: On March 31, 1968, President Lyndon Johnson tells the American people that he will not seek re-election. (Executive Office of the President of the United States Yoichi Okamoto via Wikimedia Commons)

convention, spurred by disillusionment with the Johnson administration and the party, is recognised today as one of the most graphic manifestations of the nation's turmoil.

In November, Republican Richard Nixon, former vice president during the administration of Dwight Eisenhower

and his party's nominee in the presidential election of 1960, which had resulted in a narrow defeat to John F. Kennedy, was elected President of the United States. Nixon defeated Senator Humphrey and third-party candidate George Wallace, former and future governor of Alabama.

Nixon campaigned in 1968 on the restoration of law and order, a response to the wave of riots and demonstrations that had wracked the country in recent years, as well as promising a new perspective on the prosecution of the war in Vietnam. Candidly, that perspective did not necessarily entertain the prospect of outright victory over the communists, but more so an exit strategy that turned the war over to the South Vietnamese and allowed the US to attain a nebulous notion of "peace with honor."

A month before the communists launched the Tet Offensive, they disregarded the short truce of New Year's Day as fighting broke out in Tay Ninh Province on the South Vietnamese border with Cambodia when the 271st and 272nd Regiments of the North Vietnamese Army's (NVA) 9th Division attacked elements of the US 25th Infantry Division at Firebase Burt. The communists were beaten back with the loss of 328 killed while 23 Americans died.

On January 3, an NVA regiment attacked US firebases in the Que Son Valley, south of Da Nang on the coast of the South China Sea. The NVA managed to breach the outer defences at Firebase Ross that morning but were thrown back later in the day. Situated nearby, Landing Zone Leslie came under enemy fire, and the NVA brought heavy machine guns in to harass air traffic. During the next nine days, 26 helicopters of the 1st Cavalry Division (Airmobile) were damaged and seven were shot down.

While the Tet Offensive began in earnest on January 30 and threw US and South Vietnamese authorities into temporary chaos, the tactical outcome was a serious blow to the NVA and Viet Cong. The US and South Vietnamese response to Tet restored order in South Vietnamese cities and inflicted heavy casualties on the communist infiltrators. Some observers have

BELOW: Elements of the 2nd Battalion, 4th Marines search the village of Dai Do after a four-day battle with the North Vietnamese. (Creative Commons Archives from Quantico USA via Wikimedia Commons)

and 51 American soldiers were killed. From the end of March to January 1969, the US 173rd Airborne Brigade operated in Bin Dinh Province to reestablish security against Viet Cong insurgents, killing more than 900 enemy fighters.

At the Battle of Dai Do, April 30 to May 3, on the River Cura Viet in Quang Tri Province, the fighting was hand-to-hand at times as the 1st Battalion, 3rd Marines and the 2nd Battalion 4th Marines battled two battalions of the NVA, killing 600 communist soldiers but losing 81 killed and suffering total casualties of 50%. Two Marine officers later received the Medal of Honor for the action.

ABOVE: Soldiers of the 2nd Battalion, 60th Infantry Regiment display confiscated communist weapons near My Tho, South Vietnam in April 1968.
(NARA photo 111-CCV-591-SC661666 by Brow via Wikimedia Commons)

concluded that at least temporarily the Viet Cong was gutted during Tet and ceased to be an effective fighting force.

TURNING POINT

Years later, one combat veteran of the 1st Cavalry Division (Airmobile) expressed a strong opinion regarding post-Tet media influence on the outcome of the war. "We won the Tet Offensive," he declared. "We decimated the Viet Cong. And our wonderful press made us losers. It was right at that point in time, I think, that the press fully turned on the war in Vietnam and started not necessarily generating news but generating opinions. Because we decimated the Viet Cong during Tet. We decimated the North Vietnamese Army during Tet. Had we pressed the advantage the turnout would have been different. But when you are fighting a war based on politics, stuff happens."

When the Tet Offensive began, the 77-day siege of Khe Sanh was already underway, and though it conjured up memories of the

French disaster at Dien Bien Phu in 1954, the US Marine garrison held its ground. After the siege of Khe Sanh was lifted, the US 3rd Marine Division began Operation Scotland II, nearly 10 months of campaigning against communist forces in the area. By February 1969, the Marines reported more than 3,300 enemy killed for a loss of 435 of their own. Days of ferocious urban fighting were required to clear Viet Cong and NVA forces from the provincial capital of Hue, but the communists were defeated there.

From February to September, US Marines of Task Force X-Ray fought to clear Highway 1 between Da Nang and the firebase at Phu Bai. Nearly seven months of fighting left 117 Americans dead and 702 communist troops killed. From March to August, elements of the US 9th Infantry Division, the US Navy's Mobile Riverine Force, and the South Vietnamese Army's (ARVN) 7th Division conducted Operation Truong Cong Dinh to reestablish control of the northern Mekong Delta. A total of 343 Viet Cong guerrillas

In early May, the communists launched a wave of attacks across South Vietnam sometimes referred to as 'Little Tet'. Weeks of combat followed, and once again the NVA and Viet Cong suffered thousands of killed and wounded. Even as the spring fight was taking place, representatives of the opposing sides sat down at the French Foreign Ministry in Paris for the first time to explore peace negotiations.

In late July, Secretary of State Clifford returned from a fact-finding visit to Vietnam and told his staff grimly: "We must get out of there. No way we can terminate the war militarily…Corruption runs through everything." A few days later, presidential candidate Nixon told the Republican National Convention in Miami Beach, Florida, that he intended to "bring an honorable end to the war in Vietnam."

Meanwhile, the fighting and dying in Southeast Asia continued. In August, the communists launched a third offensive against population centres in South Vietnam but were again defeated with heavy losses. On November 1, President Johnson called Operation Rolling Thunder, the sustained bombing campaign against North Vietnam, to an end after more than three years in anticipation of peace talks.

Five days after Nixon took the oath of office as President on January 20, 1969, American diplomats flew again to Paris to meet with representatives of North and South Vietnam and the Viet Cong. The Paris Peace Talks would stop and start for the next four years.

BELOW: Presidential candidate Richard Nixon (left) meets with President Lyndon Johnson at the White House in the summer of 1968. (Executive Office of the President of the United States via Wikimedia Commons)

BED-INS FOR PEACE

I t was a gesture to promote world peace. A most unusual gesture to be sure, and it was aimed directly at the war in Vietnam.

John Lennon of the Beatles and multimedia artist Yoko Ono married in Gibraltar on March 20, 1969. Both were passionate peace activists, and the war in Vietnam was raging. Considering the opportunity to make a bold statement – or put on a publicity stunt – the couple came up with an innovative way to bring attention to their anti-war message.

They went to bed.

Five days after their wedding, the couple checked into the presidential suite at the Amsterdam Hilton, and quite publicly climbed into bed, attracting tremendous attention from the media. "We're going to stay in bed for seven days," John told reporters. "Instead of having a private honeymoon, it's a private protest."

Yoko echoed: "For the violence that's going on in the world, instead of making war, let's stay in bed." Lennon followed, "And grow your hair! Let it grow until peace comes!"

And so it was that the famous newlyweds stayed in bed from March 25 to March 29, 1969. The media was welcomed between 9am and 9pm each day, and the couple answered questions and mused on the condition of the world.

ABOVE: John Lennon and Yoko Ono, joined by Tommy Smothers (back to camera) and Timothy Leary (centre) prepare to record *Give Peace a Chance* in 1969. (Creative Commons Roy Kerwood via Wikimedia Commons)

ABOVE: John Lennon and Yoko Ono entertain the media during their bed-in for peace in Amsterdam, March 25, 1969. (Creative Commons Dutch National Archives Eric Koch/Anefo)

Years later in the multimedia retrospective *The Beatles Anthology*, Lennon remembered: " We sent out a card: 'Come to John and Yoko's honeymoon: a bed-in, Amsterdam Hotel…We knew whatever we did was going to be in the papers. We decided to utilise the space we would occupy anyway, by getting married, with a commercial for peace. We would sell our product, which we call 'peace,' and to sell a product you need a gimmick, and the gimmick we thought was 'bed.' And we thought 'bed' because bed was the easiest way of doing it, because we're lazy."

The bed-in was staged just weeks after the inauguration of Richard Nixon as

President of the United States, and a new round of peace negotiations had just gotten underway in Paris. The event did gain a vast audience, and John and Yoko considered it so successful that they staged a second bed-in, this time at the Queen Elizabeth Hotel in Montreal from May 26 to June 1, 1969.

The second bed-in had been planned for New York City, but Lennon was not granted entry into the United States because of a conviction for possession of marijuana a year earlier; however, the experience in Montreal provided inspiration for writing the hit song *Give Peace a Chance*. Written during the bed-in, the song was recorded live on June 1, 1969, as a crowd of students, Hare Krishnas, and celebrity friends joined in. Among the famous participants were anti-war activists Timothy Leary, Allen Ginsberg, Dick Gregory, and Tommy Smothers, who played acoustic guitar along with Lennon.

In early July, *Give Peace a Chance* was released as a single by the Plastic Ono Band. It reached number two on the United Kingdom singles chart and number 14 on the US Billboard Hot 100 and perhaps became the best-known anti-war song in history.

Although the bed-ins were criticised in some quarters, they did in fact raise awareness. And John had the final word with a retort to the critics in his hit song *The Ballad of John and Yoko*. It chimes, "Drove from Paris to the Amsterdam Hilton/Talking in our beds for a week/The newspapers said, 'What are you doing in bed?'/I said, 'We're only trying to get us some peace.'"

The Ballad of John and Yoko reached number one on the UK singles chart and number eight on the Billboard Hot 100.

ABOVE: Wax figures in a Montreal museum commemorate the second bed-in of John Lennon and Yoko Ono. (Creative Commons Eliedion via Wikimedia Commons)

ONE WEEK'S DEAD

They were all young men, 37 teenagers, most in their 20s, the eldest 37. And they were all dead, killed in action during a single week of fighting in the Vietnam War from May 28 to June 3, 1969.

The essay in the June 27, 1969, issue of *Life* magazine mentioned that there was nothing remarkable about that week except that it included Memorial Day. Such losses had become commonplace, but then there were the names, the ages, the ranks and branches of service, and the home towns. Of 242 members of the US armed forces that died during that 'typical' week of warfare, 217 were also remembered with photographs. Their youthful faces, some gleaned from the pages of high school yearbooks, in coats and ties, graduation caps and gowns, uniformed portraits, some of them in combat gear, and quite a few wearing horn rimmed glasses, gazed from the pages.

ABOVE: A US Marine exits a transport helicopter during operations in the Plain of Reeds, South Vietnam.
(National Archives 26387449 USMC photo A188067 by SGT McVeigh via Wikimedia Commons)

ABOVE: American soldiers await the arrival of helicopters in Long An Province in the spring of 1969.
(US Government NARA photo 111-CCV-586B-CC60038 by SP4 Allen T. Rockoff via Wikimedia Commons)

The magazine's cover bore the headline, "The Faces of the American Dead in Vietnam: One Week's Toll." The haunting image on the cover was that of 20-year-old Army Specialist 5 William C. Gearing, Jr. A native of Greece, New York, he had been drafted in the spring of 1968. Something of the All-American boy, he had played on the offensive line on the varsity football team at Greece Olympia High School. In a 50th anniversary retrospective, *Washington Post* writer Michael Ruane noted that his parents and four younger siblings lived on Dewey Avenue back home. Friends and family called him 'Bill', and he had lost his life to an enemy artillery shell at a distant place called Quang Tin while serving with Detachment 3, Company B, 7th Psychological Operations Battalion (7th Psyops), 4th Psychological Operations Group.

Inside, the title page read, "VIETNAM ONE WEEK'S DEAD May 28-June 3, 1969." The 10 pages that followed were a roll call of lost youth and promise, a testimony to tragedy and waste, a sombre summation of America's loss in a single stark seven days.

Forty-five years after the dramatic publication hit newsstands and reached mailboxes across the United States, Ben Cosgrove wrote for *Life*, "To no one's surprise, the public's response was immediate, and visceral. Some readers expressed amazement, in light of the thousands of American deaths suffered in a war with no end in sight, that it took so long for *Life* to produce something as dramatic and pointed as 'One Week's Toll.' Others were outraged that the magazine was,

ABOVE: US soldiers fight the Viet Cong from a trench in Kontum Province. (US Army Center of Military History via Wikimedia Commons)

ABOVE: An American soldier of the 173rd Airborne Brigade fires a machine gun during a patrol in early 1969. (NARA photo 111-CCV-636-CC56400 by SP4 Kenneth L. Powell via Wikimedia Commons)

as one reader saw it, "supporting the anti-war demonstrators who are traitors to this country.' Still others perhaps the vast majority were quietly and disconsolately devastated…."

Regardless, it was and still is impossible to stare at the faces and read the names of these 'petals' fallen from the flower of a generation without a pang of grief. Introducing the story, a writer for *Life* noted, The faces shown on the next pages are the faces of American men killed, in the words of the official announcement of their deaths, 'in connection with the conflict in Vietnam… The numbers of the dead are average for any seven-day period during this stage of the war. It is not the intention of this article to speak for the dead. We cannot tell with any precision what they thought of the political currents which drew them across the world. From the letters of some, it is possible to tell they felt strongly that they should be in Vietnam, that they had great sympathy for the Vietnamese people and were appalled at their enormous suffering.

Some had voluntarily extended their tours of combat duty; some were desperate to come home. Their families provided most of these photographs, and many expressed their own feelings that their sons and husbands died in a necessary cause…."

Ruane interviewed Hal Buell, the retired chief of photography for the Associated Press, who commented on the article: "You saw all these incredible pictures coming out of Vietnam. But this idea of showing how many people, not just numbering, not just a list of names, but a picture of each one of these people, it had an incredible impact… the sheer enormity of the faces…It bumped history…When pictures turn up…they don't fall into a vacuum. They fall into a time and a place. Frequently, the picture affects the time, and the time affects the picture."

The individual stories of those who were killed and memorialised in the pages of the magazine run the gamut of raw human emotion, courage, and sacrifice. Five of them, Sergeant Earl Godman, Specialist 4 Dick Whitney, Specialist 4 Marvin Briss, Specialist 5

ABOVE: American soldiers await a Viet Cong attack while manning their machine gun in early 1969. (Creative Commons DannyLane1349 via Wikimedia Commons)

David Tiffany, and Lieutenant Patrick Dixon, died together in an ambush in Long An Province on May 28. The eldest was 23-year-old Dixon. With the exception of Godman, the others were pictured in the magazine.

Thirty-five-year-old Lieutenant Colonel Robert H. Carter managed a slight smile when he posed for a uniformed portrait that made the pages of *Life*. A graduate of The Citadel in Charleston, South Carolina, he had received the Silver Star medal. He was killed by a sniper while approaching a helicopter during a vicious firefight in Kantum Province on May 27. Captain Robert Sigholz, Jr., was killed in action on May 26, while fighting with the same Army 2nd Battalion, 503rd Infantry Regiment that had been under the command of his father, Colonel Robert Sigholz, Sr., two years prior.

A postscript in the pages of *Life* poignantly conveys a few glimpses of the lives of the loved and lost – different kinds of snapshots, so to speak. "On the back of a picture he sent home shortly before his death near Saigon, Sgt. William Anderson, 18, of Templeton, Pa., jotted a wry note: 'Plain of Reeds, May 12, 1969. Here's a picture of a 2-star general awarding me my Silver Star. I didn't do anything. They just had some extra ones.' His family has a few other recent photographs of the boy, including one showing him this past February helping to put a beam into place on his town's new church. His was the first military funeral held there."

Another soldier, the narrative reads, had hastily written a brief note during the battle for an otherwise piece of nondescript Vietnamese high ground. "Premonitions gripped many of the men. One wrote, 'I have given my life as have many others for a cause in which I firmly believe. You may not be able to read this. I am writing it in a hurry. I see death coming up the hill.'"

ABOVE: Tracking a wounded enemy soldier, two Americans of the 44th Scout Dog Platoon find a discarded field dressing in February 1969. (US Army SP5 Bryan K. Grigsby via Wikimedia Commons)

HAMBURGER HILL

ABOVE: A pair of US Army photographers survey the devastated landscape at Hamburger Hill after the 1969 battle. (United States Army Military History Institute via Wikimedia Commons)

Fifty years after a brigade of the US Army's famed 101st Airborne Division, the Screaming Eagles, fought a bloody battle for Hill 937 in the A Shau Valley of central Vietnam from May 13-20, 1969, veteran radio man Dennis Helms of Bravo Company, 1st Platoon, 3rd Battalion, 187th Infantry Regiment, described his recollections for the West Point Center for Oral History.

"We began to wonder about what kind of place this was and why they were defending it," said Helms. "Over the course of the battle, we made a number of assaults up the hill, and we would come back down each time because we had limited space to move in, and it seemed as if all their weapons were trained on the clearing, and we just couldn't seem to get past that. Every assault was a somewhat different scene but had the same outcome. It just depended on where they wanted to hit us when we first came in the clearing or got past the clearing. The noise level was also so unbearable."

After the fight was over and the North Vietnamese Army's (NVA) elite 29th Regiment had withdrawn, Hill 937, identified on military maps according to its height in metres, would forever be known as 'Hamburger Hill'. The Vietnamese have always called it Dong Ap Bia, or "mountain of the crouching beast."

The 101st's 3rd Brigade, commanded by Colonel Joseph Conmy, had come to Hamburger Hill during Operation Apache Snow, an effort to sweep the A Shau Valley clear of strongpoints and bases that facilitated communist infiltration from Laos and enhance the security of the cities of Hue and Da Nang,

ABOVE: Specialist Joe Leber of the 3rd Battalion, 187th Regiment, stands with the US flag on the summit of Hamburger Hill. (Department of Defense Sgt. Sarah Scully via Wikimedia Commons)

a centre of American military logistics. Hill 937 was little more than a mile from the Laotian border, and the three battalions of American airborne troops, 3rd Battalion, 187th Regiment (3/187), 2/505, and 1/506, reached the high ground where the communists had fortified the slope, neighbouring ridges, and draws with bunkers, booby traps, machine-gun nests with interlocking fields of fire, and a network of tunnels on May 10.

An early attack by 3/187 was driven back with heavy casualties on the same day. The terrain was inhospitable to say the least, steeply sloped along the hillside and surrounded by dense jungle. American officers had incorrectly believed Hamburger Hill

would be in their possession within hours, but the tenacious defenders held their positions grudgingly. When the North Vietnamese finally pulled out, documents found on the bodies of enemy dead confirmed that the 3rd Brigade had been up against the 29th Regiment, veterans of the Tet Offensive and known as the 'Pride of Ho Chi Minh'.

On May 14, the 3/187 tried again to take Hamburger Hill. Again, the airborne troopers were thrown back. As the fight wore on and casualties mounted, supporting American air strikes and artillery fire pounded NVA positions. Helicopters brought in ammunition and supplies and evacuated the wounded and dead. Several were damaged or shot down by enemy rocket-propelled grenades and small-arms fire. Aircraft dropped 142 tons of napalm and 1,088 tons of bombs. More than 30,000 rounds of 20mm ammunition were fired, and 513 tons of tear gas were expended in the vain effort to choke the NVA out of their fortifications.

HAMBURGER MACHINE

During a pause in the agonising series of uphill assaults, 19-year-old Sergeant James Spears answered a reporter's question. "What was it like? Have you ever been inside a hamburger machine? We just got cut to pieces by extremely accurate machine gun fire." Another soldier who participated in nine of the attacks up the hill offered, "I've lost a lot of buddies up there. Not many guys can take it much longer."

The news media covered the fight at Hamburger Hill extensively, and the American public consumed television and newspaper accounts as the savage fight unfolded. Associated Press reporter Jay Sharbutt graphically described what he saw. "The paratroopers came down the mountain, their green shirts darkened with sweat, their

ABOVE: Soldiers of the 101st Airborne Division pick their way across the shattered slope of Hamburger Hill shortly after the 10-day battle. (United States Army Military History Institute via Wikimedia Commons)

ABOVE: Wounded soldiers of the 101st Airborne Division are evacuated by helicopter during Operation Apache Snow.
(United States Army Military History Institute via Wikimedia Commons)

to surround the enemy and seeking to assault the hill from the sides and front simultaneously, there was one frontal assault after another, killing our boys who went up Hamburger Hill."

Some historians regard the decision to abandon Hamburger Hill as a reflection of a changing US government perspective on the war. Khe Sanh had been abandoned nearly a year earlier after a hard siege during the Tet Offensive, and the anti-war movement was steadily evolving into a force on the home front. Politicians began to assert more control over military operations, often to the dismay of professional soldiers.

Operation Apache Snow continued through June 7, 1968, and was declared successful as its limited objective of curtailing communist infiltration in the A Shau Valley appeared to have been accomplished, at least temporarily. A total of 113 Americans had died in the effort that lasted four weeks. After Hamburger Hill, it was clear that the role of US ground forces in Vietnam was to be diminished. A day after Apache Snow concluded, President Richard Nixon announced his policy of 'Vietnamisation'.

weapons gone, their bandages stained brown and red with mud and blood."

By May 20, General Melvin Zais, commander of the 101st Airborne Division, had dispatched the 2/505 and the 1/506 to assist in the capture of Hamburger Hill. Finally, after a dozen attempts, the Americans reached the crest, only to discover that the NVA had faded into the jungle and reached safety in their Laotian sanctuary. Though the high ground had been taken, there was palpable consternation as the Americans realised many enemy troops had managed to slip away. The 101st had lost 72 killed in action and 370 wounded, while NVA casualties were estimated at 630 killed. The 3/187 had been particularly hard hit, and among its four companies casualties were staggering, from 50 to 75%.

Ironically, Hamburger Hill was ultimately assessed to have no real strategic or tactical value. General Zais commented: "The only significance of the hill was the fact that your North Vietnamese (were) on it…" On June 5, 1969, scarcely two weeks after the 3rd Brigade, 101st Airborne Division had emerged from the fight bloodied, battered, but victorious, Hamburger Hill was abandoned.

On Capitol Hill in Washington, D.C., the reaction to the heavy casualties at Hamburger Hill was swift and scathing. Senator Edward Kennedy of Massachusetts called the situation "madness." He angrily declared: "I feel it is both senseless and irresponsible to continue to send our young men to their deaths to capture hills and positions that have no relation to ending this conflict."

Ohio Congressman Stephen Young lamented: "Our generals in Vietnam acted as if they had never studied Lee and Jackson's strategy. Instead, they fling our paratroopers piecemeal in frontal assaults. Instead of seeking

ABOVE: US Marines fire 105mm howitzers at Firebase Razor in support of Operation Apache Snow on May 4, 1969.
(Defense Department Photo (Marine Corps) A800625 by M. C. Patterson via Wikimedia Commons)

ABOVE: In this 2011 photo, Hamburger Hill rises above the floor of the A Shau Valley. The Vietnamese called the high ground 'mountain of the crouching beast'. (Creative Commons Bac Trau via Wikimedia Commons)

VIETNAM AND THE MEDAL OF HONOR

Specialist 5 John J. Kedenburg was 21 years old when he boarded a helicopter on June 13, 1968, at Forward Operating Base 2 along with a detachment of South Vietnamese soldiers, their mission to conduct anti-Viet Cong operations in neighbouring Laos.

Kedenburg had joined the Army in 1965, and three years later he was a Green Beret of the 5th Special Forces Group serving as an advisor to the South Vietnamese with MACV-SOG (Military Advisory Command Vietnam – Special Operations Group). Soon after insertion, the situation began to unravel. The heavily outnumbered detachment was attacked and surrounded by a battalion-strength unit of the North Vietnamese Army (NVA) and fighting for its collective life.

Born in Brooklyn, New York, Kedenburg grew up in the quiet suburbs on Scotch Pine Drive in Central Islip. He enlisted to serve his country and to find direction for his life. That day in the jungle of Laos, he freely forfeited that life so that others

ABOVE: President Barack Obama presents the Medal of Honor to Command Sergeant Major Bennie Adkins at the White House in 2014. (US Army Staff Sgt Bernardo Fuller via Wikimedia Commons)

might live. He organised the defence against the overwhelming NVA force, called for air support, and led a breakout. Then, with the enemy fire sufficiently suppressed for a time, he vectored a pair of evacuation helicopters into the area. But one man was missing.

The hovering helicopters dropped slings to pull the men up, and after half had been extracted, Kedenburg and the three men with him on the ground strapped themselves into their slings while bullets zipped all around them. Suddenly, the missing man appeared. Without hesitation, Kedenburg gave up his sling, and the four men were hoisted to safety. The young soldier remained on the ground, firing at the enemy until he was overwhelmed and killed. When his body was recovered, six dead NVA soldiers were sprawled nearby.

John Kedenburg's selfless act of heroism earned him a posthumous Medal of Honor, and he rests today in Long Island National Cemetery, Farmingdale, New York.

Such stirring stories of heroism and sacrifice are extraordinary, even in

ABOVE: Green Beret Specialist 5 John Kedenburg received a posthumous Medal of Honor for sacrificing his life during a mission in Laos on June 13, 1968.
(US Army via Wikimedia Commons)

ABOVE: Marine PFC James Anderson, Jr, covered an enemy hand grenade to protect his fellow Marines and received a posthumous Medal of Honor.
(US Marine Corps photo via Wikimedia Commons)

ABOVE: US Air Force pilot Merlyn Dethlefsen wears the Medal of Honor in this portrait. (US Air Force via Wikimedia Commons)

wartime. During the Vietnam conflict from 1955 to 1975, countless such incidents of individual bravery occurred. A total of 268 Medals of Honor for valour in Vietnam have been presented, 235 during the war and 33 in the ensuing years, 159 of them posthumously.

Sergeant First Class Bennie Adkins fought like a lion for 38 hours in the A Shau Valley in March 1966. Marine Corps Private First Class James Anderson died when he covered an enemy hand grenade near Cam Lo on February 28, 1967, absorbing the blast to save fellow Marines from injury. Air Force Captain Merlyn H. Dethlefsen repeatedly braved heavy anti-aircraft fire over North Vietnam, executing air strikes in his damaged Republic F-105 Thunderchief fighter-bomber during a mission in the spring of 1967. Navy Hospital Corpsman Robert R. Ingram, badly wounded himself, continued to treat wounded Marines during

a vicious firefight in Quang Ngai Province, March 28, 1966.

THE REAL FORREST GUMP

Private First Class Sammy L. Davis of Dayton, Ohio, enlisted in the US Army right out of high school, foregoing his senior trip to New York City. At age 21, he was assigned to C Battery, 4th Artillery, 2nd Battalion, 9th Infantry Division. Along the banks of the River Mekong near the village of Cai Lay, Davis and his battery mates occupied positions at Firebase Cudgel on November 18, 1967. CH-47 Chinook helicopters laden with artillery shells and with 105mm howitzers slung under their bellies followed them in.

"A Huey (helicopter) came in that afternoon, and a major got out and gathered 42 of us kids around there and said the probability of us getting hit that night was 100 percent," Davis remembered. "We thought what he meant was a few mortar rounds and some automatic weapons fire and that would be it."

However, the desperate fight that followed was nothing like the American artillerymen had previously experienced. Enemy mortar rounds began to fall around 2am. "…They were raining down," Davis remembered. "At exactly 2:30, they stopped and there was a strange, eerie silence. From across the river, we could hear people yelling, 'Tonight you die, GI!' We could see 150 to 200 people formed up to make a mass assault."

The artillerymen loaded their howitzers with beehive rounds, each containing 18,000 small darts, and essentially turning their weapons into big shotguns. When Davis pulled the lanyard, firing his weapon's first round, a communist 57mm recoilless rifle fired at his gun's muzzle blast and disabled his weapon. His sergeant, James Gant, was seriously wounded. Davis was hit as well, blown halfway out of his foxhole. He was hit by friendly fire when a neighbouring gun loosed a beehive round

ABOVE: Although badly wounded, US Navy Corpsman Robert Ingram continued to treat wounded Marines and received the Medal of Honor. (US Navy via Wikimedia Commons)

against enemy soldiers trying to turn Davis's howitzer on them.

Despite his wounds, Davis regained consciousness, grabbed his M-16 rifle, and expended 12 clips of ammunition against the surging enemy soldiers climbing up the riverbank. He then fired 500 rounds with an M60 machine gun he relocated from an adjacent foxhole. He also managed to single-handedly fire several damaging rounds from his disabled howitzer, assembling the rounds, loading them into the breech, and then firing. Throughout the harrowing experience, Davis showed disregard for his own safety – particularly when he observed Specialist 4 Gwendell Holloway, an infantryman of the 5th Battalion, 60th Infantry Regiment, wounded across the river.

"In the light of a flare, I saw a buddy on the other side of the river and said, 'I've got to go get him!'" said Davis. "He had a hole in his head I could lay two fingers in and was shot in the back and had shrapnel wounds."

When he reached the other side of the river on an inflatable air mattress, Davis discovered two other wounded soldiers. Praying for the strength to carry all three, he managed to get them across the river to safety. Miraculously, all these men, Sergeant Gant, and Davis survived the engagement. The following morning, only 12 of the original complement of 42 artillerymen were still standing, including Davis, who had wounds from the 57mm round that disabled his gun and the beehive round his fellow soldiers had fired. One dart had lodged in a kidney. His fourth lumbar vertebra was fractured. Ribs were crushed, and the vertebra completely broken when he discharged his gun from underneath, and it fell on him. He had also been hit in the thigh by a round from an enemy AK-47 assault rifle.

But the enemy attack had been bloodily repulsed.

Davis refused medical treatment at first. But when he passed out, he was loaded

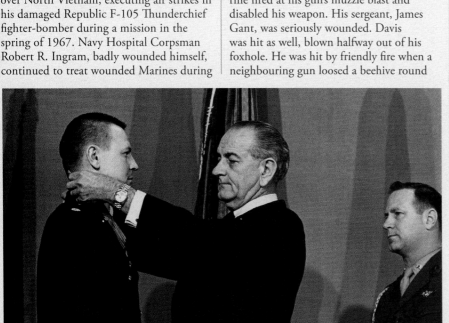

ABOVE: President Lyndon Johnson presents the Medal of Honor to Captain Merlyn Dethlefsen in 1968. (Executive Office of the President of the United States via Wikimedia Commons)

ABOVE: Medal of Honor recipient Sergeant Sammy L. Davis speaks to a group in 2009. (US Army via Wikimedia Commons)

Lieutenant Commander Joseph Robert Kerrey, a 25-year-old officer of the elite US Navy SEALS, deployed to Vietnam as assistant commander, Delta Platoon, SEAL Team One, in January 1969. Two months later, on March 14, Kerrey led elements of SEAL Team One in a raid on Viet Cong installations on Hon Tre Island in near Nha Trang Bay, Khanh Hoa Province. After coming ashore, Kerrey's team scaled a 350ft cliff to position themselves above the suspected enemy positions. He divided the team in half for the descent. As the SEALs approached their objective, a torrent of enemy fire erupted. A hand grenade exploded at Kerrey's feet, shredding the lower part of his right leg.

Despite the serious wound, Kerrey maintained command. His Medal of Honor citation reads in part: "…Kerrey called in the second element's fire support which caught the confused Viet Cong in a devastating cross fire. After successfully suppressing the enemy's fire, and although immobilised by his multiple wounds, he continued to maintain calm, superlative control as he ordered his team to secure and defend an extraction site. Lieutenant (jg) Kerrey resolutely directed his men, despite his near-unconscious state, until he was eventually evacuated by helicopter. The havoc brought to the enemy by this very successful mission cannot be overestimated. The enemy who were captured provided critical intelligence to the allied effort…."

ABOVE: Former Navy SEAL and Medal of Honor recipient Senator Bob Kerrey posed for this official portrait.
(US Congress via Wikimedia Commons)

aboard a dust-off helicopter. He woke up hours later in a hospital in Japan. A year later, Davis and four other soldiers received the Medal of Honor from President Lyndon Johnson in a ceremony at the White House. Today, Davis travels extensively and speaks to a variety of school and civic groups. Film footage of the Medal of Honor ceremony was used in the 1994 film *Forrest Gump*, the head of actor Tom Hanks superimposed on Davis's body. Since the film's release, Davis has referred to himself as the 'real' Forrest Gump.

President Richard Nixon presented the Medal of Honor to Kerrey on May 14, 1970, and the distinguished officer was medically discharged from the navy due to his injuries. In 2001, reports surfaced in the media regarding a raid by a swift boat team under Kerrey's command that occurred on February 25, 1969. Kerrey received the Bronze Star for the raid, but controversy swirled around a number of civilian deaths, including women and children. He denied allegations of

ABOVE: Sammy Davis, the 'real' Forrest Gump, stands at centre during the Medal of Honor ceremony on November 19, 1968. (Executive Office of the President of the United States via Wikimedia Commons)

ABOVE: Senator Bob Kerrey (third from left) sits with other Medal of Honor recipients during ceremonies in 2007.
(US Navy photo by Mass Communication Specialist 1st Class Brien Aho via Wikimedia Commons)

involvement in any intentional killings of civilians and countered the story told by another member of his SEAL team with the comment, "…it's not my memory of it."

Kerrey went on to serve as governor and senator from the state of Nebraska. He remains active in politics and business.

ROY BENAVIDEZ

Staff Sergeant Roy Benavidez was a veteran. He had enlisted in the military during the Korean War, and now at age 32 he was serving a second tour of duty when the most harrowing day of his life occurred, May 2, 1968. Benavides later referred to the experience as "six hours in hell."

The radio at the US Special Forces base at Loc Ninh, South Vietnam, near the border with Cambodia, crackled with frantic calls for assistance from a 12-man team from Fifth Special Forces Group Detachment B-56. Their mission to slip across the Cambodian frontier and retrieve a North Vietnamese truck as proof that the communists were using the neutral territory as a sanctuary and to infiltrate into South Vietnam had gone terribly wrong, and they were surrounded by a full NVA battalion, at least 1,000 soldiers.

One rescue attempt had failed, the helicopter driven away by enemy anti-aircraft fire. Several members of the beleaguered team were already dead. As the 240th Assault Helicopter Company organised another rescue attempt, Benavidez rushed to assist. As one wounded 19-year-old helicopter door-gunner gasped and died in his arms, he asked the pilot: "Who are those people on the ground?"

When the pilot replied that Sergeant First Class Leroy Wright and his detachment were the ones in extreme danger, Benavidez yelled, "I'm coming with you!" He owed a tremendous debt to Wright. Three days earlier during a similar mission, Benavidez and another soldier were being extracted by rope from a hovering helicopter. When the ropes became tangled, the friction threatened to snap the lifelines. Wright descended on another rope, freed the tangled lines, and probably saved the lives of Benavides and the other soldier.

So, Benavidez climbed aboard carrying only a Bowie knife and a hmedical kit. No stranger to tough situations, Benavidez had recovered from serious wounds suffered when he stepped on a land mine during his first tour of duty. After being told he was permanently disabled, he walked out of a Texas hospital in July 1966. Now he was aboard a rescuing Huey heading into a literal firestorm. The landing zone was hot, and the helicopter could not set down, so Benavidez lowered himself 10ft to the ground by rope. Immediately, a round from a communist AK-47 slammed into his right leg. Undeterred, he covered the 75 yards to the surrounded soldiers. Four men were already dead, including Wright, but Benavidez distributed water and ammunition and used his call sign 'Tango Mike Mike' to bring in supporting air strikes. Within minutes, another bullet had ripped into his right thigh.

Bleeding profusely, Benavidez managed to pick up an enemy rifle lying nearby and fired back as he crawled along, dragging wounded men toward a helicopter that had set down in a hail of enemy fire. But the pilot was dead. Pulling wounded crewmen out of the downed Huey, Benavidez had also retrieved a bag of codes, call signs, and documents from around Wright's neck. Another Huey came close, and Benavidez realised it was his last chance. He carried wounded toward it, killing an enemy soldier with his knife and sustaining yet another wound. He shot two more NVA soldiers charging the helicopter as he loaded men aboard.

By the time Roy Benavidez was pulled aboard the Huey, he had suffered 37 bullet, bayonet, and shrapnel wounds. Miraculously, he survived to receive the Distinguished Service Cross. However, after years of effort by several individuals on his behalf, including another survivor of the ordeal of B-56 and a former special forces officer, Benavidez received the Medal of Honor from President Ronald Reagan at the Pentagon on February 24, 1981.

Benavidez had devoted the remainder of his life to teaching young people the virtues of patriotism and citizenship and advocating for veterans benefits. He died of complications of diabetes and respiratory failure at age 63 on November 29, 1998.

These are only a few of the stories of remarkable heroism that led to the presentation of the Medal of Honor during the Vietnam war. Countless other acts of bravery have, no doubt, passed into history without notice or commendation.

ABOVE: Master Sergeant Roy Benavidez stands between Secretary of Defense Caspar Weinberger (left) and President Ronald Reagan during his Medal of Honor ceremony in 1981. (Ron Hall, US Air Force via Wikimedia Commons)

ABOVE: Roy Benavidez wears the rank of master sergeant and the Medal of Honor at his throat.
(US Army via Wikimedia Commons)

STATE OF CONFLICT
1969-1970

BELOW: Bell UH-1 Iroquois 'Huey' helicopters of the 170th and 189th Helicopter Assault Companies wait for troops to load before taking off on a mission. (National Archives and Records Administration via Wikimedia Commons)

ABOVE: A US Marine carries a shredded Viet Cong flag near Da Nang after a communist guerrilla attack in 1969. (Official USMC photo by Gunnery Sergeant Chuck Lane from the Jonathan Abel Collection (COLL/3611), Marine Corps Archives & Special Collections via Wikimedia Commons)

The election of Richard Nixon as President of the United States ushered in a new perspective on the conflict raging in Vietnam. When he took office on January 20, 1969, the American people were war weary. Casualty lists had lengthened, and American troop strength in Southeast Asia had peaked at 543,000. With promises to end the war and a commitment to quell the civil unrest that had been an unwelcome byproduct of it, Nixon worked both overtly and covertly to achieve his political goals.

Headwinds, however, emerged. The North Vietnamese and Viet Cong appeared more interested in using the Paris Peace Talks for propaganda purposes than to achieve a lasting peace that would allow the US to exit with honour. And the fighting dragged on. The enemy still seemed capable of sowing moments of chaos, and in early January Dr Le Minh Tri, the South Vietnamese Minister of Education, was assassinated when two communist guerrillas threw a grenade into the open window of the car in which he was riding. In the same month, Viet Cong infiltrators planted a bomb inside the US base camp at Cu Chi. The explosion killed 15 Americans and two Vietnamese kitchen workers.

Meanwhile, in mid-January the apparent futility of the talks in Paris was characterised by the ridiculous disagreement over the shape of the conference tables and the seating arrangement for the delegates. Among the most vocal of the objectors was South Vietnamese Vice President Nguyen Cao Ky, whose

obstinance delayed the talks for six weeks. At long last, the two sides agreed to a pair of rectangular tables with a round table in the centre and the delegations distinctly separated.

US and South Vietnamese search and destroy missions continued in the midst of a surge of violence in February that some observers referred to as 'Tet 1969'. However, this North Vietnamese Army

(NVA) and Viet Cong offensive was rapidly defeated during battles around the sprawling American installations at Da Nang and the air base at Bien Hoa, where respectively 500 and 264 communist troops were killed.

Continuing to pressure the communist stronghold in the A Shau Valley, American and South Vietnamese Army (ARVN) forces launched Operation Massachusetts

ABOVE: One of the communist PT-76 light tanks destroyed at Ben Het sits abandoned after the 1969 battle. (US Army via Wikimedia Commons)

ABOVE: Demonstrators make peace signs for the camera during the 'Moratorium to End the War in Vietnam'. (US News and World Report Library of Congress via Wikimedia Commons)

Striker in late February, and the nine-week foray resulted in 223 NVA and 59 Americans killed. Simultaneously, a security campaign dubbed Operation Iron Mountain was initiated in the coastal Quang Ngai Province. Destined to last for the next two years, its death toll included nearly 4,600 NVA and Viet Cong and 440 Americans.

In March, one of the few armoured clashes of the Vietnam war occurred when the NVA 66th Regiment hit the US special forces camp at Ben Het near the convergence of the Vietnamese frontier with Cambodia and Laos. American M-48 Patton tanks of the 1st Battalion, 69th Armored Regiment destroyed two Soviet-made PT-76 light tanks and a BTR-50 armoured personnel carrier. At the end of the month, President Nixon authorised Operation Menu, the sustained bombing of communist supply routes, bases, and training camps inside neutral Cambodia, in a prelude to the controversial April 1970 ground incursion. The NVA returned to Ben Het in May, pounding the base with artillery fire, and besieging the garrison. After 55 days, ARVN reinforcements and US air power had broken their grip.

A SHAU VALLEY

The A Shau Valley was a hotbed of anti-communist military activities during a continuing series of search and destroy missions that led to the heavy battle at Hamburger Hill in May-June during Operation Apache Snow. The clash saw four weeks of fighting in difficult terrain often against strongly entrenched communist units. The battle at Hamburger Hill was roundly criticised in the halls of the US Congress and considered too costly an operation for the results achieved, particularly after the bulk of the NVA defenders had successfully withdrawn. Elements of the US 173rd Airborne Brigade also abandoned the high ground following such a difficult fight when it was assessed to have no particular strategic or tactical value.

ABOVE: US Marines pass a destroyed North Vietnamese truck during a 1969 search and destroy mission. (Official USMC photo by Sergeant Ray Bribiesca from the Jonathan F. Abel Collection (COLL/3611) at the Archives Branch, Marine Corps History Division via Wikimedia Commons)

On June 10, 1969, the North Vietnamese announced the formation of the Provisional Revolutionary Government of the Republic of South Vietnam, a shadow government, or as the communists called it a 'government in exile'. Established to assume control in South Vietnam when communist forces achieved victory, it was an obviously provocative affront to the existing government of South Vietnam and evidence of resistance among North Vietnamese diplomats to participating in meaningful peace negotiations.

Three days later, US Secretary of Defense Melvin Laird announced that the first American troops to be withdrawn from South Vietnam, 900 combat infantrymen of the 9th Infantry Division, would be coming home soon. President Nixon's promise to draw down US troop strength in Southeast Asia was coming true even though the first peacetime draft lottery since World War Two would take place in December.

At the end of July, President Nixon held a press conference on the island of Guam in the Pacific. Formally announcing his programme of Vietnamisation, the 'Nixon Doctrine' stated plainly the basis of US policy toward Southeast Asia. The president told reporters:

"I believe that the time has come when the United States, in our relations with all of our Asian friends, be quite emphatic on two points: One, that we will keep our treaty commitments…but, two, that as far as the problems of internal security are concerned, as far as the problems of military defense…that the United States is going to encourage and has a right to expect that…the responsibility for it taken by, the Asian nations themselves."

However, the handover of military operations to the South Vietnamese and the extrication of US military forces from the conflict in Vietnam would prove to be a daunting task, more time consuming and costly, perhaps, than envisioned. Realising that the Paris negotiations were virtually dead in the water, Nixon ordered national security advisor Henry Kissinger to attempt to open direct secret negotiations with the North Vietnamese.

On September 2, Ho Chi Minh, the heart and soul of the communist/nationalist movement in North Vietnam, died of a heart attack in Hanoi at age 79. A quarter million people attended his funeral service a week later.

On September 5, Lieutenant William Calley was formally charged with six counts of murder in the wake of the horrific My Lai massacre that had occurred in March. American citizens recoiled in disgust when images of slaughtered Vietnamese women and children, their bodies heaped along roadsides and in fields, were published around the world two months later. Calley was convicted but eventually released from prison.

Massive anti-war demonstrations across the US, collectively called the 'Moratorium to End the War in Vietnam', occurred on October 15, and 250,000 demonstrators took to the streets of Washington, DC, alone. In response to the unrest and keeping with his campaign commitment to restore order, President Nixon took to the airwaves on November 3 to deliver his *Silent Majority* speech. A subsequent Gallup poll indicated that 77% of Americans were in favour of his conduct of the war to date.

Although the communists offered a 72-hour truce with the new year of 1970, US and South Vietnamese forces, still smarting from the surprise of Tet in 1968, observed only one day. On January 8, the Viet Cong 409th Battalion used the cover of torrential monsoon rains to launch a vicious assault

ABOVE: US Special Forces sit aboard their helicopter prior to the Son Tay Raid, an attempt to free American POWs. (US Military via Wikimedia Commons)

ABOVE: A US 105mm M2 howitzer sits in its firing position at firebase Mai Loc as a soldier strengthens the position. (National Archives and Records Administration via Wikimedia Commons)

against Firebase Ross in the Que Son Valley. The attackers fired mortars, sent sappers to clear paths through barbed wire obstacles, and penetrated the outer defences before the 1st Battalion, 7th Marines beat them back at a cost of 38 guerrillas and seven Marines killed.

On April 7, President Nixon presented 21 posthumous Medals of Honor to the families of service personnel killed during acts of exceptional valour in Vietnam. Polling revealed that the favourable opinion of the conduct of the war had eroded. Forty-eight percent of those responding still approved, but 41% did not. In light of continuing Viet Cong hit-and-run attacks and guerrilla activities that were supported from bases in Cambodia, Nixon discussed options to deal with the communist havens in the neutral country with members of the National Security Council on April 22.

INTO CAMBODIA

A week later, American ground troops were fighting in Cambodia after the President gave the go-ahead to the incursion while keeping some key advisors in the dark as to his intentions. Nixon addressed the tactic on nationwide television on the evening of April 30, and for many Americans his promises to decrease US military operations rang hollow. The Cambodia venture appeared to be a widening of the war. A wave of protests flashed across the country and precipitated the rioting that resulted in the deaths of four students at Kent State University in Ohio when National Guardsmen fired on a crowd on May 4.

During the predawn hours of May 9, Nixon looked out through a White House window and saw demonstrators gathering near the Washington Monument. He called for a car and driver, made his way to the Lincoln Memorial, and just after 4:30am, tried to engage some of the students in conversation. Reports later surfaced that the President was under no illusions that a breakthrough in communication might occur. But for the next hour he explained his position to those who

would listen. He later said that he told them: "I hope that [your] hatred of the war, which I could well understand, would not turn into a bitter hatred of our whole system, our country and everything that it stood for. I said that I know probably most of you think I'm an SOB. But I want you to know that I understand just how you feel."

In later years, some journalists revealed that few demonstrators remembered the visit in the same way that the President had. White House Chief of Staff H.R. Haldeman recalled that he was concerned about Nixon's condition and that it had been "the weirdest day so far." Haldeman wrote: "…He has had very little sleep for a long time and his judgment, temper, and mood suffer badly as a result….there's a long way to go, and he's in no condition to weather it."

The Cambodia dustup continued well after American troops were withdrawn from the neutral country in June and President Nixon pronounced that "all our military objectives" had been achieved. Repercussions on Capitol Hill were not long in coming as the Senate voted to repeal the Gulf of Tonkin Resolution on June 24.

On September 3, after peace talks had been suspended for months, North Vietnamese diplomats led by Xuan Thuy returned to Paris but stated bluntly that their positions had not changed. They still demanded unconditional US withdrawal and severing of support for the government of South Vietnam. Secret negotiations between Kissinger and North Vietnamese politburo member Le Duc Tho began four days later.

In October, while combat operations and communist terror attacks continued, President Nixon announced a five-point plan

ABOVE: Marines of Company B, 1st Battalion, 7th Marines move out during a search and destroy mission. (Department of Defense Photo (USMC) via Wikimedia Commons)

for peace, including a truce and release of all prisoners held by both sides as a prelude to earnest negotiations. The North Vietnamese immediately criticised the overture but did not reject it outright. At the end of the month, American war weariness was reflected in *New York Times* reports on the sagging morale of US troops in Vietnam, and senior command in country noted that 25 service personnel had died of drug abuse in 1970.

On December 22, North Vietnam released its first accounting of American POWs in the entire war, stating that 368 prisoners were being held. As the year closed, nearly 55,000 Americans had been killed in Vietnam War, although fatalities in 1970 total 6,173, nearly half those of the prior year and one-third that of 1968.

ABOVE: Marines of the 1st Battalion, 5th Marines stand near an airlift helicopter as they depart Hill 510 in the Que Son Mountains. (DEFENSE DEPT. PHOTO (MARINE CORPS) A373799 by Sgt Menge via Wikimedia Commons)

KENT STATE

ABOVE: This 2007 photograph depicts the memorial to Jeffrey Miller, one of four Kent State students killed on May 4, 1970. The image perspective is generally that of photographer John Filo on the fateful day. (Mws77 via Wikimedia Commons)

One of the most tragic and polarising events of the Vietnam War era occurred on May 4, 1970, on the campus of Kent State University in northeastern Ohio. Four students were killed when troops of the Ohio National Guard opened fire during demonstrations against the war in Vietnam and particularly the widening of the conflict with the recent incursion into Cambodia that had been sanctioned by the administration of President Richard Nixon.

Unrest had spread rapidly among college campuses in the days following President Nixon's authorisation for American soldiers to cross the frontier from Vietnam into Cambodia, a nominally neutral country. In the days preceding the 'Kent State Massacre', demonstrations had increased steadily, spreading into the nearby town of Kent. Protests began on May 1, the day after the news of the Cambodian incursion became public. A large group of students had congregated on the commons, an open area where previous gatherings had occurred, and two rallies were held. That night students and police brawled in the streets of Kent as bottles and rocks were thrown, and more than a dozen demonstrators were arrested.

On May 2-3, the violence increased. Students set fire to the ROTC (Reserve Officers Training Corps) building while numerous state and local leaders characterised many of the protesters as outside agitators bent on destabilising the university population and the lives of average citizens. The mayor of Kent, Leroy Satrom ordered local bars closed in a vain attempt to suppress gatherings of students and dissidents, but the move actually drove more people into the street and exacerbated the situation. More than 1,000 National Guardsmen arrived on the scene, most of them in their early 20s, aged similarly to those protesting. When the protesters blocked city streets, the guardsmen dispersed them at bayonet point and with tear gas.

Although demonstrations had been banned, at least 3,000 students gathered for another protest on the morning of May 4. By 11am, approximately 100 guardsmen were deployed to maintain order. They were armed with M-1 rifles, and the weapons were loaded. While the ruins of the ROTC building smouldered nearby, bullhorns blared warnings for the crowd to disperse. Still, the group continued to protest, and the guardsmen were ordered to advance. The demonstrators fell back, some throwing rocks as they went. Tear gas billowed from canisters.

The guardsmen pushed the demonstrators back across the commons and over nearby Blanket Hill, but when the opposing groups reached the football practice field, the guardsmen found themselves inside a fenced area with the mob continuing to hurl rocks and shout threats. The guardsmen began to withdraw over Blanket Hill, but as they topped the crest eyewitnesses saw 28 of them turn, crouch, and open fire.

CHAOS

In a flash, four students were killed and nine wounded. Some witnesses recalled that the firing was brief, only about 13 seconds, while others believed it continued for up to a minute or more. The guardsmen fired 70 rounds, and chaos reigned. There was disbelief among the demonstrators, most of whom could not comprehend that they would actually have been shot at. Investigations followed, and several guardsmen testified that they had fired because they feared for their lives. Several years later, the Ohio National Guard settled a lawsuit filed by injured students.

The shock of the Kent State massacre reverberated across the United States, and in retrospect the Ohio National Guard officially released a statement that the incident should not have occurred. Photographer John Filo captured a Pulitzer Prize-winning photograph of 14-year-old runaway Mary Ann Vecchio kneeling in anguish over the body of dead student Jeffrey Miller.

Canadian singer/songwriter Neil Young saw photos of the tragic massacre in *Life* magazine and wrote the anti-war song *Ohio* in an hour. Recorded by Crosby, Stills, Nash, and Young 17 days after the incident, the song is renowned as a classic of the period.

Another horrific incident occurred on the campus of Jackson State College in Jackson, Mississippi on May 15, 1970, when Mississippi State Police opened fire on a crowd of student demonstrators, killing two and wounding 12.

ABOVE: Kent State student Alan Canfora waves a black flag before Ohio National Guardsmen just prior to the shootings of May 4, 1970. (Student John Filo 15 May 1970 edition of LIFE magazine via Wikimedia Commons)

ABOVE: Mary Ann Vecchio kneels over the body of Jeffrey Miller at Kent State University, May 4, 1970. (Student John Filo The Post-Crescent. 5 December 1976 edition via Wikimedia Commons)

THE MONTAGNARDS

ABOVE: Montagnard tribesmen pose during training for anti-communist operations in 1962.
(US Army via Wikimedia Commons)

They were different. The indigenous inhabitants of the central highlands of Vietnam did not share the same lineage as the people that lived in urban centres and coastal areas of the country. These were 30 tribes, more than a million people, speaking different dialects and languages, and clinging to their own culture.

The French had named them collectively the 'Montagnards', translating to English as 'Mountain Dwellers'. The European colonialists had not treated them well, but they had made promises of an autonomous land in Indochina, where the Montagnards could govern themselves free from persecution by the mainstream Vietnamese, who called them derisively 'moi', or 'savages'.

But the French had gone.

In the wake of the European departure, the government of South Vietnam had continued the same ill treatment of the Montagnards, hostility at worst and neglect at best. The mountain dwellers distrusted the leaders in Saigon. However, they were also wary of the communist regime in the north and of the Viet Cong guerrillas. Many of the Montagnards had converted to Christianity during the colonial period, and they knew such faith invited communist persecution. They were also aware that the eventual occupation of their native lands, either by settlers directed there from Saigon or seizure by the Viet Cong and North Vietnamese, loomed during the turbulent years of the Vietnam War.

Then, in the autumn of 1961, the Americans came. Assisted by the Central Intelligence Agency (CIA), the Green Berets, the elite special forces of the US Army, sent advisors to Vietnam. In a relatively short period of time, the American soldiers and the Montagnards forged a bond. The Green Berets brought in food, medicine, and basic healthcare; they built roads and schools. At the same time, they recruited the Montagnards to work together against the threat of communism.

Both the Americans and the communists actively recruited among the Montagnards, and some did in fact side with the Viet Cong guerrillas. However, the majority of the indigenous people were quite friendly to the Americans, aware that when the communist fighters visited a village professing friendship they were just as likely to return days later to terrorise and rob the poor people of rice, clothing, and other necessities.

The Green Berets set about training their Montagnard friends with modern weapons and tactics, and the warrior tradition of their students made them fast learners. As the Vietnam war escalated, the Montagnards proved themselves tenacious fighters time after time. They were well-known for their own brand of night terror against the communists, coming back from nocturnal patrols with dozens of ears severed from the heads of their Viet Cong victims.

ABOVE: Two Montagnard scouts conduct a long-range reconnaissance patrol in support of the 1st Cavalry Division (Airmobile) in 1968. (Icemanwcs via Wikimedia Commons)

Meanwhile, the Americans, largely supplied by the clandestine Air America operation secretly owned by the CIA, initiated a program not only to improve the living standard of the Montagnards but also to provide security against communist guerrilla operations. They called it the Buon Enao Experiment. The establishment of the Village Defense Program (VDP) brought some degree of assurance that the improvements in agriculture, education, and infrastructure were going to last. Initially, teams of a dozen special forces soldiers trained 1,300 Montagnards from approximately 40 villages in the central highlands. An elite group of about 300 Montagnards were selected to form 100-man strike units called 'Mike Force'. In time an estimated 61,000 Montagnards would

ABOVE: US Rangers train Montagnard guerrillas in the central highlands of Vietnam. (US Army via Wikimedia Commons)

ABOVE: An American advisor briefs Montagnard fighters prior to an operation against Viet Cong guerrillas.
(US Army via Wikimedia Commons)

serve alongside the Americans during the Vietnam conflict, and they were affectionately nicknamed the 'Yards'.

FRONTIER FORCE

Not only were the Montagnards important to the anti-communist effort due to their fighting prowess. They also inhabited territory that skirted the frontiers with neighbouring Cambodia and Laos, near the Ho Chi Minh Trail, the primary conduit of weapons, supplies, and reinforcements for the communist insurgency in South Vietnam. The Montagnards knew the terrain and the countryside well. When cooperative operations were undertaken, they served as infantry support, interpreters, and scouts in the fight against the Viet Cong and later the North Vietnamese Army (NVA). They also formed the Civilian Irregular Defense Groups (CIDG), militia detachments that protected the VDP settlements and other civilian and military locations.

But it was in combat that the Montagnards showed their true mettle. One veteran of the Green Berets 5th Special Forces Group remembered: "They were never defeated. They may have been overrun,

but they always took it back. We had full faith in the Montagnards."

During one particularly vicious firefight in the remote mountains of the central highlands, K'Sao Krajan, a Montagnard fighting alongside the Green Berets, responded when the Americans were ambushed by the Viet Cong. According to author Matt Fratus, the intrepid Montagnard was dressed to resemble an enemy guerrilla and went alone into a labyrinth of tunnels and caves deep in the side of a mountain. He moved quickly and stealthily forward, killing Viet Cong along the way, and locating the enemy firing positions at the mouth of a cave. When he had silenced the Viet Cong machine guns, he appeared at the cave entrance and waved to the Americans below that the way was

open. For his heroism K'Sao Krajan received the Bronze Star medal.

Such bravery among the Montagnards was not an isolated incident, and many Green Berets returning from the central highlands proclaimed that their trusted comrades had saved their lives in combat. One of them declared: "There is no Special Forces Vietnam veteran who does not owe his life to a Montagnard. I know I do."

For all their trust in the Americans and the bravery they often exhibited in battle, the story of the Montagnards remains one of tragedy – or as some would characterise it, betrayal. When US forces began to withdraw from South Vietnam, thousands of Montagnards fled into remote areas hoping to escape communist reprisals for their assistance to the Americans. Some of them

ABOVE: Montagnards and US Army soldiers prepare to move out of their base camp in South Vietnam.
(US Army via Wikimedia Commons)

ABOVE: US Special Forces advisors to the Montagnards take a moment to relax at their command post in the central highlands. (National Archives and Records Administration via Wikimedia Commons)

formed the Hauts-Plateaux Montagnard (FLHPM), an armed resistance against the communist government in Hanoi and the ruling Khmer Rouge in Cambodia.

Even as they were withdrawing, some American soldiers tried to assist the Montagnards in escaping the communists. A relative few successfully reached the United States to start new lives, but many remained in dire straits as the communists waged a steady campaign to eradicate them. When the Vietnam conflict was over, an estimated 200,000 Montagnards, including women and children, had been killed, and much of their homeland was occupied.

During the quarter century after the war only a few thousand Montagnards were able to emigrate to the United States. In 1989, Congress passed legislation that allowed more Montagnards to emigrate to America, where many settled in North Carolina near Fort Bragg (now Fort Liberty), the home of their lifetime friends in the US Army Special Forces.

CAMBODIA INCURSION

ABOVE: A Bell AH-1 Cobra gunship lands to refuel at a forward base during the fighting in Cambodia. (National Archives and Records Administration via Wikimedia Commons)

Even as the first American combat troops were withdrawn from South Vietnam in the summer of 1969 and President Richard Nixon's programme of Vietnamisation was undertaken, concerns regarding communist forces using sanctuaries and staging areas in Cambodia for operations in South Vietnam persisted.

Since March, American bombers had been conducting clandestine air raids against communist supply routes along the Ho Chi Minh Trail, which coursed through Laos into Cambodia and then to distribution points for infiltration into South Vietnam. Although these secret missions, dubbed Operation Menu, had been revealed in the pages of the *New York Times* two months later and brought widespread condemnation, Nixon was further willing to commit US troops along with units of the South Vietnamese Army (ARVN) to a ground campaign that would clear the communists out of their bases.

The elimination of these sanctuaries would provide more time for Vietnamisation and assist Cambodian General Lon Nol, a pro-American leader who had recently replaced Prince Norodom Sihanouk as head of state, in the stabilisation of his new government. Under Sihanouk, Cambodia's weak regime was nominally neutral and had been unable or unwilling to deal with the communist

ABOVE: American soldiers prepare to destroy a communist stockpile of bicycles discovered in Cambodia, 1970. (US Army via Wikimedia Commons)

North Vietnamese Army (NVA) and Viet Cong insurgents that were active in the country. At the same time, the communist-backed Khmer Rouge were on the cusp of engaging in a bloody civil war with Cambodian government troops.

Nixon was painfully aware that an incursion into Cambodia would appear to be widening the war, contradicting the stated American policy of withdrawal and de-escalation. He expected opposition from members of Congress, as well as an immediate groundswell of demonstrations at home as the anti-war movement became enraged. He got both.

Willing to take the calculated risk, Nixon authorised the limited invasion of Cambodia on April 28, 1970. Two days later, he appeared on national television and told the American people that the operation would "strike at the heart of the trouble" caused by the communists and vowed it "…puts the leaders of North Vietnam on notice that…we will not be humiliated. We will not be defeated."

The ground operation made good progress, and large caches of communist supplies, weapons, and ammunition were discovered. In early May, ARVN troops supported by air strikes, artillery, and tanks severed an area known as the Parrot's Beak that protruded into South Vietnam. Light opposition was encountered as US and ARVN units linked up in a region called the Fishhook. One centre

ABOVE: American soldiers load communist documents seized during the Cambodia incursion aboard a helicopter. (National Archives and Records Administration via Wikimedia Commons)

ABOVE: President Richard Nixon points to a map of Cambodia during his television address to the American people, April 30, 1970. (National Archives and Records Administration via Wikimedia Commons)

of communist activity covering more than a square mile came to be known as 'the city' due to the elaborate network of bunkers, gun emplacements, hospitals, training grounds, and support facilities that were found. ARVN forces continued to operate in Cambodia through July 22, although US forces were withdrawn at the end of June. Some estimates indicate that enough weapons, ammunition, and foodstuffs to support 55 battalions of troops were confiscated or destroyed.

Small unit actions took place during the invasion, but the bulk of the NVA and Viet Cong withdrew deeper into Cambodia, avoiding a pitched battle. Overall, the operation was deemed successful, although ARVN forces failed to perform to their potential when US military advisors were not present with them. Nevertheless, communist operations emanating from Cambodia were curtailed for some time. American bombing of Cambodia continued through to the end of US military involvement in Southeast Asia in 1973.

PROTESTS

When news of the Cambodia incursion broke, it created a veritable firestorm of protest on college campuses across the United States. Administrative buildings were occupied, and some were put to the torch. Thousands of students rallied in common areas and on football fields. They marched in the streets of nearby towns, disrupting traffic and clashing with local police forces. At Kent State University, four students were shot dead by Ohio National Guardsmen during a May 4 demonstration. At least 400 schools experienced student walkouts or strikes, while more than 200 were compelled to shut down completely in attempts to quell the violence.

Within his own administration, Nixon fomented a wave of mistrust. He had authorised the Cambodia operation without the knowledge of either Secretary of Defense

ABOVE: South Vietnamese armoured personnel carriers roll down a dirt road in Cambodia during the 1970 incursion. (US Department of Defense via Wikimedia Commons)

Melvin Laird or Secretary of State William Rogers. Both had been strong advocates for the reduction of American military involvement in Vietnam, and Nixon knew they would oppose the offensive military move. Instead, the President instructed General Earle Wheeler, chairman of the Joint Chiefs of Staff, to inform General Creighton Abrams, commander of US forces in Vietnam, that the mission was authorised by 'a higher authority'.

Three members of the staff of National Security Advisor Henry Kissinger resigned their posts in opposition to the de facto invasion of 'neutral' Cambodia, but it was only the beginning of the whirlwind of opposition that came from Congress. In an effort to contain the uproar, Nixon held a press conference on May 8, attempting to justify his actions and pledging to withdraw up to 150,000 troops within the year. Sceptics continued to question the progress of Vietnamisation, and the Cambodian venture became a touchstone of the war in Vietnam.

Powerful members of Congress were determined to curb the authority of the President to commit US combat troops on his own initiative. According to the US Constitution, the authority to declare

war is reserved for the legislative branch of government. However, during the course of American history several Presidents had taken the liberty of sending military forces into action without Congressional approval, blurring the line between presidential power and an official declaration of war.

Subsequently, a series of Congressional initiatives were undertaken to restrict the President's authority to further deploy troops in Southeast Asia. In June 1970, the Senate repealed the Gulf of Tonkin Resolution of 1964, which had granted sweeping power to the President, by a vote of 81 to 10. Also prominent among the legislative actions was the Cooper-Church Amendment, sponsored by Senators Frank Church of Idaho and John Sherman Cooper of Kentucky, which passed both houses of Congress in December 1970 after an earlier version had been approved in the Senate but failed in the House of Representatives.

In November 1973, Congress passed the War Powers Act over the veto of President Nixon. The act requires the President to inform Congress when military forces are deployed and limits any such deployment to 60 days unless Congressional authorisation has been received. The limits of the War Powers Act have been tested on several occasions since.

One significant and unintended consequence of the Cambodian incursion was the propaganda tool provided to the communists. With the support of the NVA and Viet Cong, the insurgent Khmer Rouge occupied large areas of Cambodia while using the invasion as a recruiting tool. Some observers have concluded that the invasion hastened the communist victory in the five-year civil war in Cambodia that concluded in 1975. After the Khmer Rouge seized power, their barbarous government embarked on a reign of terror, killing an estimated two million people.

ABOVE: An M-551 Sheridan tank follows a US Army engineer team clearing mines along a road in Cambodia. (US Army via Wikimedia Commons)

OPERATION LAM SON 719

The effectiveness of the US policy of Vietnamisation, begun three years earlier, was an open question in the spring of 1971. Operation Lam Son 719 was the first major ground operation of the Vietnam war undertaken by the Army of the Republic of South Vietnam (ARVN) without direct involvement of American units or embedded advisors.

General Creighton Abrams, commander of US forces in South Vietnam, conceived the idea for a large-scale raid across the frontier of South Vietnam into neighbouring Laos to disrupt North Vietnamese Army (NVA) logistical preparations for an anticipated offensive. Successful interdiction of the flow of supplies along the Ho Chi Minh Trail and a sweep of two centres of communist activity known as Base Areas 604 and 611 would boost the morale of the ARVN troops and deliver a blow to the enemy.

The ARVN 1st Infantry and 1st Airborne Divisions, the 1st Ranger Group, and the 1st Armoured Brigade, roughly 20,000 strong, would execute the mission with US air support, including helicopter airlift and tactical strikes by fighter-bombers. The Rangers would be inserted by helicopter to supporting fire bases north and south of Route 9, covering the flanks of the advance, while the infantry, airborne, and armour would proceed 25 miles along Route 9 from Khe Sanh to the Laotian village of Tchepone, a nexus of NVA command, supply, and training.

After several delays, Operation Lam Son 719 commenced on February 8 and met strong NVA and Marxist Pathet Lao opposition from roughly 36,000 troops under

ABOVE: US Army Bell AH-1 Cobra attack helicopters operate over Laos in 1971. (US Army via Wikimedia Commons)

the capable command of General Le Trong Tan. In the event, ARVN and NVA troops engaged in numerous sharp firefights, while some NVA weapons and supply caches were found and destroyed. The ground column was attacked along Route 9 about halfway to its objective and never reached Tchepone, stalling on the dirt road for three weeks. NVA artillery pounded the fire bases occupied by the ARVN Rangers, and NVA troops mounted sustained attacks against them, overrunning at least one while others were abandoned.

However, South Vietnamese President Nguyen Van Thieu ordered an airmobile assault into Tchepone, possibly attempting to claim a sort of victory by asserting that ARVN troops had entered the town while also

earning popular support during an election year. In early March, Thieu ordered ARVN troops to begin withdrawing from Laos. Predictably, once they became aware of this movement, the NVA stepped up their attacks, and the ARVN withdrawal became a calamity.

Meanwhile, the heavy losses among US helicopters that were engaged in transport, evacuation, fire support, and resupply shocked the American military planners. More than 100 helicopters were destroyed, while the 101st Airborne Division alone had more than 400 damaged. The failure of Lam Son 719 precipitated a reassessment of US airmobile tactics.

On March 25, 1971, the book was closed on the mission. The results were grim. ARVN casualties topped 1,600 killed and wounded, while the Americans lost more than 200 dead and the NVA approximately 500. The ARVN defeat may be substantially attributed to poor planning and lack of competence among its officers despite the fact that they had worked beside American advisors for some time. Just two weeks after the Lam Son 719 debacle, President Nixon asserted that Vietnamisation had succeeded.

ABOVE: US helicopters and supply vehicles stage at Khe Sanh to support Operation Lam Son 719.

(Official United States Marine Corps Photo No: 1W16-196-2-71 (L) by Sgt Gregg Sloat via Wikimedia Commons)

ABOVE: North Vietnamese Army troops swarm into Fire Support Base Lolo during Operation Lam Son 719.

(US Army via Wikimedia Commons)

AUSTRALIANS AT LONG KHANH

After an eight-hour firefight over June 7-8, 1971, the 3rd Battalion, Royal Australian Regiment finally occupied a labyrinth of well-concealed bunkers that had been stubbornly defended by elements of two North Vietnamese Army and Viet Cong battalions. The enemy fought tenaciously, but the Battle of Long Khanh stymied an expected communist offensive aimed at nearby Phuoc Tuy Province.

The Australians and their New Zealander partners, prominent among the allied forces that fought alongside the US and South Vietnamese during the Vietnam conflict, had conducted successful operations in Phuoc Tuy beginning in late 1969, inflicting heavy losses on the communists and compelling them to withdraw to lick their wounds. When intelligence reports indicated the enemy's intent to move into the province once again, the Australians launched a pre-emptive strike code named Operation Overlord to thwart their plan.

Overlord began on June 5, 1971, with the positioning of blocking forces consisting of the 4th Battalion, Royal Australian Regiment (ANZAC) and a contingent of supporting American troops that would cut off the retreat of any communist forces that might attempt to flee the attack of the 3rd Royal Australian Regiment. Helicopters and armoured personnel carriers of the Australian 3rd Cavalry Regiment transported the Australians to the border between Phuoc Tuy and Long Khanh Province in the vicinity of the Courtenay Rubber Plantation.

The aerial insertions of the 3rd and 4th battalions were greeted by intense small-arms fire, which slackened after a few minutes, allowing the Australians to secure their

ABOVE: Australian soldiers wait to be picked up by American helicopters after a mission in 1967.
(Australian War Memorial Michael Coleridge via Wikimedia Commons)

landing zones. Tanks from the 1st Armoured Regiment, artillery of the 12th Field Regiment, and sappers from the 1st Field Squadron were poised to assist if needed.

Two days of jungle patrolling followed, and on the morning of June 7, the 5th Platoon, 3rd Battalion attacked enemy positions that had been located the previous afternoon just inside the boundary of Long Khanh Province. Within minutes, the platoon was pinned down along the perimeter of a well-hidden and elaborate system of enemy bunkers. One sergeant recalled: "In the initial burst of fire the platoon took a few casualties, the most serious being Private Mitchell who was shot through the throat. The platoon deployed; we realised we were in deep…The platoon was receiving fire from the front as well as the flanks."

Without orders, three Centurion tanks and an armoured recovery vehicle of 5th Troop, C Squadron, 1st Armoured Regiment rolled toward the trapped platoon roughly 875 yards distant. Already low on ammunition, the tankers fired selectively at the bunkers which were visible; however, when they tried to move on top of the tunnels and collapse several, they found them built strongly enough to withstand the weight of a Centurion. As necessity begged for innovation, the tankers moved from above, and intrepid crewmen leaned outside to toss grenades into vents and firing slits.

At midday, helicopters were called in to deliver ammunition and evacuate wounded,

ABOVE: Australian soldiers prepare for a patrol in company with an M113 armoured personnel carrier.
(Australian War Memorial Bryan Rupert Dunne via Wikimedia Commons)

and one of the UH-1s was shot down. Still, American helicopter gunships and the artillery of the 12th Field Regiment helped the Australians gain the upper hand. They held the hard-won bunkers through the tense overnight and cleared the rest of the complex the following morning.

The Australians had forced the communists to withdraw at the cost of three killed, two of them crewmen aboard the downed helicopter, and six wounded. Enemy casualties were unknown, and though only six bodies were discovered, thought to be heavy.

Operation Overlord concluded on June 14, 1971, with the successful suppression – at least temporarily – of the communist attempts to re-enter Phuoc Tuy. Ten Australian soldiers had been killed and 24 wounded. Australian units operated in Vietnam from 1966 to 1972, reaching peak strength of nearly 8,000. A total of 523 died and 2,400 were wounded before the last Australian unit was withdrawn in June 1973.

ABOVE: Armed with a .30-calibre M60 machine gun, a tired Australian soldier turns toward the camera in Vietnam. (US Army via Wikimedia Commons)

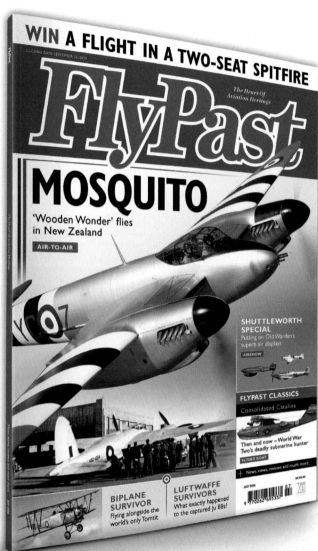
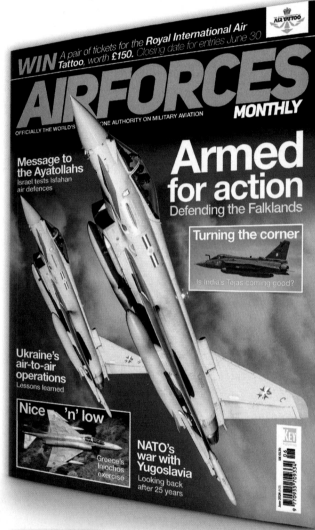

495/24

SUBSCRIBE TODAY!

SPECIAL ISSUE: 132-PAGE D-DAY 80 COMMEMORATIVE EDITION

BRITAIN'S BEST-SELLING MILITARY MONTHLY

BRITAIN AT WAR

ISSUE 206

V1 IN WT1
The flying bomb that killed London's famous female 'bobby'

OVERLORD UNLEASHED

- **YEOMAN GUNNERS' DESPERATE CHARGE**
- No.4 COMMANDO'S CASINO SCRAP
- **HOW 12,000 AIRCRAFT SHIELDED THE INVASION**

A SURPRISE RETURN
Will retired Falklands Type 21 frigate become museum ship?

Heavies on the beaches	Trapped under fire	Fledgling flyers
Myth-busting the Churchill AVRE and its Flying Dustbin	British troops besieged in forgotten 1920 Iraqi revolt	The eyes guiding Botha's push into German colony

Britain at War - dedicated to exploring every aspect of the involvement of Britain and her Commonwealth in conflicts from the turn of the 20th century through to the present day.

HARBOUR AIR THE FIRST ALL-ELECTRIC AIRLINE?

AVIATION NEWS

www.Key.Aero

The past, present and future of flight

ARRIVEDERCI AMX
Italian AF retires 'Ghibli' ground attack maestro

BRITTEN-NORMAN AT 70
How Hatfield classmates became Isle of Wight innovators

PLUS
USMC IN NORWAY
REGISTER REVIEW
WHAT'S ON GUIDE
AIRPORT MOVEMENTS
EXERCISE INIOCHOS
TACTICAL AIR MEET 1978

June 2024 £5.80

DIAMOND FORMATION
The RAF Red Arrows' 60th display season

GOING FOR A CHINESE
We take a trip on a Shanghai-built ARJ21

Aviation News is renowned for providing the best coverage of every branch of aviation.

from our online shop...
collections/subscriptions

Free 2nd class P&P on all UK & BFPO orders. Overseas charges apply.

THE POW ORDEAL

ABOVE: POW Jeremiah Denton blinks 'TORTURE' in Morse Code during a press conference in Hanoi.
(North Vietnam Government Propaganda Film The Central Intelligence Agency via Wikimedia Commons)

BELOW: US Navy Commander A.C. Brady is guarded by a North Vietnamese soldier in this 1969 photo. (National Museum of the US Navy via Wikimedia Commons)

Commander Jeremiah Denton would have none of it. His North Vietnamese captors wanted to use Denton and other American prisoners of war as propaganda tools. During the July 1966 press conference before a gathering of international news media in Hanoi, the officer answered questions – but not as the North Vietnamese wanted.

Denton, a US Navy pilot shot down over North Vietnam on July 18, 1965, while leading 28 Grumman A-6 Intruder attack planes from the aircraft carrier USS *Independence*, told astonished reporters that he supported the US government and: "…I will continue to support it as long as I live." While motion picture cameras rolled and flash bulbs popped, the captive officer committed another act of defiance, one that the North Vietnamese probably never got wise to until Denton was awarded the Navy Cross for bravery in 1974. As he answered questions, Denton blinked the word "TORTURE" in Morse Code. American intelligence analysts picked up the message, and they knew that the condition of the POWs was horrendous.

"They beat you with fists and fan belts," Denton told the *Los Angeles Times* in a 1979 interview. "They warmed you up and threatened you with death. Then they really got serious and gave you something called the rope trick." He went on to describe being bound by ropes until his circulation was cut off, rendering his limbs useless for long periods and causing intense pain. "In the early morning hours, I prayed that I could keep my sanity until they released me. I couldn't even give in to their demands because there were none. It was pure revenge."

Denton spent more than seven years in captivity, much of the time in a fetid, windowless cell at the Hoa Lo Prison in Hanoi, an infamous hellhole that the

POWs nicknamed the Hanoi Hilton. He demonstrated tremendous leadership among the prisoners, 52 of whom endured a horrific march through the streets of Hanoi in July 1966. Handcuffed in pairs, the POWS were subjected to the wrath of an angry mob. Civilians beat and stoned them without mercy.

ABOVE: US Navy Captain Jeremiah Denton addresses a crowd after being released from captivity in North Vietnam, 1973. (US Military via Wikimedia Commons)

Denton was released from prison on February 12, 1973, and addressed a gathering at Clark Air Base in the Philippines with the military bearing he had maintained throughout his ordeal. "We are honoured to have had the opportunity to serve our country under difficult circumstances," he said. "We are profoundly grateful to our commander-in-chief and to our nation for this day. God bless America." Denton went on to serve in the US Senate and wrote a book about his POW experience titled *When Hell Was In Session*.

During American involvement in the Vietnam conflict, nearly 800 US military and civilian personnel were taken prisoner by the North Vietnamese and Viet Cong. More than 80% of these were pilots and aircrew of the US Air Force, US Navy, and US Marine Corps, whose aircraft had been shot down during missions over enemy-occupied territory. As many as 65 prisoners died in captivity, while 687 were repatriated beginning with Operation Homecoming in early 1973 after the signing of the Paris Peace Accords.

MISSING IN ACTION

At the end of the war, roughly 2,500 American personnel were listed as missing in action (MIA), and the effort to account for them is ongoing. However, through the years the endeavour has been slow and painstaking due to the sometimes strained relations between the US and the governments of Vietnam, Cambodia, and Laos, difficult

ABOVE: Lieutenant Commander Richard A. Stratton of the US Navy sits in a North Vietnamese prison cell in this photo from October 1969. (National Museum of the US Navy via Wikimedia Commons)

jungle and mountainous terrain in country, and the fact that Americans did not occupy the land where the men went missing. In October 2022, a total of 1,582 men remained unaccounted for.

Controversy once swirled around the question as to whether all American POWs were actually repatriated. Some Americans were sceptical, and several groups of concerned citizens were formed to push for closure on as many of the MIA cases as possible. Even Hollywood films were produced surrounding the theme. Some believed prisoners were secretly sent to the Soviet Union or the People's Republic of China. Supposed sightings of Americans still in Southeast Asia occurred, and from 1991 to 1993, the US Senate investigated and held hearings, ultimately reaching the conclusion that no substantial evidence existed to support the claims.

The North Vietnamese refused to comply with the terms of the 1949 Geneva Conventions, to which their country was a signatory. The conventions specified the humane treatment of prisoners of war, but North Vietnam contended that their American captives were perpetrators of war crimes and had been captured in an undeclared war. And they saw the POWs as a bargaining chip. The prisoners were systematically brutalised, coerced to make statements against the war or supposedly confessing to their criminal behaviour. They were brought before the international media in a sham effort to show the world that they were being treated well.

Under extreme duress, some POWs did succumb to torture. Pushed beyond the limits of human endurance, they complied with the demands of the North Vietnamese. However, the US government declined to prosecute any who had been tortured and

forced to cooperate; the lone exception was a proceeding against a former US Marine who returned to the United States in 1979. Most of the US POWS were officers, many of them highly-trained and well educated. Their refusal to cooperate with their captors confounded the North Vietnamese, but the reprisals were horrific. The prisoners were starved and often held in solitary confinement. Medical care was inadequate, and the squalid cells were rife with rats and cockroaches. Communist propaganda speeches regularly blared over loudspeakers.

At a camp nicknamed Alcatraz, one of the most notorious, prisoners were regularly beaten and deprived of food. Air Force Colonel Robbie Risner spent 10 months in solitary confinement there, and Colonel Gordon 'Swede' Larson endured a similar period of isolation. Navy Lieutenant Harry Jenkins was shackled for 85 days after being caught communicating with another POW.

RESCUE MISSION

American POWs were held in more than a dozen camps and prisons, most of them in or near Hanoi. One of these was known as Camp Hope, near the town of Son Tay located 23 miles northwest of the North Vietnamese capital city and opened in May 1968 to ease overcrowding in other prisons. Intelligence reports indicated that 55 Americans were being held at Son Tay, and in November 1970, special forces and other military personnel undertook Operation Ivory Coast, a high-risk raid intended to free the POWs.

The raid was executed with tactical precision, but no POWs were found. In 27 minutes on the ground, the raiders suffered only two casualties, one with a broken

ABOVE: US Navy Lieutenant Robert Frishman, his arm in a sling, was photographed while a POW of the North Vietnamese. (National Museum of the US Navy via Wikimedia Commons)

ankle and another with a minor wound. After-action reports indicated that dozens of enemy soldiers were killed or wounded. Although the prisoners at Camp Hope had been relocated months earlier, the raid was successful in that the North Vietnamese were wary of future such operations and concentrated prisoners more closely together. News of the Son Tay Raid filtered into the prisons, boosting POW morale. One remembered later: "The Son Tay rescue attempt dispelled all doubt – we were not forgotten; our country cared."

For the POWs, resistance to their captors took many forms. Some attempted to escape, but reports indicate that only about 30 were

ABOVE: An American prisoner of war sorts through mail in this photo from October 1969. (National Museum of the US Navy via Wikimedia Commons)

ABOVE: US Navy pilot John McCain stands at right with squadron members just prior to the mission during which he was shot down in 1965.

(US Navy Library of Congress via Wikimedia Commons)

successful during the course of the war. German-born US Navy Lieutenant Dieter Dengler was one of them. Flying from the aircraft carrier USS *Ranger* on February 1, 1966, Dengler's Douglas A-1 Skyraider attack plane was shot down over Laos. He was captured by the communist Pathet Lao, tortured, and handed over to the North Vietnamese. In late June, he managed to escape along with several other prisoners, including two Americans who were both later lost. After 23 days in the jungle, Dengler was picked up by a rescue helicopter. He remained in the navy for a year afterward. In 1977, he returned to Laos and was greeted warmly by Pathet Lao leaders.

Other escape attempts ended in tragedy. At a prison dubbed the 'Zoo' southwest of Hanoi, US Air Force captains John Dramesi and Edward Atterberry escaped in May 1969 with the help of other POWs. They were recaptured only a few miles from the prison and subjected to terrible torture. The North Vietnamese beat Atterberry to death and subjected Dramesi to 38 days of horrendous flogging with a fan belt. He was allowed no sleep, often tied with ropes that cut into his flesh, required to sit for hours on a small stool, and allowed only two tiny pieces of bread and two cups of water per day.

Those who had assisted in the escape were brutalised. One POW was suspended upside down and shocked with an automobile battery. Another was beaten and tortured savagely over a two-week period, enduring 700 belt strokes, electric shocks, and the excruciating manipulation of a fractured arm during interrogation. The depravity of the prison guards was routinely excessive.

Among the high-profile individuals who survived captivity in North Vietnam was future Arizona Senator and 2008 US presidential candidate John McCain, son of legendary US Navy Admiral John S. McCain, Jr. When he took off from the deck of the carrier USS *Oriskany* on October 26, 1967, on his 23rd combat mission, Lieutenant Commander McCain had recently recovered from serious injuries sustained in an accident aboard the carrier USS *Forrestal*. His Douglas A-4 Skyhawk attack plane was shot down over Hanoi by an enemy surface-to-air missile.

McCain parachuted earthward over Hanoi and nearly drowned in Truc Bach Lake before he was hauled to shore by civilians, one of them shattering his shoulder with a rifle butt. He had suffered two broken arms and a broken leg after ejecting from his plane and he spent six weeks in a hospital and was not expected to recover. In March 1968, McCain was placed in solitary confinement for two years.

When his father was named Commander-in-Chief Pacific Command and commander of US forces in theatre, Lieutenant Commander McCain was offered early release as a communist propaganda ploy. He refused unless all other POWs captured prior to his own date were released as well. After months of physical and psychological abuse, the North Vietnamese extracted a 'confession' from McCain. He regretted the incident later and commented: "I had learned what we all learned over there. Every man has his breaking point. I had reached mine." McCain was released in March 1973 after more than five years in captivity.

US Navy pilot Captain James Stockdale, captured after 200 combat missions when his A-4 was shot down on September 9, 1965, spent nearly eight years as a POW, much of that time at the Hanoi Hilton. He was the highest-ranking navy officer held by the North Vietnamese and remained defiant under terrible torture. After release, Stockdale received the Medal of Honor for heroism, reached the rank of vice admiral, and ran unsuccessfully for vice president of the United States alongside independent presidential candidate Ross Perot in 1992.

ABOVE: American POWs stand in line just prior to being turned over to an American delegation in North Vietnam.

(National Archives 6504309 photo by TSGT Eddie Boaz via Wikimedia Commons)

ABOVE: Former POWs cheer as their plane becomes airborne while leaving the North Vietnamese capital of Hanoi.

(National Archives and Records Administration)

STATE OF CONFLICT
1971-1972

On January 6, 1971, US Secretary of Defense Melvin Laird made an announcement that many Americans had long hoped to hear. Vietnamisation, he said, was running ahead of schedule, and the US combat mission in Vietnam would draw to a close by the summer.

Laird's announcement was welcomed, but in reality, complete US military disengagement hinged on the ability of the South Vietnamese Army (ARVN) to fight on its own. Within a month of the secretary's speech, ARVN forces launched Operation Lam Son 719, an invasion of Laos by 20,000 troops intended to disrupt the flow of communist supplies on the Ho Chi Minh Trail.

Although some ARVN units performed well, the operation disintegrated in the face of strong North Vietnamese Army (NVA) and Viet Cong counterattacks. The South Vietnamese retreated in disorder, and only the presence of US military advisors and the introduction of US air power prevented the debacle from being worse. In order for the South Vietnamese government to save face and deliver a 'victory' to the people, the largest airmobile assault of the war was launched on March 6, as 276 helicopters transported two ARVN battalions to capture the town of Tchepone, believed to be the centre of Viet Cong Base Area 604, a command and control hub.

ABOVE: A communist mortar rounds explodes near US Marine Cobra attack helicopters at the Khe Sanh combat base.
(Official U. S. Marine Corps photo 92-71 by Cpl. Sergio Ortiz via Wikimedia Commons)

Clearly, Vietnamisation had a long way to go. To underscore the uncertainty of the programme, the *New York Times* printed an account of the battle at Ranger North in Laos, asserting that ARVN Rangers, supposedly elite troops, had panicked under fire. Some of them had discarded their weapons and pushed aboard medevac helicopters although they were uninjured.

Domestic terror reared its ugly head on March 1, 1971, when a bomb exploded at the US Capitol Building. At 1:32am, the detonation rocked an area of several blocks in Washington, DC. Although no one was injured, the blast caused $300,000 in damage. The Weather Underground, a subversive group, claimed responsibility and indicated that the bombing was in protest at the ARVN invasion of Laos.

In mid-March, *Newsweek* magazine published an article titled *The Helicopter War*, illustrating the use of the aircraft in regular Vietnam operations and describing the hazard of communist anti-aircraft fire that was regularly encountered. A Loach and Cobra gunship made the *Newsweek* cover. On the 17th, MACV, the US military command in Vietnam, cautioned the White House that the withdrawal of US assets from the country was being driven more thoroughly by shortages of manpower and budgetary constraints than by the progress of Vietnamisation.

By the end of March, Lam Son 719 was seen as a fiasco, and national security advisor Henry Kissinger told President Richard Nixon

ABOVE: The colours are cased as elements of the US 23rd (Americal) Infantry Division prepare to withdraw from Vietnam. (National Archives and Records Administration via Wikimedia Commons)

ABOVE: American aircraft spray defoliant while flying over the dense jungle of Vietnam. (US Air Force via Wikimedia Commons)

ABOVE: A Marine stands watch in an observation tower during action at Hill 950 in 1971.
(National Archives and Records Administration via Wikimedia Commons)

that it had ended "…clearly as not a success." On the heels of that pronouncement, the *New York Times* reported that the morale of ARVN soldiers who had fought in Laos during Lam Son 719 was shattered.

Despite compelling evidence that Vietnamisation was struggling, President Nixon went on national television on the evening of April 6 and told the American people: "Tonight I can report that Vietnamisation has succeeded." He further advised that 100,000 American troops would be exiting Vietnam between May and November 1971. Still, Americans were dying in country. From April 8 through July 11, the US 1st Brigade, 5th Infantry Division, conducted Operation Montana Mustang, a search and destroy mission also intended to boost Vietnamisation

in Quang Tri Province. Fifty-seven Americans and 91 NVA soldiers were killed.

US Navy Lieutenant John Kerry, a member of Vietnam Veterans Against the War, candidly told the US Senate Foreign Relations Committee on April 22: "Someone has to die so that President Nixon won't be – and these are his words – 'the first president to lose a war.' How do you ask a man to be the last man to die in Vietnam? How do you ask a man to be the last man to die for a mistake?"

A decorated veteran, Kerry would later become a US senator from the state of Massachusetts and serve as US Secretary of State. He would also become one of the foremost proponents of establishing diplomatic ties with Vietnam after the war. A day after Kerry's testimony, members of Vietnam Veterans Against the War tossed more than 700 medals on the west steps of the Capitol Building as approximately half a million anti-war demonstrators marched through the streets of Washington, DC.

DUPLICITY

Communist duplicity was demonstrated at the negotiating table in Paris in May. When the United States asserted that full withdrawal of its forces would not be possible until all NVA troops were pulled out of South Vietnam, Cambodia, and Laos, the North Vietnamese insisted that they had no troops outside their own country.

Deception, however, was not only a component of North Vietnamese policy; it had become standard procedure in the US government. On June 13, the *New York Times* published excerpts from a Department of Defense report that came to be known as the Pentagon Papers. The disclosure provided details of the conduct of the Vietnam war through 1967 that were quite contradictory to the facts previously presented in the news media. Daniel Ellsberg, a former US Marine officer, and analyst working for the State Department and the Rand Corporation,

leaked the excerpts and set off a torrent of criticism of the government, eroding the public trust significantly.

Ellsberg and an accomplice were indicted on criminal charges including espionage, conspiracy, and unlawfully taking government property. The charges were dropped after the disclosure that a team of 'plumbers' had broken into the office of Ellsberg's psychiatrist in an attempt to find information that might publicly discredit the whistleblower. Later, the same burglars, G. Gordon Liddy, and E. Howard Hunt, were implicated in the notorious Watergate break-in at Democratic National Headquarters, which ultimately brought down the Nixon presidency.

By early 1972, the number of US ground troops in Vietnam had decreased to roughly 157,000, while troops from allied countries totalled approximately 54,000. In the coming weeks, further reductions would draw those numbers down further. On January 2, President Nixon announced continuing reductions that would leave only about 35,000 Americans, most administrative and advisory personnel, in Vietnam, while Australia, New Zealand, and Thailand withdrew their combat units as well.

In February, Nixon made a historic trip to China, visiting with Chairman Mao Tse-tung in the first face-to-face meetings between a US President and the communist nation's head of state. North Vietnamese leaders worried that warming relations between the two countries might marginalise their own agenda for an end to the war.

On March 10, elements of the 101st Airborne Division, the last full US combat division in Vietnam, left the country. Already, however, it appeared that the NVA and Viet Cong were marshalling forces for a spring offensive.

EASTER OFFENSIVE

General Creighton Abrams, commander of US forces in Vietnam, had warned the White House in January that: "the enemy is preparing and positioning his forces for a major offensive…There is no doubt this is to be a major campaign." Indeed, the communists launched their three-pronged Easter Offensive on March 30, surprising numerous ARVN garrisons and initially gaining substantial territory. However,

ABOVE: A damaged helicopter lies amid debris after a typhoon made landfall near the Chu Lai combat base in 1971. (US Army via Wikimedia Commons)

ABOVE: A US Air Force B-52 Stratofortress bomber lands at an air base in Thailand during the bombing campaign against North Vietnam. (National Archives and Records Administration via Wikimedia Commons)

ABOVE: General Frederick C. Weyand replaced General Creighton Abrams in command of US forces in Vietnam in June 1972. (US Army via Wikimedia Commons)

ground defences stiffened with tactical air support, and on May 9, President Nixon authorised Operation Linebacker, a sustained bombing campaign to interdict the flow of supplies to NVA troops in the South.

The Easter Offensive eventually ended in frustration for the NVA, whose thrusts were stopped in the north in Quang Tri Province and further south at Kontum and Pleiku, while the defence of An Loc thwarted a drive toward the South Vietnamese capital of Saigon.

While US air power was decisive in defeating the Easter Offensive, President Nixon had also authorised stepped up raids against Hanoi and the port of Haiphong in North Vietnam under Operation Linebacker. The Soviet Union protested, and demonstrations against the air assault broke out across the US, but the bombing sent a clear message to the North Vietnamese. Secretary of Defense Laird said publicly that the bombing of North Vietnam would continue until the North Vietnamese halted their invasion of the South.

He also warned that mining of harbours in the North was a possibility. A short time later, mining operations got underway. Soviet cargo ships en route to Haiphong were diverted to other destinations, although Soviet Navy warships and submarines were observed operating 200 miles off the Vietnamese coast near the Paracel Islands.

Keeping its Vietnamisation effort on track, the US initiated Operation Enhance in mid-May to replace weapons and equipment lost or depleted during the repulse of the communist offensive. Operation Enhance Plus followed in October with the US sending an additional $750m in weapons and equipment to South Vietnam.

Despite increasing tensions between the two countries, President Nixon travelled to Moscow at the end of May. The weeklong summit with Premier Leonid Brezhnev was intended to improve relations with

ABOVE: The cruiser USS *Newport News* fires at communist coastal defences during naval action in 1972. (US Navy via Wikimedia Commons)

the Soviets and, in concert with Nixon's successful February visit to China, exert additional pressure on the North Vietnamese to pursue peace negotiations more earnestly.

As the communist Easter Offensive was blunted, the US 196th Infantry Brigade, the last full American combat brigade in country, departed Vietnam on June 29. The following day, General Frederick C. Weyand assumed command of US forces in Vietnam from General Abrams, and after a 10-week halt the Paris Peace Talks resumed on July 13.

On the morning of August 12, elements of the 3rd Battalion, 21st Infantry Regiment, and other units of Task Force Gimlet became the last American combat troops to withdraw from South Vietnam. They had concluded the final US offensive ground sweep of the war two days earlier, sustaining two men wounded by booby traps.

By October, the North Vietnamese and US delegations in Paris had agreed to peace terms that would allow NVA troops to remain in South Vietnam. Although rumours of a cease-fire swirled, South Vietnamese President Nguyen Van Thieu rejected this provision along with any notion that a coalition government in South Vietnam might be acceptable. Thieu lashed out: "The communists could only hope to win if our ally betrays us and sells us out, but our main ally will never betray us. He has invested so much blood and money."

While US bombing raids on targets in North Vietnam continued, President Nixon won re-election in a landslide in November, carrying 49 states and receiving more than 60% of the popular vote. Meanwhile, he assured President Thieu that the United States would stand by South Vietnam if peace terms were accepted. Nevertheless, the peace talks were suspended without a full agreement on December 13.

To compel the North Vietnamese to return to the negotiating table, President Nixon ordered an intensification of the bombing campaign against North Vietnam. Operation Linebacker II, better known as the 'Christmas Bombing', began on December 18. Despite widespread protests and condemnation, the air offensive achieved its purpose. On December 30, as peace talks were set to resume on January 8, 1973, Nixon suspended the bombing of North Vietnam above the 20th parallel. The President cautioned the North Vietnamese that more widespread bombing would resume if the negotiations failed again.

ABOVE: An American bomb explodes on a target in North Vietnam during Operation Linebacker, 1972. (US Navy via Wikimedia Commons)

VIETNAM WAR IN FILM AND TELEVISION

ABOVE: Actor Richard Basehart narrated the documentary television series *Vietnam: The Ten Thousand Day War*. (CBS Television via Wikimedia Commons)

P erhaps the most thoroughly documented armed conflict of the 20th century, the Vietnam war, from the 1940s to the 1970s, is analysed, remembered, criticised, vilified, and memorialised in film and television.

Americans, and indeed people around the world saw the conflict unfold in stark, virtually real-time colour and black and white footage as correspondents reported from the front lines and their broadcasts were absorbed, provoking thought and response with such immediacy as had never been experienced previously.

Even today, camera footage of the fighting is often unnerving. One television reporter holds a microphone before a young US Army officer just after a vicious firefight and asks about "feelings." The response is captivating. "I don't know…I've got one KIA…." In another, American soldiers sit in groups as one strums a guitar and sings folk songs. Others smoke marijuana through the barrel of a shotgun. While such images have found their place in the history of the war, they speak to viewers today, even as Vietnam veterans age into their 70s and beyond.

Aside from the realism of weeknight news reporting, the television documentary has lifted the veil from the Vietnam war, providing viewers with analysis and imagery that conveys its raw emotion – horror amid death and destruction to anxiety and relief at having survived another patrol into the jungle. Among the best-known Vietnam war documentaries, the 1982 CBS News presentation *The Uncounted Enemy: A Vietnam Deception* was immediately controversial in alleging that General William Westmoreland, commander of US forces in Vietnam, had deliberately manipulated reports of communist strength to deceive his government and the American people into believing that the US and South Vietnam were winning the war. The presentation prompted Westmoreland to file a lawsuit.

Vietnam: The Ten Thousand Day War, written by Peter Arnett and narrated by Richard Basehart, was produced in 1980 and aired by the Canadian Broadcasting Corporation (CBC) as a 26-part presentation. US audiences watched a condensed 13 hours of programming, and in one of the most detailed presentations to date, viewers became more familiar with the conduct of the war itself on the battlefield, in the jungle, and in the halls of power.

Acclaimed filmmaker Ken Burns and Lynn Novick directed the 10-part documentary *The Vietnam War*, which aired on the Public Broadcasting Service (PBS) in the United States in 2017. Narrated by Peter

ABOVE: Filmmaker Ken Burns led the development of *The Vietnam War* documentary that premiered in 2017. (Creative Commons Library of Congress Life via Wikimedia Commons)

ABOVE: Oliver Stone, a Vietnam war veteran, directed a memorable trio of Vietnam themed films. (Creative Commons Towpilot via Wikimedia Commons)

Coyote, the documentary includes interviews with 79 individuals who experienced the conflict firsthand. Burns did not seek high-profile eyewitnesses to history, but rather the recollections of people who saw the war from its grittiest perspectives.

Hearts and Minds received the Academy Award for Best Documentary of 1974, and when he stood onstage to accept the Oscar on April 8, 1975, co-producer Bert Schneider was well aware that the final drama of the war was unfolding in South Vietnam. He remarked: "It's ironic that we're here at a time just before Vietnam is about to be liberated…." Schneider then read a telegram from Dinh Ba Thi, a representative of the Viet Cong Provisional Revolutionary Government and delegate to the Paris Peace Talks that simply conveyed: "Greetings of friendship to all American people," and further thanking the anti-war movement for its contribution to ending the conflict. It was an emotionally-charged and controversial moment.

Among many other Vietnam war documentaries, PBS aired a 13-episode exploration of the conflict in 1983 with *Vietnam: A Television History. Dear America: Letters Home from Vietnam* was released in 1987. Its poignant content includes readings of letters from American soldiers serving in

ABOVE: John Wayne poses with actress Irene Tsu in a still photo promoting *The Green Berets*.
(PD-US Warner Bros. via Wikimedia Commons)

Southeast Asia, and among the readers are actors Robert De Niro, Robin Williams, and Sean Penn. In 1997, actor Louis Gossett, Jr, hosted a perspective on the evocative power of the traveling replica of the Vietnam Memorial wall titled *The Wall That Heals*. Presenting a thought provoking mid-war milieu, the 1967 documentary *Far from Vietnam* included the work of seven well-known directors. *Into Harm's Way* delivered a stirring chronicle of the Vietnam experiences of the West Point Class of 1967, which graduated from the US Military Academy and soon became immersed in the crucible of war.

TV SERIES

The Vietnam war has also served as context for numerous made for television entertainment series. In the US, two of the most memorable originated in the 1980s and ran for more than one season. *China Beach* depicts the day-to-day experiences of staff and supporting characters in an evacuation hospital that receives battle casualties regularly. Actress Dana Delaney received two Emmy Awards as Best Actress in a Drama Series in 1989 and 1992 for her portrayal of nurse Colleen McMurphy. The fictional 510th Evac Hospital is the setting for 61 episodes and one pilot film that aired from 1988 through 1991.

The series *Tour of Duty* aired from 1987 through 1990 and chronicles the wartime experiences of a platoon of US soldiers in country. Second Platoon, Bravo Company is depicted on patrol slogging through rice paddies, engaged in brisk firefights with a shadowy enemy, and coping with life and death far from home. The series received one Emmy Award in 1988 for Outstanding Sound Mixing for a Drama Series.

Both *China Beach* and *Tour of Duty* were among numerous television series that were produced following the release of director Oliver Stone's Academy Award-winning feature film *Platoon* in 1986. Other Vietnam war themed series include 1980's two-episode *A Rumor of War* based on the 1977 autobiography of Philip Caputo, the Australian production *Vietnam*, which aired in five episodes in 1987 and starred Nicole Kidman, Barry Otto, and Nicholas Eadie, and *Vietnam War Story*, a series of independent fictionalised variations on real soldier experiences that aired in 1987-1988. *Fortunate Son*, focusing on an American living in British Columbia, Canada, in 1968 has aired via the CBC since 2020.

THE CINEMA

Feature films have presented the Vietnam war in varied contexts, from patriotic themes to those lamenting the waste of war, the struggles of returning veterans, the transition of military men from warriors to vocal opponents of the war, heroism, sacrifice, futility, friendly fire, anti-hero action presentations, and more.

ABOVE: Robert De Niro starred in the 1978 Oscar-winning film *The Deer Hunter*. (Creative Commons Georges Biard via Wikimedia Commons)

Actor John Wayne starred as Colonel Mike Kirby in the 1968 film *The Green Berets*, highlighting the training, combat prowess, and dedication of the US Army special forces. The film offers such memorable sequences as the identification of weapons and ammunition supplied by several communist countries for the benefit of a sceptical reporter played by David Janssen to the defeat of Viet Cong guerrillas who have overrun an American base. When an AC-47 gunship, nicknamed *Puff the Magic Dragon*, is called in to suppress the enemy breakthrough, Wayne sardonically quips, "I think Puff broke their back!"

The 1978 film *The Deer Hunter* depicts the stories of three friends from a Pennsylvania steel town who return from Vietnam as changed men. The film stars Robert De Niro, Christopher Walken, John Savage, John Cazale, and Meryl Streep. *The Deer Hunter* won Academy Awards for Best Supporting Actor (Walken), Best Director (Michael Cimino), Best Picture, Best Film Editing, and Best Sound. In the same year, *Go Tell the Spartans* depicted US Army advisors in Vietnam during the early days of American involvement, and *Coming Home* starred Jane Fonda, Jon Voight, and Bruce Dern in the drama of a love affair between a paralysed veteran and the wife of a US Marine officer. The film won three Oscars, Voight for Best Actor, Fonda Best Actress, and Best Screenplay.

In 1979, Director Francis Ford Coppola brought an adaptation of Joseph Conrad's novella *Heart of Darkness* to the big screen in the epic *Apocalypse Now*, starring Martin Sheen, Marlon Brando, and Robert Duvall. The film garnered eight Academy Award nominations and won for Best Cinematography and Best Sound. That year, Vietnamese director Nguyen Hong Sen brought *The Abandoned Field: Free Fire Zone* to the big screen with a harrowing depiction of life under fire aboard a helicopter in the Mekong Delta.

Throughout the 1980s, anti-hero John Rambo is portrayed by actor Sylvester Stallone, a veteran suffering from post-traumatic stress disorder. The series, based on the 1972 novel *First Blood* by David Morrell, debuted in 1982. In five instalments, Rambo fights at home and back in Vietnam. The finale, titled *Last Blood*, was released in 2019. Chuck Norris starred in the 1984 film *Missing In Action*, which explored the persistent theme that Americans remained missing in Vietnam and possibly still imprisoned by the communists. The action film was followed in 1985 by *Missing in Action 2: The Beginning* and 1988 by *Braddock: Missing in Action III*.

Oliver Stone's *Platoon* depicts the story of a young US Army recruit portrayed by Charlie Sheen and the struggle between two non-commissioned officers, Sergeant Barnes (Tom Berenger) and Sergeant Elias (Willem Dafoe) who personify decency and evil.

ABOVE: Actress Meryl Streep played a leading role in the Vietnam-era film *The Deer Hunter* released in 1978.
(Creative Commons Montclair Film via Wikimedia Commons)

ABOVE: Veteran and anti-war activist Ron Kovic leads a demonstration at the 1972 Republican National Convention in Miami, Florida. (Tony Schweikle via Wikimedia Commons)

The film is based on Stone's own experience as a combat infantryman in Vietnam and garnered eight Oscar nominations, winning Best Picture, Best Director, Best Sound, and Best Film Editing. *Platoon* is the first of a Stone trilogy of films on the Vietnam war, followed by *Born on the Fourth of July* in 1989, and *Heaven & Earth* in 1993.

In *Born on the Fourth of July*, Tom Cruise portrays Ron Kovic, an idealistic star high school athlete who joins the Marine Corps, receives a paralysing wound in Vietnam,

and returns home to become a leader of the anti-war movement. The film received eight Academy Award nomination, winning Best Director and Best Film Editing. *Heaven & Earth* stars Tommy Lee Jones and is based on Stone's military service experience.

Director Stanley Kubrick described the life of a US Marine and his platoon in *Full Metal Jacket*, released in 1987. Matthew Modine, Adam Baldwin, Vincent D'Onofrio, and R. Lee Ermey star. The Marines complete boot camp and fight for control of the provincial capital of Hue during the 1968 Tet Offensive. Along the way, they lose buddies as their perspective on life and death is altered. Also in 1987, Coppola's *Gardens of Stone* told the story of a sergeant played by James Caan serving with the honour guard at Arlington National Cemetery; Robin Williams starred in Barry Levinson's *Good Morning Vietnam* about the life of deejay Adrian Cronauer; and John Irvin's *Hamburger Hill* was an adaptation of the epic fight for high ground in the A Shau Valley of Vietnam.

In 2002, Randall Wallace directed *We Were Soldiers*, based on the book *We Were Soldiers Once…and Young*, written by journalist Joe Galloway and Lieutenant General Harold 'Hal' Moore. Mel Gibson portrays Moore, while Barry Pepper stars as Galloway, and Sam Elliott and Greg Kinnear add strong support in the film based on the Battle of the Ia Drang, the first major combat between US Army and North Vietnamese Army troops of the Vietnam war.

Among many other films that include elements of the Vietnam war experience are *Air America* (1990), *Forrest Gump* (1994), *The Last Full Measure* (2019), *Da 5 Bloods* (2020), and more, while *Miss Saigon*, a theatrical adaptation of the Giacomo Puccini opera *Madame Butterfly*, debuted in London in 1989 and on Broadway in 1991. Lea Salonga, Jonathan Pryce, and Hynton Battle received Tony Awards for their work in *Miss Saigon*, one of Broadway's longest running musicals.

ABOVE: Actor Barry Pepper portrayed journalist Joe Galloway in the 2002 film *We Were Soldiers*.
(Philkon Phil Konstantin via Wikimedia Commons)

ABOVE: Lieutenant General Harold 'Hal' Moore is portrayed in *We Were Soldiers* by actor Mel Gibson.
(US Army via Wikimedia Commons)

COMMUNIST EASTER OFFENSIVE

A ware of the US drawdown of its ground forces in Vietnam and the ongoing programme of Vietnamisation that handed the South Vietnamese greater responsibility for their own national security, The North Vietnamese Army (NVA) and Viet Cong launched their largest conventional offensive of the war in the spring of 1972.

General Vo Nguyen Giap, whose prior offensives during the Tet lunar new year of 1968 and at Khe Sanh during the same period had cost the communist military dearly in terms of casualties, prevailed upon his government to authorise a three-pronged invasion of the South. Giap knew that US ground troops in South Vietnam had been reduced from their peak of more than half a million in 1969 to only about 95,000.

Giap believed the time was ripe to inflict a decisive defeat on the South Vietnamese, whose combat effectiveness was questionable while US advisors remained in country and American air power had been reduced by approximately two-thirds. The communist objectives included gaining as much territory in the South as possible to strengthen the bargaining position of North Vietnamese negotiators at the Paris Peace Talks, possibly induce the US to withdraw its remaining troops in Southeast Asia entirely, and

BELOW: South Vietnamese soldiers ride atop a North Vietnamese tank captured during Easter Offensive fighting at Dong Ha. (US Army via Wikimedia Commons)

perhaps even influence the US presidential campaign of 1972 and prevent the re-election of Richard Nixon.

Although American and South Vietnamese intelligence reports had indicated a buildup of NVA and Viet Cong forces ahead of

the 'Nguyen Hue Offensive', which the communists had named after an 18th century military hero, they discounted the probability of a major conventional Soviet-style offensive. South Vietnamese Army (ARVN) forces were taken by surprise when the NVA unleashed heavy artillery fire on positions near the Demilitarized Zone (DMZ) and the border between North and South Vietnam on March 30, 1972, in the area noted by the US command as Military Region I. Approximately 40,000 troops supported by tanks and armoured vehicles rolled into

ABOVE: North Vietnamese soldiers fire 122mm artillery at South Vietnamese positions around Kon Tum. (US Army Center of Military History via Wikimedia Commons)

ABOVE: ARVN M-48 Patton tanks hold positions near the River Dong Ha close to Highway QL-9 during the Easter Offensive of 1972. (NARA photo 111-CCV-319-CC81751 by SP5 Michael Laley via Wikimedia Commons)

ABOVE: An ARVN soldier keeps watch on the defensive line at My Chanh during the communist Easter Offensive of 1972. (NARA photo 111-CCV-64-CC82549 by SSG Richard Hiwa Jr. via Wikimedia Commons)

Quang Tri Province, intending to capture Quang Tri City and drive further on the ancient city of Hue. The NVA and Viet Cong took advantage of bad weather that kept American aircraft from interfering for a while.

To the south in Military Region II, the communists sent roughly 20,000 troops from bases in Laos and Cambodia toward the cities of Pleiku and Kontum in Binh Dinh Province. If successful in capturing Pleiku, the NVA would cut South Vietnam in half and take control of the entire north of the country. In Military Region III to the south, the communists waited until April 8 to attack with three divisions along QL-13, the main highway toward the South Vietnamese capital of Saigon. The fall of Saigon might well signal the end of the war and confirm communist victory.

In Quang Tri Province, General Giap sent three divisions across the River Ben Hai to strike the inexperienced ARVN 3rd Division, forcing the South Vietnamese to fall back to Dong Ha and then a defensive line along the River My Chanh. ARVN Marines and Rangers reinforced the beleaguered 3rd Division, and the attackers were stopped by stiffening ground resistance and heavy raids by US Air Force B-52 bombers. The NVA occupied Quang Tri City, but resupply efforts were crippled by American tactical air strikes. Slowly, the ARVN troops wrested the initiative from the NVA and set about retaking Quang Tri City. Fighting at times was hand to hand, and after 48 days of combat the communists were driven out of the walled Citadel, the heart of the city.

Striking at Kontum in Military Region II, the NVA 2nd and 10th Divisions surrounded the city and attacked repeatedly. However, General Ly Tong Ba, commander of the ARVN 23rd Division, committed his armoured reserve to halt the enemy. The ARVN troops in Kontum were resupplied by air, and US fighter bombers pounded the enemy troop concentrations and armoured formations. B-52s dropped tons of bombs on NVA supply lines, and when communist tanks came into the open, US and South Vietnamese attack helicopters took a heavy

toll with anti-tank missiles. Street by street, ARVN soldiers wiped out the communist troops that made it into Kontum, while the NVA failed to capture Pleiku.

AN LOC

In the south, the fight at An Loc became the lynchpin of the Easter Offensive. Communist forces drove toward Saigon along QL-13, taking the district town of Loc Ninh on April 7. After this initial reversal, US and South Vietnamese commanders realised that An Loc would have to be defended at all costs, or Saigon itself was vulnerable.

The initial assaults against the South Vietnamese garrison at An Loc, numbering fewer than 6,400 troops, began on April 13. Three full NVA infantry divisions, a division of artillery, and mobile anti-aircraft guns and missile launchers ringed the city. The hazardous aerial resupply of the besieged garrison succeeded after much trial in bringing ammunition and food in along with the reinforcing ARVN 1st Airborne Brigade and 81st Airborne Commando Group.

While North Vietnamese delegates to the Paris Peace Talks crowed that An Loc would soon fall and become the capital of the Viet Cong government in the south, the defenders of the city fought with dogged determination. The NVA soon found that their armour and infantry were vulnerable when separated from one another. On more than one occasion, NVA tanks were caught in the open or in city streets and destroyed in detail by US air assets or ARVN shoulder-fired anti-tank missiles.

The strongest NVA assaults against An Loc took place on May 11, and two thrusts were stopped just 300 to 500 yards from the ARVN command post inside the city. Fighting raged in the streets of An Loc, but gradually the NVA strength waned, and it became apparent that ARVN troops would hold firm. Operations to lift the siege began quickly as the enemy cordon was broken. Adequate resupply, absolute US air superiority, and successful interdiction of communist supply lines forced the NVA back. By early June, the ARVN 21st Division

ABOVE: An ARVN soldier scans the distance during the defence of An Loc. At his right are several M-72 LAW shoulder-fired anti-tank weapons. (US Air Force via Wikimedia Commons)

and the supporting 9th Armored Cavalry Regiment and 15th Regiment, 9th Division, had fought their way along QL-13 to link up with the An Loc defenders and lift the siege.

All three major communist offensive efforts had failed to achieve their primary objectives, although the NVA did manage to retain some of the ground it had traversed. The butcher's bill for General Giap was substantial with an estimated 40,000 killed and 60,000 wounded. NVA armoured strength had been decimated.

Prior to the Easter Offensive, ARVN troop strength approached a million men. The best trained and equipped ARVN units, particularly those with US advisors in company, fought well. However, some observers asserted that without US air power the outcome of the Easter Offensive might have been quite different.

General Creighton Abrams, commander of US forces in Vietnam, commented: "I doubt the fabric of this thing could have been held together without US air, but the thing that had to happen before that is the Vietnamese, some numbers of them, had to stand and fight. If they do not do that, 10 times the air we've got wouldn't have stopped them [the NVA and Viet Cong]."

Even so, the communists bided their time, re-armed and re-equipped, and recovered from their significant casualties. In the spring of 1975, without US air support and advisors, the end for South Vietnam would come swiftly.

ABOVE: US Air Force F-111 and F-4 fighter bombers sit at an airbase in Thailand. American air power was decisive during the Easter Offensive. (US Air Force via Wikimedia Commons)

SIEGE OF AN LOC

Situated astride the paved highway known as QL-13, the city of An Loc held great significance during the North Vietnamese and Viet Cong Easter Offensive of 1972. A city of roughly 15,000 people, An Loc was only 90 miles from the South Vietnamese capital of Saigon. If the communists could take An Loc, the road to Saigon might indeed lie open.

As fighting raged to the north in Quang Tri Province and the Central Highlands near Kontum, another communist thrust was launched on April 5, south from Cambodia and into Binh Long Province. Three divisions of the North Vietnamese Army (NVA), roughly 35,000 troops, advanced, capturing the town of Loc Ninh after a two-day fight with South Vietnamese Army (ARVN) Rangers. With the communists poised to strike An Loc, the ARVN 5th Division was ordered to the town.

By this stage of the Vietnam war, American troop withdrawals had significantly reduced the number of US ground units in country. However, experienced US advisors accompanied the ARVN division, outnumbered nearly five to one, into An Loc. Swiftly, the NVA overran ARVN outposts and swept up the soldiers who occupied them. Once communist artillery was positioned, the attackers loosed a 15-hour barrage of roughly 7,000 heavy-calibre shells and rockets on the city.

The NVA launched a strong assault against the northern edge of An Loc the following morning, and within hours had gained control of a substantial area. Some ARVN soldiers fled in panic at the sight of communist tanks. However, the ARVN troops had been supplied

ABOVE: South Vietnamese troops board a helicopter while under enemy fire early in the siege at An Loc.
(US Department of Defense via Wikimedia Commons)

with the US-made, shoulder-fired M-72 LAW (Light Anti-tank Weapon), which proved effective against the Soviet-supplied NVA tanks. Once the ARVN troops realised that they could fight the enemy armour, resistance stiffened. Nevertheless, the communists gained ground, and by April 13, An Loc was surrounded. QL-13 was cut, and a regiment of anti-aircraft guns was positioned to interdict aerial resupply efforts. Still, the defenders repulsed heavy attacks that day and then again on April 15.

At one time the area under ARVN control was reduced to roughly one square kilometre, but the defenders of An Loc fought doggedly. Resupply was hazardous, and numerous aircraft were damaged or shot down.

Although greatly outnumbered, the US and ARVN forces possessed a trump card. The American advisors called in highly effective air strikes. Bell AH-1 Cobra helicopter gunships unleashed rockets with deadly accuracy, actually disabling the first and last of a dozen enemy tanks in one column strung out along QL-13 and allowing tactical sorties by fixed-wing fighter bombers to finish off the 10 armoured vehicles trapped in between. Heavy Boeing B-52 Stratofortress bombers pounded communist positions, flying 30 sorties, and dropping 375 tons of bombs in a single day.

Repeated efforts to take An Loc were thrown back until the enemy shot its bolt in three separate failed bids from May 10-14. By early June, some ARVN relief troops had fought their way toward An Loc, and US helicopters airlifted 1,400 reinforcements into the city by May 14. With renewed strength, ARVN forces pushed forward from An Loc, and by June 18, the 66-day siege was lifted. Nearly 2,300 ARVN soldiers had been killed in the fighting, while US estimates of NVA casualties reached 10,000 dead and 15,000 wounded.

The ARVN victory at An Loc prevented a communist advance on Saigon; however, it also demonstrated that the South Vietnamese remained highly dependent on US air power and advisors on the ground.

ABOVE: This aerial view of An Loc taken in 1972 depicts the ground around which the lengthy siege swirled.
(ZubenelgenubiA2L Own Work via Wikimedia Commons)

ABOVE: A communist tank, probably a Soviet-made T-54, lies knocked out and abandoned at An Loc. (US Air Force via Wikimedia Commons)

JANE FONDA'S ACTIVISM

ABOVE: Actress and activist Jane Fonda is shown during an appearance at the 2007 Cannes Film Festival.
(Creative Commons George Biard via Wikimedia Commons)

In 1971, actress Jane Fonda won her first Academy Award for her role in the film *Klute*. The daughter of beloved actor Henry Fonda and socialite Frances Ford Seymour had also starred in the films *Cat Ballou*, *Barefoot in the Park*, *Barbarella*, *They Shoot Horses, Don't They?*, and numerous others.

All the while, she leveraged her fame in support of social change in America. Her vocal advocacy of the civil rights movement, the Black Panthers, and the rights of Native Americans, and her opposition to the Vietnam war made headlines. Her second husband, Tom Hayden, was one of the defendants in the famous trial of the Chicago Seven, charged by the US Department of Justice with inciting unrest during the 1968 Democratic National Convention in Chicago.

Fonda was outspoken in her anti-war stance. She demonstrated publicly against the war and in 1971 formed the counter-culture Free The Army tour along with actor Donald Sutherland and political organiser Fred Gardner to contrast the famed USO tours presented by actor Bob Hope.

Fonda's activism was always noteworthy and at times quite polarising, but nothing else approached the response to her visit to North Vietnam and the capital city of Hanoi in the summer of 1972. At the time, American troops were fighting and dying in Vietnam, but Fonda made the trip to emphasise her opposition to the war and ostensibly to survey the damage to non-military targets inflicted by the continuing US bombing of North Vietnam. During the two-week visit, she made radio broadcasts and toured hospitals, schools, and other facilities that had been damaged, denouncing the American government and its participation in the war.

One photo opportunity made a lasting impression and contributed to her derogatory nickname of 'Hanoi Jane'. The actress was invited to pose with the crew of a North Vietnamese anti-aircraft gun, and the sequence of photos depicts her smiling and laughing with the gunners. When the photos were published, many Americans considered them an affront to

ABOVE: Jane Fonda and activist husband Tom Hayden walk with their son Troy in Santa Monica, California, 1976.
(Creative Commons William S. Murphy, Los Angeles Times via Wikimedia Commons)

ABOVE: Jane Fonda discusses Vietnam at a press conference in the Netherlands in 1975.
(Creative Commons Verhoeff, Bert / Anefo via Wikimedia Commons)

the families of those serving in Vietnam and especially those who had suffered and died. Some lawmakers called for her to be tried for treason.

Years later, Fonda apologised for the incident and explained the sequence of events that led to the famous – or infamous – photos. She recalled: "It happened on my last day in Hanoi…The translator told me that the soldiers wanted to sing me a song…The soldiers asked me to sing for them in return…I memorised a song called Day Ma Di, written by anti-war South Vietnamese students. I knew I was slaughtering it, but everyone seemed delighted that I was making the attempt. I finished. Everyone was laughing and clapping, including me…someone (I don't remember who) led me towards the gun, and I sat down, still laughing, still applauding. It all had nothing to do with where I was sitting. I hardly even thought about where I was sitting. The cameras flashed…."

To this day, many, although not all, Vietnam war veterans resent Fonda's anti-war activism. The images with the gun crew remain particularly evocative of the turbulent times. Fonda has since continued an acting career that includes two Academy Awards and seven nominations as well as advocacy for various causes.

STATE OF CONFLICT
1973-1975

ABOVE: Former prisoners of war rejoice aboard the 'Hanoi Taxi' as they are flown out of North Vietnam to freedom.
(US Air Force via Wikimedia Commons)

On January 23, 1973, President Richard Nixon addressed the American people. He told the television audience that at long last their nation's military involvement in the Vietnam war was over.

"The following statement is being issued at this moment in Washington and Hanoi:

At 12:30 Paris time today, January 23, 1973," Nixon said, "the Agreement on Ending the War and Restoring Peace in Vietnam was initialled by Dr Henry Kissinger on behalf of the United States, and Special Adviser Le Duc Tho on behalf of the Democratic Republic of Vietnam.

The agreement will be formally signed by the parties participating in the Paris Conference on Vietnam on January 27, 1973, at the International Conference Center in Paris."

In a somewhat ironic sidenote, former President Lyndon Johnson, whose presidency was mired in the war, died just a day before the historic announcement of peace. He was 64 years old.

The accords provided specifically for a ceasefire between the armed forces of North and South Vietnam to take effect on January 27. American troops remaining Vietnam would begin a 60-day withdrawal period, and North Vietnam would release all American prisoners of war then being held. South Vietnamese President Nguyen Van Thieu had been reluctant to agree to the terms, primarily because North Vietnamese troops then in the South would be allowed to remain there.

Nixon, however, made promises to come to the aid of South Vietnam militarily in the event of a major breach of the ceasefire by the North Vietnamese. But in the months that followed, Nixon was disgraced by the Watergate Scandal and resigned from office while President Gerald Ford was restricted by a reluctant Congress and waning support from the war-weary American people in providing further such aid to South Vietnam.

In actuality, much of the hopeful language in the accords rang hollow. North and South Vietnam never actually stopped fighting. Both sides repeatedly violated the treaty, and the North Vietnamese government soon covertly committed to a continuation of large-scale strategic raiding operations in the South in careful preparation for the final major offensive that they expected would require up to two years to unite Vietnam.

Operation Homecoming began on February 12, with the first of 591 former POWs flying out of Vietnam. Forty freed Americans were aboard the Lockheed C-141 Starlifter transport plane that was soon dubbed the 'Hanoi Taxi', and through April 4, a total of 54 flights airlifted the former captives to freedom.

Lieutenant Colonel William B. Nolde was killed by a communist artillery shell near An Loc on January 27, just hours before the cease-fire went into effect – he was the last US soldier to lose his life before hostilities were to cease. American military withdrawals continued, and by the end of March fewer than 250 US soldiers, sailors, Marines, and airmen remained in country as the last combat troops pulled out. MACV (Military Assistance Command Vietnam) ceased operations on March 29 and was replaced by the Defense Attache Office (DAO), headed by General John Murray.

KHMER ROUGE

American bombers struck for the last time in Southeast Asia on August 15 as B-52s

ABOVE: Former President Lyndon Johnson died of a heart attack at his Texas ranch on January 22, 1973. He was 64 years old. (Frank Wolfe US Government via Wikimedia Commons)

ABOVE: The famed Lockheed C-141 Starlifter nicknamed 'Hanoi Taxi' flies over the National Museum of the US Air Force at Wright-Patterson Air Force Base in Ohio.
(US Air Force via Wikimedia Commons)

targeted communist Khmer Rouge troop concentrations that threatened Phnom Penh, the capital city of Cambodia. Within months, Phnom Penh fell, and the Khmer Rouge were masters of the war-ravaged country.

Through the rest of the year, fighting ebbed and flowed in Vietnam. On August 30, Viet Cong artillery shells hit a schoolyard in the Cai Lay District of South Vietnam, killing seven South Vietnamese (ARVN) soldiers and wounding at least 20 more people, including civilians. In late September, North Vietnamese Army (NVA) troops overran the ARVN Ranger camp at Plei Djereng, killing or capturing 200 while only 93 Rangers escaped. On December 3, Viet Cong guerrillas attacked the fuel depot at Nha Be, the largest facility of its kind in South Vietnam, which held roughly 80% of the country's storage capacity. The guerrillas destroyed 600,000 barrels of fuel. On the 15th, US Army special forces Captain Richard Morgan Rees was killed in a Viet Cong ambush while taking part in a joint US-South Vietnamese search for the remains of persons listed as missing in action (MIA).

Meanwhile, in October Dr Henry Kissinger, national security advisor to President Nixon and chief US negotiator in Paris, assumed the post of Secretary of State, replacing William Rogers. On the 23rd, Kissinger and Le Duc Tho, chief North Vietnamese negotiator in Paris, were jointly awarded the Nobel Peace Prize.

On March 27, 1974, the last major ARVN offensive action against the NVA commenced. It concluded five weeks later with the Battle of Svay Rieng, a victory for ARVN troops along the South Vietnamese frontier with Cambodia as 1,200 NVA were killed and 65 captured for the loss

ABOVE: The North Vietnamese Army's 203rd Tank Brigade prepares for offensive operations after US forces pulled out of Vietnam. (Nguyen Huu An via Wikimedia Commons)

ABOVE: President Gerald Ford and Secretary of State Henry Kissinger meet with South Vietnamese Ambassador Tran Kim Phuong in Washington, DC. (National Archives and Records Administration Gerald R. Ford Library via Wikimedia Commons)

ABOVE: Former President Richard Nixon gestures to the crowd and television cameras as he departs the White House following his August 1974 resignation. (Executive Office of the President of the United States via Wikimedia Commons)

of fewer than 100 ARVN soldiers. From May through November, fighting raged in the Iron Triangle, a region where sporadic combat had occurred since 1965, and after key towns changed hands more than once the fighting temporarily stalemated. From July to early October, combat centred on the village of Duc Duc in Quang Nam Province left 4,700 soldiers of the ARVN 3rd Division killed or wounded. Although the exact number of NVA casualties is unknown, they were believed heavy as the communists gained some territory in keeping with their policy of conducting strategic raids.

President Nixon resigned from office on August 9, and as President Ford met strong opposition to proposals for increased aid to South Vietnam, military and political leaders in the North sensed an opportune time for bolder military action. In December 1974, NVA and Viet Cong forces attacked the city of Phuoc Long in Binh Phuoc Province, 75 miles from Saigon, the capital of South Vietnam. On January 6, 1975, Phuoc Long became the first South Vietnamese provincial capital permanently occupied by the communists.

During the period of strategic raids and the fall of Phuoc Long, the North Vietnamese had worried that the United States would make good on Nixon's promise to intervene militarily on behalf of South Vietnam. However, no military response was forthcoming from the Ford administration. The President condemned continuing communist offensive operations, but there was no indication that US aircraft would resume heavy bombing or ground support missions. Therefore, two days after taking Phuoc Long, the North Vietnamese politburo endorsed a campaign to destroy the ARVN as a combat force.

ABOVE: President Gerald Ford listens to comments from Ambassador Graham Martin, General Frederick Weyand, and Secretary of State Henry Kissinger during a March 25, 1975 meeting. (Gerald R. Ford Presidential Library via Wikimedia Commons)

On February 5, General Van Tien Dung assumed command of NVA and Viet Cong forces in South Vietnam. A month later he launched Campaign 275 with the objective of seizing Ban Me Thuot, a provincial capital in the central highlands. The assault on Ban Me Thuot began on the morning of March 10, and by nightfall communist troops had occupied the heart of the city. Fighting in the area subsided by March 18, and the ARVN 23rd Division absorbed such heavy casualties that it ceased to be an effective fighting force. Many South Vietnamese soldiers deserted, concerned not only for their own safety, but also for family members who lived nearby.

President Thieu and his closest military advisors recognised that the central highlands could not be held and ordered the cities of Pleiku and Kontum evacuated. The only open highway was Route 7B, and the withdrawal disintegrated into a panicked jumble of soldiers and civilian refugees. The flight became known as the Convoy of Tears, and NVA artillery and small-arms fire added to the peril. Of roughly 27,000 ARVN soldiers who began the withdrawal, only about 6,000 remained combat worthy after reaching safety. Roughly one-third of 180,000 civilians who started along Route 7B are believed to have reached temporary havens near the coastline.

By mid-March, NVA troops occupied the northern city of Quang Tri, and ARVN forces had evacuated An Loc, the scene of their great stand against the communist Easter onslaught three years earlier. On March 24, the North Vietnamese initiated the Ho Chi Minh Campaign, seizing the moment to achieve total victory, although communist leaders were astonished by the rapid disintegration of ARVN resistance. After a week of fighting, the ARVN base at Chon Thanh, west of Saigon, was abandoned to the communists on April 1.

ABOVE: US Marines secure a helicopter landing zone during the evacuation of American personnel from Cambodia in Operation Eagle Pull.

(Department of Defense Photo (USMC) via Wikimedia Commons)

DA NANG
In the north, the NVA and Viet Cong pushed forward along the coast, occupying Hue, the scene of bitter fighting during the 1968 Tet Offensive. When the communists arrived, the ARVN defenders and civilians had already been in the process of abandoning the old city. These refugees were headed toward Da Nang, the second largest city of South Vietnam roughly 50 miles south of Hue. At the end of the month, at least half a million civilians and deserting soldiers commingled in the streets of Da Nang trying to escape by any means possible, plane, boat, or 250 miles further south to the former US military installations at Cam Ranh Bay. The NVA surrounded Da Nang and then occupied the city on March 29. Three days later, Qui Nhon, the third-largest city of South Vietnam, was taken with little resistance, while Lon Nol, the US-backed former leader of Cambodia, fled into exile in the United States.

On April 3, President Ford announced the commencement of Operation Babylift, an evacuation of Vietnamese orphans, more than half of them two years old or younger. Nearly 2,600 were flown to safety. However, the following day the first Babylift flight resulted in tragedy as the Lockheed C-5

Galaxy aircraft crashed, killing 128 people, dozens of them Vietnamese children.

After the US declined a plea from Thieu to resume bombing against the communists, the greatest glimmer of ARVN courage under fire occurred April 9-21 at the town of Xuan Loc, 50 miles east of Saigon. In the last major battle of the Vietnam war, the ARVN defenders stood firm against repeated NVA attacks and finally pulled out after the majority of communist forces had bypassed the stronghold.

President Thieu resigned on April 21, and Tran Van Huong was named President of South Vietnam. A subsequent proposal of a ceasefire and negotiations fell on deaf communist ears.

As the NVA and Viet Cong drew closer to Saigon, the evacuation of Americans and South Vietnamese who had worked closely with them in the capital city got underway in earnest. As of April 23, two military flights per hour were taking off from Tan Son Nhut air base, and 7,000 people per day were brought out. Soon enough, the communists reached the outskirts of Saigon, and artillery shells were lobbed into the air base at Bien Hoa, just 19 miles northeast.

Corporal Charles McMahan and Lance Corporal Darwin Judge became the last two US service personnel killed in Vietnam as NVA rockets shut down Tan Son Nhut to fixed-wing aircraft on April 29. Hours later, Operation Frequent Wind, the hasty helicopter evacuation of US and Vietnamese personnel from Saigon, was underway. More than 30 US Navy ships, including five aircraft carriers, had taken station off the coast to receive the refugee-laden helicopters.

Huong resigned as president on April 27 and was replaced by Duong Van Minh with directions from the South Vietnamese National Assembly to seek peace. When a Viet Cong tank famously crashed through the gate of the presidential palace in Saigon on April 30, Minh was waiting. He ordered ARVN forces to surrender.

Within a few days, all resistance to the communist forces ended. The long Vietnam war was finally over, but difficult days and years lay ahead for a country finally unified by the proverbial sword.

ABOVE: A Viet Cong Soviet-made T-54 tank that crashed through the gate of the presidential palace in Saigon on April 30, 1974, sits in the Vietnam Military History Museum. (Creative Commons 3144228 via Wikimedia Commons)

THE FINAL OFFENSIVE

On the morning of April 30, 1975, a communist tank with the Viet Cong flag flying from its turret crashed through the gates of the presidential palace in Saigon. The long, bloody journey of the Vietnam war was fast ending.

The last American combat troops had exited South Vietnam in 1973, leaving the South Vietnamese Army (ARVN) and other military forces without their experienced and highly-trained US advisors on the ground. Although the ARVN numbered more than a million soldiers, many of these had been deployed to supposedly protect rural villages and bases across the countryside. Therefore, numerical superiority against the North Vietnamese Army (NVA) and the Viet Cong was threadbare at approximately three to one.

Conventional analysis had often indicated that suppression of an insurgency required a superiority of 10 to one. Compounding the ARVN issue with manpower was the inclusion among the communist forces of well-equipped, highly-trained, and motivated NVA divisions and the lack of motivation and poor leadership that were commonplace within the ARVN.

ABOVE: Confronted with communist military victories, South Vietnamese President Nguyen Van Thieu resigned on April 21, 1975. (Yoichi R. Okamoto US Government via Wikimedia Commons)

Though the Paris Peace Accords had provided an exit for the United States from the war, the communists and ARVN forces were still fighting. Communist leaders were wary of the promise of President Richard Nixon to South Vietnamese President Nguyen Van Thieu that the US would stand behind South Vietnam and direct massive air power, specifically waves of big B-52 Stratofortress bombers, against any major armed offensive launched by North Vietnam.

However, by late 1974 the situation had changed dramatically. Nixon, whose presidency had collapsed under the weight of the Watergate scandal, had resigned from office. His successor Gerald R. Ford faced a dilemma if and when the North Vietnamese tested his resolve to defend South Vietnam and that of the US Congress as well.

North Vietnamese leaders bided their time, augmenting their forces and conducting so-called 'strategic raids' into South Vietnam to retake control of territory previously lost to ARVN troops around the conclusion of the Peace Accords in January 1973. These raids began in the spring of 1974 and continued into November, none

ABOVE: President Gerald Ford tells a gathering at Tulane University in New Orleans, Louisiana, that US involvement in the Vietnam war is over. (Gerald R. Ford Presidential Library National Archives and Records Administration via Wikimedia Commons)

ABOVE: Vietnamese refugees, having fled communism by boat, are hauled aboard a US Navy ship on April 3, 1975. (National Archives and Records Administration US Navy via Wikimedia Commons)

ABOVE: A Viet Cong armoured vehicle rolls down a highway in South Vietnam on April 19, 1975.
(Creative Commons Tommy Japan via Wikimedia Commons)

of them scaled to be so provocative as to provoke American military retaliation.

By December, however, the time had come. The NVA and Viet Cong launched a major attack against the provincial capital of Phuoc Long, 75 miles northeast of Saigon. From their bases in Cambodia, the communists struck with two infantry divisions, an attached infantry regiment, heavy artillery, and anti-aircraft units. The fighting for Phuoc Long lasted 24 days, December 13, 1974, to January 6, 1975, and the city became the first provincial capital in South Vietnam occupied permanently by communist forces. More than 5,400 ARVN troops had been defending Phuoc Long, and only 850 retreated to safety. The remainder had been killed, captured, or simply deserted or switched sides.

Phuoc Long was a bitter harbinger of things to quickly come. At first, the North Vietnamese hesitated to initiate further military operations. They waited for a reaction from President Ford, but nothing other than a hollow denunciation materialised. No B-52s were overhead raining destruction.

Ford's hands were effectively tied. There was little support in Congress or among the American people to re-engage in Vietnam militarily. In fact, Congress had approved the War Powers Act to restrict the free actions of the President to commit military forces anywhere without forthcoming legislative approval. Later, as the final communist offensive unfolded, Ford went to Congress on April 11, 1975, asking for nearly a billion dollars in emergency aid for South Vietnam, $722m in military aid and $250m for economic and humanitarian purposes. The request stalled in Congress, and the Senate approved $200m on April 18 while the topic of further assistance remained divisive.

Pleased with the success at Phuoc Long and the apparent reluctance of the US to commit military assets to the continuing war, the North Vietnamese launched Campaign 275 in March 1975. The NVA objective was the provincial capital of Ban Me Thuot in the long-disputed central highlands. The battle for the city opened on March 10, and soon a flood of refugees was heading out of Ban Me Thuot, restricting the

ABOVE: South Vietnamese General Nguyen Xuan Thinh is shown aboard a US Navy ship after his evacuation in 1975.
(US Navy via Wikimedia Commons)

ARVN response. NVA troops captured the town of Phuoc An, 20 miles from Ban Me Thuot, and with that all of Darlac Province was under communist control.

President Thieu sent a delegation to Washington, DC, to plead for US assistance but received only the cold and empty comfort of promises to send further aid as President Ford continued his vain attempts to persuade Congress to act decisively in favour of South Vietnam. Meanwhile, Thieu and his generals decided to abandon the cities of Pleiku and Kontum to reinforce Ban Me Thuot. The communists swept up these prizes and Ban Me Thuot fell to the NVA on March 18.

Thieu ordered his forces to abandon the central highlands and to take up better defensive positions in the south. However, as the poorly led ARVN formations began their tactical withdrawal, it soon devolved into a rout. The North Vietnamese and Viet Cong continued to press their advantage from the north and west, while the US government declined to intervene militarily.

FINAL VICTORY

Surprised with the relative ease of the campaign, the North Vietnamese government had planned on an offensive that would last up to two years. Instead, its military forces were now presented with a golden opportunity to achieve final victory.

On March 24, the communist forces launched the Ho Chi Minh Campaign. Quang Tri, Hue, and Da Nang fell quickly to the advancing NVA, and the evacuation

of Da Nang at the end of March was a helter skelter affair. Major communist reinforcements streamed into the coastal areas for the southward push, but for two weeks, from April 9 to 22, the ARVN put up a tough resistance at the town of Xuan Loc. The communists eventually bypassed the town en route to Saigon, and the ARVN 18th Division had suffered heavy losses in defence but managed to escape encirclement.

At the same time, neighbouring Cambodia came under communist domination as the bloodthirsty Khmer Rouge captured the capital of Phnom Penh on April 17. In December, the communist Pathet Lao would take complete control of the government in Laos.

President Thieu resigned on April 21 and later made a radio broadcast condemning the United States for abandoning his country. He fled to Taiwan and lived in the US until his death in 2001 at the age of 78.

The NVA and Viet Cong juggernaut proceeded toward the South Vietnamese capital and by April 27, Saigon was surrounded. As ARVN resistance collapsed, evacuation of American personnel and Vietnamese staff members, diplomats, and family members who would be targeted by the communists, was underway. For several years, many Vietnamese refugees fled communism by sea and were later collectively termed the 'boat people'. This humanitarian crisis peaked in the 1980s, and an estimated 139,000 refugees eventually reached the United States.

During the first week of May 1975, military operations in South Vietnam ground to a halt. Two South Vietnamese generals commanding virtually intact forces in the Mekong Delta southwest of Saigon committed suicide as resistance to the NVA sputtered to an ignominious close.

The victorious communist offensive ended in complete victory after only 55 days.

ABOVE: A banner in the Vietnamese capital of Hanoi commemorates the April 30, 1975, victory in the Vietnam war. (Creative Commons Dragfyre via Wikimedia Commons)

OPERATION FREQUENT WIND

ABOVE: US Marine helicopters land on the grounds of the US Defense Attaché Office in Saigon, April 1975.
(Department of Defense US Marine Corps via Wikimedia Commons)

Armed Forces Radio announced a cryptic statement. "The temperature in Saigon is 105 degrees and rising," it said. Then, the familiar Bing Crosby song *White Christmas* began playing over and over. For those who knew the meaning, the end of their sojourn in Vietnam was at hand.

In keeping with the terms of the Paris Peace Accords, the United States had withdrawn what remained of its combat forces from Vietnam in 1973. However, the communist North Vietnamese Army (NVA) and Viet Cong were still at war with South Vietnam. The communists used an interim period to make good on losses in manpower and reequip their forces. Their leaders believed correctly that the US would not interfere militarily when their offensive operations resumed.

President Richard Nixon had responded to the communist Easter Offensive of 1972 with heavy bombing that inflicted tremendous casualties on the NVA and proved decisive in the strategic failure of the offensive. However, by the spring of 1975 Nixon was embroiled in the Watergate scandal and had resigned from office. The American people were tired of war, and in a practical sense there would be no support for renewed bombing to save the South Vietnamese again.

In the spring of 1975, the final communist offensive of the Vietnam conflict was initiated.

Through March, the NVA and Viet Cong had rolled from victory to victory against the crumbling South Vietnamese Army (ARVN) resistance. The signs were ominous for the Americans who remained in Vietnam, administrative personnel, diplomats, family members, and the handful of Marine guards that stood watch at US facilities including the embassy in the South Vietnamese capital of Saigon and four consulates at Nha Trang, Da Nang, Bien Hoa, and Can Tho.

As communist forces advanced, more than 5,000 Americans were still in South Vietnam, and several thousand more South Vietnamese who had worked with them, loyal and committed individuals, were at risk of capture and even death in the event of communist takeover. To prepare potential evacuees, the US embassy issued a 15-page pamphlet titled SAFE (Standard Instruction and Advice to Civilians in an Emergency) describing the procedures to exit the country and revealing the coded messages to be broadcast on Armed Forces Radio.

As the communists advanced steadily, they cut the land evacuation routes in the south. On April 3, President Gerald Ford had ordered Operation Babylift, an air operation which eventually delivered 2,600 Vietnamese orphan children to safety in the United States. The evacuation of Da Nang had been particularly frenzied. In the first week of April, the invaders occupied South Vietnamese bases at Nha Trang and Cam Ranh Bay. And during those chaotic days, the US government did evacuate large numbers of US citizens and South Vietnamese who applied for visas. Commercial airlines under contract to fly these individuals out of the country operated regularly. That is, until the sprawling Tan Son Nhut air base outside Saigon came under communist artillery fire on April 29.

President Gerald Ford declined to intervene militarily and authorised Operation Frequent

ABOVE: A South Vietnamese C-130 Hercules transport aircraft burns on the ground at Tan Son Nhut air base, April 29, 1975. (US Marine Corps via Wikimedia Commons)

ABOVE: Carrying just a few personal belongings, Vietnamese refugees make their way aboard a US Navy ship during Operation Frequent Wind.
(US Department of Defense via Wikimedia Commons)

Wind, the final evacuation of American and South Vietnamese personnel from Saigon. The shutdown of other air bases across the country and the shelling of Tan Son Nhut rendered further operations by fixed-wing aircraft too hazardous, and seaborne evacuation routes were blocked as well. Further evacuations would require the use of helicopters. Two Americans were killed in the communist bombardment at Tan Son Nhut, and one Marine assigned to the security detail of Ambassador Graham Martin told the *Chicago Tribune*: "It was an absolute mess. We knew immediately when we saw that airfield that the fixed-wing operation was done."

PUBLIC PANIC

While an evacuation control centre had been established in Saigon on April 1, the US Navy's Task Force 76 took station off the coast of Vietnam to provide air cover and receive the helicopters flying from the capital. By the end of the month, the situation had deteriorated rapidly. As the citizenry panicked, roughly 10,000 South Vietnamese waited anxiously in line to receive evacuation clearance, and thousands more had crowded into the embassy grounds as the guards

attempted to secure the gates. Although the original evacuation plan had made provision only for American citizens to leave South Vietnam, Ambassador Martin directed that Vietnamese government officials and embassy staff should be brought out as well. Some desperate Vietnamese attempted to climb the walls of the embassy compound, while others begged desperately for Marine guards just to take their babies to safety.

During the 19 hours that followed the initiation of Frequent Wind, 81 US helicopters transported a total of 1,373 Americans and 5,595 Vietnamese to safety while communist forces raced toward the South Vietnamese capital city. Frequent Wind, according to analysts, remains the largest helicopter operation of its kind in history.

When the defence attaché building and grounds came under attack, the embassy remained the only location where helicopters

ABOVE: US Navy sailors push a helicopter over the side of the amphibious assault ship USS *Okinawa* during Operation Frequent Wind. (US Marines via Wikimedia Commons)

could operate during Frequent Wind, and the aircraft landed on the roof at 10-minute intervals. Some of the pilots flew for the entire 19-hour evacuation period without rest, and at sea when helicopters crowded the decks of US Navy aircraft carriers and other vessels, they were emptied of evacuees and then, if necessary, pushed over the side and into the ocean to make room for more helicopters laden with evacuees.

Deputy Chief of Mission Wolfgang Lehmann described his harrowing escape from Saigon to a waiting ship as the NVA closed in on the heart of Saigon. He recalled: "We could see the lights of the North Vietnamese convoys approaching the city… The chopper was packed with the rest of the staff and remaining civilian guards…and it was utterly silent except for the rotors of the engine. I don't think I said a word on the way out and I don't think anybody else did. The prevailing emotion was tremendous sadness."

Two weeks after the completion of Operation Frequent Wind, *Newsweek* magazine reported in its May 12, 1975, edition that the end of the Vietnam war had emphatically come. "Eleven Marines crouched on the flat roof of the US Embassy, nervously fingering their M-16 rifles," it read. "From time to time, shots rang out from below, where thousands of Vietnamese milled about angrily in the embassy courtyard. Other Vietnamese were already rampaging through the lower floors of the six-storey building, trying to make their way up tear-gas-filled stairwells. Suddenly, the whine of a helicopter could be heard in the distance and the Marines fired a red-smoke grenade to mark their position. As the US CH-46 Sea Knight touched down on the roof, the Marines piled into the chopper. The last man scrambled aboard with the embassy's American flag – neatly folded and stuffed inside a brown-paper bag…."

At 7:53am on April 30, 1975, the last American helicopter lifted skyward and turned toward the sea. Within hours, Saigon and all of South Vietnam would be in communist hands.

ABOVE: Vietnamese refugees exit a helicopter aboard a US Navy ship during Operation Frequent Wind, April 30, 1975. (US Department of Defense via Wikimedia Commons)

ABOVE: Helicopters crowd the flight deck of the aircraft carrier USS *Hancock* as refugees come aboard during Operation Frequent Wind. (US Marine Corps Dirck Halstead via Wikimedia Commons)

VIETNAM POSTSCRIPT

"Let the days when we talk past each other be gone for good. Let us acknowledge our importance to one another. Let us continue to help each other heal the wounds of war, not by forgetting the bravery shown and the tragedy suffered by all sides but by embracing the spirit of reconciliation and the courage to build better tomorrows for our children…May our children learn from us that good people, through respectful dialogue, can discover and rediscover their common humanity and that a painful, painful past can be redeemed in a peaceful and prosperous future…."

President Bill Clinton spoke these words on November 17, 2000, before a crowd at Vietnam National University in Hanoi. Clinton was the first US president to visit Vietnam since Richard Nixon in 1969, when the nations were embroiled in a terrible war. Clinton came to Hanoi five years after the United States and the Socialist Republic of Vietnam formally established diplomatic relations.

The war in Vietnam left a legacy of bitterness, tremendous suffering, and irretrievable loss, and when the last helicopter carrying Americans out of war-torn Saigon cleared Vietnamese airspace in the spring of 1975, no one could conceive that any hope of diplomatic rapprochement could be in the future. Massive destruction lay in the wake of the war, and differences ran deep. The US placed a trade embargo on Vietnam, and the nation was isolated, its economy struggling for years to gain a solid footing.

Meanwhile, the country became involved in regime change in Cambodia and in 1979 fought a brief, month-long border war with China, its colossal neighbour to the north. In the US, the accounting of approximately 2,600 personnel listed as missing in action (MIA) became a political priority. Mistrust on both sides prevented real progress in establishing good relations for years. The US believed that Vietnam had blatantly disregarded some critical terms of the Paris Peace Accords of 1973, including the failure to fully account for MIAs. The Vietnamese expected US foreign

ABOVE: The US flag flies on the grounds of the American ambassador's residence in the Vietnamese capital of Hanoi.
(US Department of State via Wikimedia Commons)

ABOVE: President Barack Obama passes an honour guard during a visit to Vietnam in 2016.
(Executive Office of the President of the United States via Wikimedia Commons)

ABOVE: President Bill Clinton greets a friendly crowd during his visit to Hanoi in 2000. (National Archives and Records Administration via Wikimedia Commons)

aid of approximately $3.3bn – promised by President Nixon prior to the signing of the peace accords – to assist in rebuilding their country's shattered infrastructure. For years, these issues obstructed real progress.

While Vietnamese troops remained in Cambodia and the Vietnamese government closely aligned with the Soviet Union, the US remained reticent toward Vietnam due to concerns that positive overtures would damage relations with China. However, when Chinese troops invaded Vietnam, the Soviet Union hesitated to offer support to Vietnam beyond providing weapons, supplies, and intelligence while massing some troops along the Russo-Chinese frontier. The Vietnamese hope to bind the Soviets to a mutual military agreement while improving relations with

the US as twin buffers to future Chinese interference failed to materialise.

By the time a transitional government was installed in Cambodia with United Nations supervision in 1991, Vietnam veterans themselves had taken some of the first steps toward healing the wounds of war, visiting Vietnam within a few years of their personal trials and experiences in wartime. The Vietnamese people welcomed them. Among them were Senator John McCain, a former POW, Senator Bob Kerrey, a former Navy SEAL and recipient of the Medal of Honor, and Senator John Kerry, a decorated veteran of the US Navy riverine force, future US Secretary of State, and presidential candidate. The senators advocated for improved relations with Vietnam, and their effort proved worthwhile.

ABOVE: The names of more than 58,000 American service personnel who lost their lives in Vietnam are etched on the black granite memorial in Washington, DC. (Creative Commons David J. Jackson via Wikimedia Commons)

More than 2.7 million Americans served in Vietnam. Their average age was 19, and since the war's end many Vietnam veterans continue to experience serious challenges. When they returned home, veterans were often scorned and vilified just for doing their duty. They were forgotten, and the welcoming parades and fanfare that had greeted returning soldiers in prior wars were conspicuously absent. Veterans have continually dealt with health issues surrounding the use of the toxic Agent Orange defoliant and other chemicals, and many have suffered with drug addiction and varying degrees of post-traumatic stress disorder. A survey conducted in 1990 revealed that roughly one-third of those who served experienced PTSD. As the years have passed, Vietnam veterans has received greater recognition for their service and sacrifice, but their comprehensive experience is unique in American history.

On November 13, 1982, the Vietnam Veterans Memorial designed by architect Maya Lin was dedicated on the National Mall in Washington, DC. Inscribed on the V-shaped black granite wall are the names of 58,318 Americans who died in Vietnam. The wall remains a place of reflection and reverence. On November 11, 1984, a statue titled The Three Servicemen, depicting combat soldiers of the Vietnam era, was added to the memorial. Vietnamese deaths during the long war are estimated at more than two million.

The US government formally lifted travel restrictions to Vietnam in 1991. Two years later, the US State Department and Vietnamese Foreign Ministry opened consular offices in Hanoi and Washington, DC. In 1994, President Clinton lifted the longstanding trade embargo, and on July 11, 1995, two decades after the fall of South Vietnam, the two nations normalised diplomatic relations.

ECONOMIC REFORMS

In the mid-1980s, the Vietnamese government had initiated some economic reforms, moving toward a more market economy and opening the country to foreign investment. Another major step forward occurred with a bilateral trade agreement concluded between the US and Vietnam in 2001, as Vietnam was granted conditional most favoured nation trade status, which facilitated its entry into the World Trade Organization in 2007. Since then, trade between the two countries has expanded steadily, increasing from $451m in 1995 to $60bn in 2018 and $90bn in 2021. The US has become Vietnam's second-largest trading partner behind China, and Vietnam ranks ninth on the US list.

Through the years, cooperation on resolving both American and Vietnamese POW and MIA issues has continued, and emerging

ABOVE: US Agriculture Secretary Tom Vilsack and Vietnamese Deputy Prime Minister Hoang Trung Hai meet in 2011. (US Department of Agriculture via Wikimedia Commons)

security concerns have brought the two countries closer together. When President Clinton visited Hanoi, he delivered more than 300,000 pages of documents that might assist the Vietnamese in accounting for their own missing, while more joint teams of American and Vietnamese personnel ventured into remote areas across Vietnam in search of MIA evidence. The United States has also pledged to work in the cleanup of chemicals such as Agent Orange, used liberally as a defoliant during the war, and toxic, carcinogenic Dioxins.

The issue of human rights remains one of frequent contention. The authoritarian government in Hanoi has regularly cracked down on dissent, curbing personal liberties. International surveys have ranked Vietnam's human rights record quite low among nations, but progress has been made while Vietnam continues to further engage with the US and other countries of Asia and the Pacific.

Mutual interests concerning foreign trade and national security have engendered greater dialogue between the US, Vietnam, Japan, India, and Australia. Although Vietnamese foreign relations policy is heavily influenced by China, the countries have long been involved in a dispute over sovereignty in some areas of the South China Sea. Closer cooperation with the US and other nations will counterbalance the Chinese claims and assist in maintaining freedom of navigation in the disputed areas.

Closer military ties between the US and Vietnam have been hinted at in recent years, particularly due to the shared concerns over Chinese expansion in Asia and the Pacific. The two countries have participated in a dozen political, security, and defence dialogues, and US Navy ships have made calls in Vietnamese ports on several occasions. However, Vietnamese defence policy is guided by the 'four no's', which comprise no foreign military alliances, no foreign troops stationed in Vietnam, no joining with one foreign power to combat another, and no use of force or threat of force in international relations.

For all the progress that has been made in US-Vietnamese relations on the political, economic, and humanitarian fronts, some degree of wariness may remain due to the legacy of the conflict that ended half a century ago.

ABOVE: US Navy Commander James Jones accepts flowers during welcoming ceremonies as the guided missile destroyer USS *Mustin* visits the port of Da Nang, Vietnam in 2008. (US Navy via Wikimedia Commons)

THE UNITED STATES AND VIETNAM TODAY

Although there are lingering scars from the war that ended nearly 50 years ago, the United States and Vietnam are working today toward an ever more extensive partnership that includes closer economic, geopolitical, and humanitarian ties.

Hanoi has increased its visibility on the world stage in recent years, hosting a historic summit meeting between President Donald Trump and North Korean leader Kim Jong Un in February 2019. Following President Joe Biden's visit to Vietnam in the autumn of 2023, the Vietnamese government announced the elevation of its relationship with the United States as a "comprehensive strategic partnership," its highest level of international interaction.

During the same meeting, it was confirmed that the US Secretary of State and the Vietnamese Foreign Minister will meet annually. The US further pledged to endorse Vietnamese development in semiconductors, digital infrastructure, physical construction, and climate change mitigation, including $25m in American financial support for these initiatives. Since the signing of the first bilateral trade agreement between the two countries more than 20 years ago, economic ties have steadily increased. In fiscal year 2023, the US appropriated $197m in aid for Vietnam, up from the $185m allocated in 2022.

Since the normalisation of relations between the United States and Vietnam in 1995 and the establishment of embassies in Hanoi and Washington, DC, the office of the US Consulate General has opened in Ho Chi Minh City, and the Vietnamese Consulate General has located in San Francisco. In 2009, the US was given the opportunity to open a second consulate in Da Nang, and Vietnam was authorised to open a second consulate in Houston in 2010.

While the countries navigate through their differences, particularly US concerns for human rights in Vietnam and longtime Vietnamese concerns regarding US intentions to weaken domestic authoritarian control, common interests continue to broaden. The nations are working together today to remediate the dangers of unexploded ordnance, a legacy of the war, as well as to deal with environmental contamination due to Agent Orange and other chemicals. In 2020, the governments entered into a 10-year programme to clean up the Bien Hoa airbase site with an estimated cost of $450m. Still more emphasis is being placed on the location and recovery of those missing in action (MIA) from the war, and in recent years Congress has provided $7m to Vietnam to assist in accounting for approximately 300,000 Vietnamese MIAs.

ABOVE: President Barack Obama receives a bouquet of flowers while touring Vietnam in 2016. (Executive Office of the President of the United States via Wikimedia Commons)

ABOVE: The aircraft carrier USS *Carl Vinson* arrives at the port of Da Nang, Vietnam, in 2018. (US Navy via Wikimedia Commons)

The burgeoning influence of China in Asia and the Pacific is a concern for both nations, and in recent years the US has become a tangible partner with Vietnam in countering Chinese expansionism. In 2016, President Barack Obama lifted a longstanding embargo against the sale of arms to Vietnam. That October, the destroyer USS *John S. McCain* and submarine tender USS *Frank Cable* became the first US Navy ships to visit the Vietnamese port at Cam Ranh Bay since 1975.

In 2017, the US provided six patrol boats to the Vietnamese Coast Guard in response to mutual concerns regarding freedom of navigation in the South China Sea amid Chinese territorial assertions. In 2018, the aircraft carrier USS *Carl Vinson* visited the port of Da Nang, and interaction between US and Vietnamese naval personnel included training and cultural exchanges. After observing in 2012 and 2016, Vietnam became an active participant in the US-hosted Rim of the Pacific Military Exercises (RIMPAC) in 2018.

During the decades since the long and costly war ended, the US and Vietnam have grown closer – never forgetting the sacrifices of their two countries but choosing to look toward the promise of the future rather than to dwell upon a turbulent past.

ABOVE: President Donald Trump greets Vietnamese Prime Minister Nguyen Xuan Phuc in Hanoi, 2019. (Executive Office of the President of the United States via Wikimedia Commons)